Against all odds...

Trinity Western University: 1974 to 2006
—to the praise of His glory

by Dr. R. Neil Snider,
PRESIDENT EMERITUS

The Vision

THE BEGINNINGS—Aerial view of Seal Kap Farm property in Langley, 1961. The visionary and courageous leadership of the TWU founders along with past and present leadership is aptly reflected in this quote by John F. Kennedy.

The vision to see,
The faith to believe, and
The courage to do.

Years After the Trinity Western Opening—Aerial view of the campus taken from the southwest, showing Douglas, Fraser and McMillan Halls, RNT, the gym, library, and the construction of NBTC in the background. 1998.

Chapel Ministry

Calvin B. Hanson Chapel—the first new building constructed on campus, 1962.

Dave Rushton at the keyboard. Dave was so faithful in playing for the chapel services.

In July of 1979 the chapel's foyer and balcony were extended, and wooden pews were replaced with yellow, folding lecture-type-seats. On March 1, 1980 the Chapel was rededicated and officially named the Calvin B Hanson Chapel in honour of Trinity's first president."

Malcolm Cameron: Campus Chaplain.

As the student body continued to grow in size, chapel services outgrew the capacity of the Cal Hanson Chapel so had to move to the David Enarson Gymnasium.

University Communications

With a Heart to Serve

An example of the hundreds of men and women, staff and faculty who have served so faithfully at Trinity Western.

Allan Kotanen with wife Sylvia.

English professor Barbara Pell.

Dwight Johnson.

Dick Walters.

Faculty member Chris Cross helping a student examine a beaker filled with liquid in the chemistry lab.

Into the Marketplace

FIRST NURSING GRADS—The first graduates of TWU's School of Nursing posing in the atrium in the Reimer Student Centre, 1997.

FIRST HONORARY DEGREE—The Honourable Jake Epp, Minister of Health and Welfare, 1984 – 1989, was awarded TWU's first Honorary Degree, Doctor of Laws, on April 26, 1987.

Members of Parliament, Alumni:
Chuck Strahl ('90), Deborah Grey '97),
Diane (Broadway) Ablonczy ('68),
Grant McNally ('84).

The Snider Family

THE SNIDER FAMILY—Dean, Marlie, Dawn, Neil, Dana, shortly after their arrival at Trinity Western, 1974.

Fun Times—Neil and Marlie enjoying a skate with the students.

IN MEMORY OF MARLIE—In June 2005, the Board of Governors announced that the Pacific Rim Collegium, dedicated March 27, 2003, would be renamed the Marlie Snider Collegium.

THE MARLIE SNIDER COLLEGIUM—affectionately dubbed "The Marlie" by the students, many of whom remember her warm down-to-earth hospitality as they 'hung out' in the Snider home—A memorial to Marlie who passed into the presence of her Lord, June 11, 2005.

University Communications

Signs of Growth

NORTHWEST BUILDING—now student residences and School of Business. The dedication of Northwest Baptist Theological College (NBTC) took place on October 18, 1991. In 2000 the School discontinued its undergraduate programs and focused on seminary training. TWU's Board of Governors approved the purchase of the Northwest Building in December, 2000. *TWU Archives*

On April 20, 2005 ground breaking was held for the new Music Building. This facility, provided for by a generous donor, houses music practice rooms and faculty offices. *TWU Archives*

REIMER STUDENT CENTRE—The grand opening and dedication of the Student Centre on January 20, 1997, was named in honour of Delbert Reimer, a founding and former long-time member of the University's Board of Governors. *TWU Archives*

NEUFELD SCIENCE CENTRE—The dedication of the Anna and J.G. Neufeld Science Centre was celebrated on April 8, 1994. *TWU Archives*

Marketplace Performances

Trinity Western University Choirs—Masterworks Choir (TWU's adult, alumni choir); Chamber Singers (TWU's most elite student choir); Chamber Choir (a choir of mainly music majors); and Concert Choir—performing at the Chan Centre for Performing Arts at UBC.

First CIS Women's Volleyball Game, 1999.

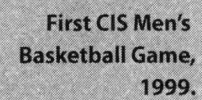

First CIS Men's Basketball Game, 1999.

President's Leadership Council

The PLC was established for the purpose of assisting the President and his staff in areas of strategic planning and development.

PLC members include: Heather Alloway, Jake & Lydia Epp, Bruce & Karen Etherington, Abe & Lillian Friesen, Jacques & Rani Gauthier, Michael & Tanja Gibney, Eric & Toni Jabs, Jim & Sharon Janz, Hugh & Sharon Little, Preston & Sandra Manning, Reg & Carol Petersen, Don & Anne Reimer, Rick & Chris Reimer, Malcolm & Marge Seath, Neil & Marlie Snider, Al & Sandra Stober, Philippe & Laura Vallerande, Don & Alma Voth.

PLC (President's Leadership Council)—5th Annual Retreat, May 12–14, 2005. (L to R) Jacques & Rani Gauthier, Abe & Lillian Friesen, Reg & Carol Petersen, Michael & Tanja Gibney, Rick & Chris Reimer, Bruce Etherington, Neil & Marlie Snider, Preston & Sandra Manning, Hugh & Sharon Little. Missing from picture: Jim & Sharon Janz, Heather Alloway.

Laurentian Leadership Centre—Home of TWU's leadership development program in Ottawa. The first group of 22 TWU students took up residence in September 2002.

Carmen Tomé attended B.C.'s prestigious Emily Carr Institute of Art and Design for three years. She has been commissioned to travel internationally and has a calling to the nations with a camera in her hand. Her photographic work has garnered over 30 awards including Photographer of the Year nationally and provincially with Professional Photographers of Canada. She is presently a member of the Master Photographers International where she has the designation of 'Master Photographer in Fine Art'. Renowned for adding painterly qualities to her photos, she says, "I am an artist who has used a camera as my medium for years." For more information on Carmen go to: www.carmentome.com

Against all odds… Trinity Western University: 1974 to 2006—to the praise of His glory

by Dr. R. Neil Snider

© 2016 by Trinity Western University

All rights reserved. No part of this publication may be reproduced, stored in a retrieval system or transmitted, in any form or by any means—electronic, mechanical, photocopying, or otherwise—without the prior written permission of

Trinity Western University
7600 Glover Road,
Langley, B.C. V2Y 1Y1
CANADA

Cover photo by: Carmen Tomé
Logo designed by George Pytlick

Publication data

Author: R. Neil Snider, 1938—
Title: Against all odds… Trinity Western University,
    1974-2006: to the praise of His glory

ISBN 978-1542682022

Contents

Dedicated to the praise of God's glory. . . . . *xiii*
Introduction . . . . *xv*
Acknowledgements . . . . *xix*

PART I • BEGINNINGS 1

1 The God of grace and miracles *2*
2 Growing up with a leader *6*
3 God's preparation for leadership *8*
4 Integrating faith and learning *11*
5 How Trinity Western began *14*

PART II • CASTING A FRESH VISION 21

6 My first visits to Trinity Western College *22*
7 Arriving on campus *29*
8 Facing the future as a Christian college . . . *38*
9 Curriculum expansion takes flight *43*
10 If Aviation, why not Business? *48*

PART III • A PERIOD FOR PLANNING 53

11 Developments in the new era *54*
12 The practice of planning *62*
13 The decision *67*
14 A pastor brings TWC's first computer . . . *72*
15 Amending our two-year charter *76*
16 Seeking the right to grant degrees *79*
17 Playing politics *81*
18 Developing 'Management by Objectives' . . . *90*
19 'A great door for effective service!' *95*
20 Expanding the vision for Student Life . . . *98*
21 New growth, new pressures: 1979-80 . . . *103*
22 Our first four-year graduates *111*
23 Crafting our Mission Statement *114*
24 TW's 'paragon of planners' *121*
25 Dreams, visions and plans *125*

PART IV • TRINITY WESTERN BECOMES A UNIVERSITY 131

26 Our academic and spiritual roots *132*
27 One final step to academic acceptance . . *139*
28 Meeting the AUCC in Toronto *143*
29 Perseverance pays off *151*
30 TWC becomes TWU *156*

PART V • BRINGING THE VISION INTO FOCUS 159

31 TWU as a faith-filled academic community . . *160*
32 CTP: our 'Critical Time Period' *164*
33 Dr. Don Page comes to TWU *167*

PART VI • LEARNING THROUGH TRAGEDY 173

34 Our aviation disaster *174*

PART VII • GROWTH THROUGH GRADUATE PROGRAMS 179

35 Graduate pastoral and theological programs . . *180*
36 ACTS: a bond of love, a passion for ministry . . *184*
37 Preparing Student Life for the 21st century . . *188*
38 Realizing 'Total Student Development' . . *193*
39 Athletics and leadership *197*
40 Launching the Nursing Program *202*
41 TWU's MA in Leadership *211*
42 TWU rated 'foremost in leadership development' . . *215*
43 TWU as a 'national learning laboratory' in Leadership Development *221*
44 TWU's Laurentian Leadership Centre . . *223*
45 TWU's scholarly research in the Dead Sea Scrolls . . *232*
46 Septuagint studies land in Langley *238*
47 'Christian Leaders in Residence' program . . *240*

PART VIII • MEETING NEW CHALLENGES 243

48 The Legal Challenge *245*
49 Stating our case *250*
50 The Court of Appeal *255*
51 'On the bird' *258*
52 'The heart of the king is in the hand of the LORD' . . *260*
53 A bridge to the future *271*

PART IX • EPILOGUE 275

Epilogue *277*
In the words of others… *281*
54 Remembering DRIME *282*
55 Redeemer Pacific College at TWU *285*
56 Canadian Institute of Linguistics at TWU . . *291*
57 Student, alumnus, administrator *295*
58 'Learning about myself by learning about Him' . . *297*

Gracing the entrance to the campus are the fountains in the pond beside the Salmon river that runs by the campus.

Dedicated to the praise of God's glory

When I retired from Trinity Western University in 2006, many friends told me: "You should write a book about the three decades when you were president of Trinity Western."

A few years later, many others, including some of the people who had caught the vision of "Total Student Development" with me at Winnipeg Bible College, and had also decided to come to Trinity Western College in 1974, who had worked and prayed with me as we watched God bring about the many miracles that allowed Trinity Western University to materialize—"against all odds"—began again to say, "Neil, you should write a book about those years."

By then, I'd had nearly a decade to reflect, and to see more clearly the pattern of God's plan at work.

God still has a plan. As always, He sought people through whom to execute His plan. But first, He needed to groom those people, to form them into instruments He could use in fulfilling His plan. Then He called them into something that He'd been preparing for a long, long time. Slowly at first, but then accelerating rapidly, it all began to come together.

As you will learn, especially in the later chapters, this school—Trinity Western University—has been carried by God far beyond anything we anticipated in the early days: in several important respects, it has become a leader among North American universities—perhaps the most important way was the restoration of biblical principles in education to the culture of the nation… and the church.

It's also important to remember as you read this book that to us, the most important thing was not the University, but what the University produces: as our Mission Statement clearly states "godly Christian leaders… serving God and people in the various marketplaces of life."

It wasn't always easy. It didn't just "flow together"; there were often obstacles, blockages and hindrances; and there were spiritual barriers—barriers we couldn't see, but could surely feel. However, beyond every barrier was the vision—sometimes crystal clear, sometimes misty; but always strong.

There was one method we relied upon to overcome obstacles: prayer. When we were humble enough to confess: "I can't do this—*but You can!*" and submitted enough to say: "Here I am; use me for Your glory!"— things really began to happen… things that we had previously thought "impossible", and even things we hadn't even thought about, suddenly became possible.

There was an amazing spirit among the people of Trinity Western during those three decades—a God-given spirit of optimism and trust; in most things and at most times, we knew we could trust one another, because we all trusted in God.

There is, and has always been, only one God: the God of Abraham, Isaac and Jacob; the God of the Bible. And when we knew we were in His hands, we trusted implicitly that His purposes were good; and we knew that, as Job said, *"no purpose of Thine can ever be thwarted."*[1]

We knew something really good was happening, and we knew that we were blessed to be allowed to have a part in it. I hope that these recollections and reflections—in which I have been greatly helped by many people who were also eyewitnesses of the glory of God's grace—will be an encouragement and a help to others when, inevitably, they encounter challenges in their efforts to live "to the praise of His glory."

---

[1] Job 42:2 (NASB)

Introduction

The phenomenal growth and development of Trinity Western University between 1974 and 2006 can only be attributed to the gracious provision of Almighty God. Recognition, often coming in ways and arenas that had previously seemed impossible, demonstrated that the very existence of this unique institution—a biblically Christian centre of higher learning in the arts and sciences—was, from its founding, an intention of the Sovereign Lord of the universe.

From the earliest days, even before the founders of Trinity Western had located the pasture that was to become our campus, they had understood God's intention that the focus of the vision was not on the institution, but on the people it would produce.

At first, the concept was to establish a junior college that could ground university-bound students in a biblical worldview—much as Canada's Bible colleges had always done, but also teaching liberal arts and sciences courses that would enable them to transfer credits towards a university degree.

As the years passed, the vision began to unfold like a maturing flower: it became apparent that to empower our graduates to serve in the incredibly diverse social, religious, and philosophical environments of our complex world, they would need to develop a well-honed capacity to think and lead from the perspective of a thoroughly biblical worldview. They would need to unravel information from many sources, parse it, and develop strategies for responses rooted in biblical faith.

To enable that, we would have to provide a full four-year degree program. More important, we wanted our graduates not merely to be effective workers in their chosen fields of service, but *leaders*. That meant that study and training for leadership had to be embedded throughout the educational process, both in the classrooms and extending out to all the multiple activities of university life.

God instructed the prophet Habakkuk to "*Write down clearly on tablets what I reveal to you, so that it can be read at a glance.*"[1] The thought is of a herald who can proclaim a message accurately and powerfully throughout a community. The sense of purpose and vision that animated Trinity Western from the outset was eventually crystallized into a powerful statement of mission:

---
1   Habakkuk 2:2 (GNT)

> *The mission of Trinity Western University, as an arm of the Church, is to develop godly Christian leaders: positive, goal-oriented university graduates with thoroughly Christian minds; growing disciples of Jesus Christ who glorify God through fulfilling the Great Commission, serving God and people in the various marketplaces of life.*

It took the four people who gathered to produce the initial draft of this statement only a weekend to complete their work; but then, over the next full year, the whole campus community added its voice, finalizing the Mission Statement that to this day guides the University. It has often been observed, in the years since, that the strength of this statement arises from its focus on outcomes in the lives of graduates. The processes of education are essential, and we worked hard to make sure that these were marked with excellence as well as faithfulness; but it is the results, as lived out in careers, service, and families of those who leave an institution, that are the true measure of its success.

Still more was necessary. A statement of purpose—even one as clear as this—had to be connected to an integrated set of principles for guiding the University in implementation of that vision. We knew that to bring such an institution into being in an otherwise entirely secular educational environment would also require:

- a biblical *Statement of Faith* to shape the worldview of a community of scholars;
- community standards; not as 'rules' but as a challenge and encouragement every member of the campus community—to faculty, staff and students—to live to please God in everything, and to build up one another in every aspect of personal development;
- a philosophy of holistic personal development—TWU's *Total Student Development*—that uses the university experience to help every student grow intellectually, emotionally, spiritually and relationally;
- a unique understanding of "curriculum"—something beyond the traditional academic definition, embracing everything that affects the personal development of all who choose the "Trinity Western Way." This term, in fact, looks back to the first-century Christian believers, who were known as "people of The Way."

One further unique feature of Trinity's development must not be overlooked. It was the consistent practice of planning, beginning with intentional goal-setting. Rather than simply maintaining the status quo, every department, division, and administrator at Trinity Western was challenged to prayerfully consider, in faith, what God might want to accomplish through all of us in each coming year. The objectives and goals of the major divisions were then reviewed by leadership at every level, and finally approved by the Board of Governors. The results shaped the agenda for each year.

Early in my own practice of leadership I came to the conclusion that senior leaders in a fast-growing organization should spend up to 70 percent of their working time engaged in futuristic planning. We were convinced of God's sovereignty, intent on envisioning His purposes, and willing to act together in faith. It's always gratifying to see God's unexpected provisions, and over the years God surprised us with His goodness on many occasions. It can be even more rewarding to see well-researched plans come to fruition—prayerfully developed and then implemented with firm resolve and faith.

As I look back today, I'm amazed and humbled at how God assembled an incredible community of people—leaders and planners, scholars and teachers—who came together with energy, faith, passion, and a great deal of hard work to fulfill the plans for building Trinity Western University. He revealed to us a plan—and we give to Him the glory which is justly His alone, for the results.

To relate the many miracles that brought Trinity Western into being is, of course, a remarkable story in itself. Equally interesting is the story of how God prepared the individual men and women through whom He enacted those amazing events; and how He brought them to our beautiful Langley, B.C. campus and then sent them far beyond.

This book is an attempt to entwine these stories: the events, God's unique preparation of the people, and the researched plans. I was privileged throughout these years to know colleagues and their families intimately, and to observe and participate in the amazing, action-packed—sometimes even scary—events that shaped TWU.

I have been so very pleased to have been assisted, in bringing to light the behind-the-scenes details of those miracles, by some of the very people whom God prepared and brought to Trinity Western to be a part of our history—which is really *His story*.

Acknowledgements

Above all else, this book is about the grace of our Lord; and to Him alone belongs the glory.

In this remembrance of the years from 1974 to 2006 at Trinity Western, you'll meet many of the people whom God prepared and used in this on-going story: folks who were devoted 'to the praise His glorious grace'. If we were to include *all* the names—hundreds of faculty and staff, thousands of students—there'd be no room left for the narrative!

It has been a privilege to live through the continuing miracle years of Trinity Western, but if it weren't for the urging of my friend, Arvid Olson, I may never have written all these things down. Arvid was the first senior executive to join me at Trinity as Director of Student Affairs. He is a man of God and was a pastor to our campus community for more than a decade with a heart committed to the discipleship and personal growth of each student. He recruited the Student Life staff we hired and laid the foundation for the emphasis on student development that is unique to Trinity even today. More recently, he gathered together the people and managed the resources for the writing and production of this book. My thanks to him for his love and friendship, and his commitment to Trinity Western.

Several of the executive leaders I worked with gathered over the last few years to remember and document Trinity's fascinating history. My thanks to five senior leaders who have contributed to the planning and the writing:

Dr. Guy Saffold has been my friend and closest senior advisor for 27 years. His creativity and giftedness in strategic planning and leadership, and his ability to collaborate and communicate ideas made him invaluable to our senior leadership team as we developed plans for the growth and mission of the university.

Dr. Craig Seaton came to Trinity at a crucial time in our history and carried a bill to the legislature that would give us full university status. His account of those events is recorded in later chapters.

My friend, Dr. Ken Davis, joined us as Vice President and Academic Dean with the credentials and the capability to guide our academic growth to university level, and to prepare Trinity for membership in the Association of Universities and Colleges in Canada (AUCC). He was also a leader in shaping the vision for the formation of the Associated Canadian Theological Schools seminaries (ACTS), and gave oversight to the establishment of Trinity Western's graduate programs.

Dr. Don Page came to Trinity Western with experience in both universities and the federal government. His passion and commitment for the University's mission statement contributed greatly to the rapid expansion of our academic programs, and especially to the focus on developing leaders for every field of study. He played a major role in the establishment of the Laurentian Leadership Centre in Ottawa, giving disciplined attention to the mission's charge to develop leaders for the marketplace.

Dr. Ken Kush came to us early in his career, joining the Student Life staff in their commitment to student development. He returned to Trinity after completing doctoral studies at UBC with a clarity of vision that refined our strategy and care for students in their learning years, and then resulted in a recognizable shift in student development in universities across Canada.

A number of others graciously contributed their recollections: Allan Kotanen, John Sutherland, Tom Bulick, Mike Walrod, Tom Hamel, students whose testimonials appear throughout the book, and many more whom you will meet along the way. Dr. Simon Moore, a student intern in the President's office during my tenure, wrote reflections on his personal experience of TWU—an example of what many other students might say.

Special recognition belongs to Ron Gray, who spent hours with me reading, writing and editing. His gratitude to God and his honour of the people and the story made possible the conclusion of the project, for which I am particularly grateful. Staff friends Arvid Olson, Allan Kotanen, Hazel Campbell, Joan Gleddie, and Dwight Johnson—who are as close as family—prayed and supported, read through draft documents and pulled together photographs. And thanks especially to Sylvia Stopforth, the Trinity archivist who assisted us greatly on this project.

Thanks to the marvelous faculty and staff who wrote the story with their lives, and to our board members, president's advisory counsel, and friends who supported us. We know something of the joys and sorrows of walking submitted to God, and committing ourselves to a community that is listening for His voice at a time when many people are not.

If your name is included here, please accept my thanks for the role you played in making this story fulfill God's vision for a biblically Christian university in Canada; and if it's not, please be assured that your contribution is recorded where it matters most: in the annals of the Kingdom of Him Whose glory has no end.

Closest to me of all have been my amazing family, who all became ministers with me and to me through God's grace. My wonderful wife of 45 years, Marlie, was my greatest support, friend, love and partner, a devoted mother to our children—and in the midst of an incredibly busy family life, a gracious hostess to the hundreds of guests in our home year after year. Marlie went to be with the Lord in 2005. In addition to the great debt I owe to her for our years together, the name "Marlie Snider Collegium" honours the students' recognition of the many very significant contributions she made to TWU's development; it was they who gave her name to one of TWU's first collegia—an institution that still does so much to enrich the social development of TWU students.

My children Dawn, Dean and Dana played a unique role, not only as exemplary students, but also by serving with enthusiasm and skill as ambassadors for the University as we travelled together, sang together, and shared together in telling the story of TWU. All three were leaders, each in their own way; and they became vital parts of the TWU community. I want to say to them, "Well done! Your father couldn't possibly love you more deeply or be more proud of all that you did during those years—and your even greater accomplishments in the years since."

It is my hope and my prayer that this retelling of the story of those 32 turbulent, amazing years in TWU's history will be an inspiration to those now tasked with carrying the vision forward; and that it will also be an inspiration for all who read it: for the history of TWU should provide ample evidence that if God has given you a role in building His Kingdom on earth, He is willing and well able to equip you for the execution of your tasks, ***for the praise of His glorious grace***.

I also want to thank my wife, Myrtle, for the grace and tolerance with which she accepted the challenge that writing this book required of our time. I consider this opportunity to be one of my most rewarding endeavours.

Special thanks to professional photographer and artist Carmen Tomé, for all the work she did in searching for requested pictures. Carmen's work may be viewed at www.carmentome.com. We have attempted to acknowledge the identity of all studio photographs. Wherever these are not properly credited, please feel free to contact the author or Trinity Western University.

Thanks to Bill Glasgow for his excellent editorial and digital design work; and to Helen Secco at ASM Printers for her continuous counsel in the process of preparing this book; and to TWU archivist Sylvia Stopforth for her availability, professionalism and knowledge in obtaining information and photographs for this book. Special appreciation goes to Jennifer Watton and Wendy Lees in TW University Communications for their help in searching for pictures and for their photography assistance.

Cherry Blossom Time at Trinity Western.

Courtesy of Carmen Tomé

PART I

Beginnings

Every gardener knows the routine: you plant, you watch, perhaps you water—and you wait. And every Christian knows it's God who gives the growth: the seed puts forth shoots that become a healthy plant; the plant flowers and bears fruit. And perhaps the greatest miracle of all is that inside that fruit is at least one seed, so the cycle can be repeated until the whole world becomes a garden...

—editor

1

The God of grace and miracles

Grace and miracles. From the time I was old enough to understand, I was taught that the God we worshipped was a God of grace and loving kindness, but also of power, action and miracles. By the time I arrived at Trinity Western, I had full confidence that there was a Higher Power who was actively working at this College, and I truly expected that God would accomplish great miracles there, that would change the lives of staff, faculty and students.

That thrilling sense of expectation was a lesson that I often passed on at Trinity Western, in student chapels. I wanted these young people to look forward to their year at Trinity with great anticipation and to expect to meet the God of grace and miracles. So I told them the story of a woman known as "Happy Anne".

Young Anne and her large extended family had traveled from Hungary, by way of Germany, to settle in a small farming community in Saskatchewan. They established homesteads, cleared the land, brought in machinery and cattle, planted crops and raised chickens. Money was scarce, but although they were poor, they were happy. They were devout people who feared God, and were loyal to their church.

Anne was an effervescent and curious child, who loved school and asked lots of questions. But when she was in Grade Nine, Anne contracted a rare form of tuberculosis that attacked her spine. She was soon paralyzed from her chest to her feet, and taken to a sanitarium in Saskatoon, nearly 100 miles away.

It was the middle of the Great Depression, and the sanitarium would seem primitive by today's standards. Indeed, it must have seemed to her more like a prison than a hospital. Above her bed was a frame about nine inches wide, and she was strapped to it to keep her from falling. The frame was bent back so that her head was lower than her shoulders. Another strap attached her neck to a 16-pound weight that kept her infected spine from touching the spinal cord. She could move only her head, arms and hands. She used a mirror to see around the room and pulled the chain on a single light-bulb to provide light during the darker hours.

As a young teenage girl, she must have felt very lonely when her parents had to leave her to return to the farm. But any sadness that she felt seemed to fall away as she began to discover the strength of her spirit and a will to keep living in spite of her circumstances. So she regained hope. As such, she became somewhat of a curiosity to others in the hospital, and many wandered by her door just to catch a glimpse of this remarkable girl.

About two years later, a God-fearing couple visiting her asked if she were a Christian.

"Well yes!" she responded, "Canada is a Christian country. Isn't everybody a Christian?"

They explained to her what I know so well to be true: being a Christian means having a personal relationship with God's Son, Jesus Christ. She asked, "How could I have Jesus as my friend?" They explained that God loved her, just as He loved them; and they had a very personal relationship with Him. Best of all, they told her that she could have that very same experience; and they left her a Bible to search out the truth for herself.

Anne was an avid reader with a keen sense of discovery. She was known to search through books when she needed answers to her questions, and the hospital staff had readily accommodated her curiosity by bringing her a variety of books. But the Bible was something new, and she savoured every page she read. She quickly gained the knowledge and confidence to fully believe that God had sent Jesus Christ into this world to be her Saviour, too. She later prayed with this couple, asking God to forgive her sins and prepare her to tell others that she now believed in the death and resurrection of Jesus Christ.

Centuries before this day, the Apostle Paul had written, "*If you openly declare that Jesus is Lord and believe in your heart that God raised him from the dead, you will be saved. For it is by believing in your heart that you are made right with God, and it is by openly declaring your faith that you are saved.*"[1] Anne took that verse to heart and it wasn't long before she was telling everybody about what God had done for her. Her joy was so evident that this young, helpless invalid soon became known as "Happy Anne."

She took every opportunity to tell her family, the hospital staff and any visitors about God's love, and how it had made such a difference in how she saw her situation. She flabbergasted the nurse who was opening her blinds one morning when she exclaimed, "What a beautiful day! I'm so glad to be alive!"

The nurse looked at her in disbelief. "How can you say that?" she asked. "Here I am, able to go wherever I want whenever I want, and I can't say that!" Of course,

---
[1] Romans 10:9-10 (NLT)

Happy Anne was more than ready to tell her how God had come into her life—and how that made all the difference.

Amidst her joy, Anne didn't know that doctors had told her family members that her health was failing and that Anne might not survive. But her pain and discomfort grew stronger, and one night, she prayed that the Lord might take her to be with Him. She then turned to her Bible and allowed the pages to open at random; it opened to Luke 13:10-12:

> "One Sabbath day as Jesus was teaching in a synagogue, he saw a woman who had been crippled by evil spirits. She had been bent double for 18 years and was unable to stand up straight. When Jesus saw her, he called her over…"

At this point, Anne felt the Presence of God enveloping the room, and the rest of the words seemed to leap from the page. She read aloud what Jesus said next:

"Woman, thou art loosed from thine infirmity."

Anne immediately felt the paralysis which had bound her for the last four years move down from her shoulders, through her body and right out through her toes! She began praising and thanking God. At that moment, Anne *knew* that God had healed her!

She unfastened the buckle that held the heavy weight around her neck and it went crashing to the floor. Nurses came running as she called out, "Praise the Lord! I'm healed! *I'm healed!*"

The nurses had never seen anything like this! They laughed, cried and rejoiced with Anne, as she asked to be released from the frame that had held her for so long. They tried to slow her down, as the doctors would have to give approval for any change in Anne's situation. But they finally agreed to release the straps holding her to the frame, and she rolled onto the bed, where they could make her comfortable.

When the nurses and other attendants finally left the room, she was too excited to sleep. She hadn't stood or walked for more than four years, but she could wait no longer. She put her skinny legs over the side of the bed and stood up.

She stood. It was a miracle! When she lay down again, she slept like a baby for the first time in years.

The next morning, before leaving her shift, the head nurse came to tell her, "I came in every break I had, to see whether you were dead or alive."

Over the next few weeks, doctors from the sanitarium and the local hospitals came to see Anne and examine her. Although the doctors were happy for Anne, they clearly wanted to find some concrete medical reason for her change in health. But there was nothing; and the doctors were utterly flummoxed as they wrote the following words on her medical record: *"This is a conundrum."* (Apparently, doctors are more comfortable diagnosing a "conundrum" than a "miracle.")

They agreed that Anne was to be released, but warned her, "You might be back in a couple of weeks, worse than ever; or you might be well a long time. You must be very careful. 'Rest and sunshine' is the best cure for tuberculosis. You should avoid stress of any kind. And you'll probably never have children." It was a confounding day for the doctors, but a glorious day for Anne, as she rejoiced with her family, friends and fellow patients. Many prayers and much praise were offered up to God that day.

The doctors had warned Anne that she should not expect too much from life, but the God of grace and miracles obviously had other plans. Over the next number of years, Anne married Elmer Snider, my father, and gave birth to two children—me and my sister, Caroll. She went on to live a joyous, rich life of productive ministry with my father, and was known as Happy Anne until her death at the grand age of 93.

Thus begins the story of my Christian heritage: I grew up in a family that only came together because of the miraculous power of God; and we lived daily with the confidence that nothing was too great a challenge if it was part of God's vision and will for our lives. Years later, when God led me to become the President of Trinity Western, I not only believed in God's miracles… I *expected* them.

Is it any wonder that I always told students, after recounting my Mother's story: "Do I believe in miracles? You bet I do! I've never doubted the sovereignty of God."

2

Growing up with a leader

While my mother's healing led me to live with the expectation that God could perform miracles in our lives at any moment, my father showed me the necessity of taking action and leading others to accomplish great things for God. Elmer Snider was a quiet leader of men; and over his lifetime, he led others as they planted churches in Alberta, and later greatly expanded the camping program that was a hallmark ministry of the Canadian Sunday School Mission (CSSM).

My father became a Christian shortly after meeting Anne, his wife-to-be. They married during the Great Depression, a time of massive crop failures and general economic collapse. Businesses went bankrupt and there was widespread unemployment. Many families lost all their material goods and economic security. In some cases, they even lost family members to a dark moment of despair.

In the midst of this darkness, local churches often became beacons of hope and light. Many seized the opportunity to offer daily Bible studies and other spiritual and moral support to the unemployed and their families. As a result, my parents became avid students of the Bible, and eventually felt God's calling to undertake the Great Commission to live out their lives by sharing their faith and welcoming others into the fellowship of God's people.

In practical terms, that meant our family moved from one place to another across Northern Alberta to tell others about God's goodness and what He had done for us. By the time I entered grade school, our family had made many good friends, and my parents had led in the establishment of a church and a small Bible institute. The latter was particularly significant in terms of sustaining and growing the faith communities my parents had planted, as these institutions ensured that strong teaching and fellowship would continue once they left.

As I grew older, I came to observe that the strength of my parents' ministry transcended the words that they spoke, to include who they were as Christians. They were very real, honest and sincere. Authentic. Their actions were in line with the words they spoke, and their intimate fellowship with God was evident as they prayed—it was as though they were talking to a friend, and those who joined them in prayer knew beyond a shadow of a doubt that they were in God's presence.

We eventually moved to Saskatchewan, where Dad ultimately became the Provincial Superintendent of the CSSM. It was as if this leadership position had been created specifically for my Dad, and for our entire family. We all became active in visiting people's homes and welcoming children to summer Bible camps or Vacation Bible School.

As I began to understand and participate in my father's ministry, I witnessed his bold approach to leadership and taking action. The CSSM had a central camp to serve the whole province of Saskatchewan; and although it was well-attended, it remained far too distant for many who lived in the more sparsely populated rural areas. My father decided it was time for a change in structure, and determined that those in outlying communities could come together to develop camping programs in their own districts. Over the next 11 years, under his leadership, six new campsites were established and 18 were operating each summer. These Christian camps offered life-changing and life-enriching opportunities for hundreds of children, teens, families—and me.

As a teenager and young man, I had multiple opportunities to join my father as I took on various leadership roles in his ministries: over time, I was active as a counselor and athletic director. But I now recognize that my most valuable leadership experience was the privilege of standing by my father and observing him—not just as a dad, but as an effective leader and a man of action. He prayed, he believed, and he motivated people to get things done. Witnessing this up close was exhilarating, rewarding and most of all, transformative in my own life, as I realized that leadership is a gift from God that can accomplish great things for His Kingdom.

3

God's preparation for leadership

The year was 1959, and I'd enrolled in a liberal arts program at United College, the institution that would later become the University of Winnipeg. To me, it represented a whole new world of studies and possibilities, and I relished the adventure. Without fully understanding how much time university-level academics would require, and with a bit too much youthful enthusiasm, I eagerly enlisted in a host of extra-curricular activities: I led the local church choir, took on a leadership role with Inter-Varsity Christian Fellowship, played hockey, and even provided the music for a Saturday morning radio broadcast. My enthusiasm for all of these activities seemed endless; but when I saw my first semester grades, I quickly realized that some adjustments were necessary!

While studying at Briercrest Bible College during the previous three years, I had developed a strong friendship with a girl from Toronto named Marlie Payne. We shared most of our classes and had been involved in many of the same choirs and music groups.

As often happens, it was only after we graduated that we decided to extend our relationship beyond being friends. We were each going our separate ways for the summer, so we knew it would be difficult. But Marlie had made a commitment to work with the Hawaiian Islands Mission that summer. She loved the school and the children, and before the summer term ended, she was asked to stay on as a teacher for the next school year. It seemed an unbearable time to be apart; but I was bound for university in Winnipeg, and we had not yet made other plans.

In those days before cell phones and Skype, we began a marathon daily letter-writing campaign. One letter every day for the next eight months! It was a marvelous preparation for the shared ministry God had planned for the next forty-five years we'd have together. We were married the next September, just before my second year at university began.

The 1960 school year had barely begun when Marlie and I were asked to provide leadership for international students through Inter-Varsity Christian Fellowship; a student ministry which had, at its heart, the clear directive of Jesus: that we who are committed to Him should become disciple-makers. We sensed our responsibility to invite others into our fellowship and, as a result, we opened our hearts and our home to the more than 400 international students in our academic community.

Those were wonderful years! Perhaps the only thing more wonderful than the opportunity to share our faith with these students was the growing intimacy Marlie and I together were developing with God. J.I. Packer's classic book *Knowing God* became a best friend, as Marlie and I sought to know God so intimately that we could receive and witness His transforming power in our own lives.

Seeking our future

With my graduation from university pending in Spring of 1962, we began to pray that God would lead us to where He wanted us to serve. Marlie and I still believed the notion that truly 'spiritual' people went to the mission field; so even though we didn't feel called to go anywhere in particular, we felt obliged to let God know we were willing to do so. As a result, we applied to the then-newly-formed CUSO (Canadian University Students Overseas), a non-profit development organization that had openings for university students to teach English in Nigeria. Our application was accepted and we began to think seriously about moving to Nigeria for the following school year.

However, God had a different idea. On our way back from the Urbana Missionary Conference, held during the Christmas break, Marlie experienced the first indications that she was pregnant. A visit to the doctor confirmed this, and informed us that our first child would be born in the summer—so Nigeria was out.

We decided to seek the advice of three missionary statesmen who came through Winnipeg that year. As expected, each asked us same question: "Where do you feel called to serve?" Our response was always the same—we simply didn't feel called to go anywhere.

But we did share with them our excitement about all the things God was doing to enrich our lives right then, through the ministry opportunities in which we were already involved. After considerable discussion, they each gave us similar advice: "You seem to have a significant ministry right here. Have you thought about the field of education?"

So I enrolled in the Department of Education at the University of Manitoba; and I wasn't disappointed. I loved the teacher education program; and more than anything else, I enjoyed working with other potential teachers. I knew that God had placed me there among them, and the month I spent teaching in two different high schools confirmed the wisdom of this move.

At the same time, I continued to lead the choir during worship services and to teach a class of lively, but serious, high school seniors at church. All of this, along with the gift of our happy baby, Dawn, made for a full and rich life. God was good to us and it seemed that life couldn't get any better.

Back to school—as a teacher

I'd never before applied for a job; work opportunities had always opened up at just the right time. Even now, as I faced the challenge of finding a teaching position, I received offers before I could even send out a resumé. Both schools that had been part of my teacher training program offered me positions, so I made the decision to teach English at Churchill High, and to serve as the choral director (two nights per week) at Winnipeg Bible College. It meant that I had an exceptionally heavy workload with planning, teaching, marking, music—and a new baby at home. But it was a marvelous experience, and both Marlie and I felt that this fullness of life was from the Lord.

Although I found great satisfaction in both positions, there was a special place in my heart for preparing college students to minister through music. Beyond the choir, I led several small singing groups that served in the College's extension ministry. We never thought of ourselves as performers, but rather as ministers of God's grace, who wanted to convey to others what we ourselves had experienced.

I had just completed a series of musical programs for Easter when I received a contract renewal offer from the high school—and also the offer of a full-time faculty position at Winnipeg Bible College. The faculty position would cover teaching various subjects in the arts—such as Psychology, Sociology and Cultural Anthropology—as well as continuing to direct the choral and extension music ministries. Once again, this meant that I would carry a very full load, and that I would do so with a considerable reduction in salary. But that didn't matter to Marlie and me; we'd become part of the WBC family, and prayerful consideration gave us the calm assurance that this was what God intended for us. I knew I'd miss the high school; but hadn't He always led us clearly in the past? So I turned down the high school contract.

But I wasn't quite so sure, once I actually arrived on the college campus to set up my office. I felt insecure. I asked myself, "What's a college professor supposed to be like? Can I really manage to prepare all this course work? Can I relate to college students?" I went back outside to sit in my car and review what I was doing. I felt so small for such a big challenge! I prayed, finally asking God to "give me whatever it takes to do what You want me to do." And then I said aloud, "I'm not going to try to be anyone else, Lord. I just want to be the person You created me to be. And if that's not good enough, I guess they'll just have to find someone else!" They didn't.

4

Integrating faith and learning

I never worked so hard as I did during my early days as a faculty member at Winnipeg Bible College! I was athletic, and on many occasions had played with all my might for the duration of a practice or game; but this situation seemed to require far more effort than that, and I soon found myself working day and night.

There were classes to prepare and teach, personal interactions with students (who, at that stage of my career, were often close to my own age), relationships to develop with faculty and—not the last nor the least—my family. There was also music, and we developed an exciting program of small group and choral music, which opened the doors to a variety of schools and churches.

'Total Student Development'

The students were eager to learn; and while this made for stimulating conversation in the classroom, it also served to challenge the professor—me!—on more than one occasion. But I was also asking probing questions: How did my Philosophy and Social Science courses relate to our Christian commitment? Were we really developing a Christian worldview? Were we even asking the right questions?

I wasn't content to simply pass along data from textbooks. What did the Scriptures say? Were we seeing things from God's perspective? I was becoming very concerned about the integration of faith and learning.

I also wondered how the whole experience was helping me and my students to become the unique persons God intended us to be. Without realizing it, I was moving into developing an educational emphasis on personal development. This was a big move from the idea that education is just a matter of transmitting knowledge from the teachers and books into students' heads! I wanted my students to engage in the process of discovery, and to utilize the kind of "useful knowledge" that engenders personal growth. But I was the only full-time professor in our curricular area of general studies; and my own university studies had always been presented from a very secular perspective. I needed help.

Fortunately, in God's marvelous timing, I was then asked to serve as Dean of Students. I saw it as an opportunity to further influence the personal development of students and I accepted the challenge with one condition—that I could replace the student handbook. At this point, it was little more than a rulebook, and I recognized that it could be better utilized if framed in terms of encouraging healthy student development. Instead of a negative focus—telling students how we wanted to restrict their behaviour—we should outline positive steps that encourage them to "build up one another" in all aspects of their lives.

Few people realized how significant this was. That is, until we began to recognize that the emphasis on Total Student Development had the potential to shape personal development through the entire curriculum, and virtually everything else in the WBC community. It brought a broader definition to the concept of discipleship—going beyond only spiritual development to include the development of our minds, attitudes, bodies and social relationships for the glory of God.

My major concentration in my undergraduate studies had been Psychology, and I was pleased to teach an introductory course in it each semester. It was a popular course, and it attracted a number of students, including graduates from other Bible colleges.

The first major topic in the course syllabus was "motivation". There was a variety of known motivators, including our drives and incentives. Factors like physical, mental, chemical, or social pressures could affect our motives; but so could religious and political values. I noted that there was one motivator that was not even mentioned in the text books—God.

How does God motivate us?

It opened my eyes to a whole new world of investigation. I knew that God could and does motivate us; but I'd never really considered *how* He motivates us. I knew and had experienced God's presence—His ability to communicate with me, to extend His love, goodness, generosity and wisdom—and so much more. Indeed, I was alive only because He had miraculously healed my mother. Scripture had long ago affirmed that "*...the LORD, whose very name is 'Jealous', is a God Who is passionate about His relationship with you.*"[1] In view of all this, I was motivated to please Him in everything I did; or as the Apostle Paul put it, I wanted to live "*to the praise of His glorious grace.*"[2]

This new understanding provided an immediate benefit to my course preparations: rather than focusing only on what the textbook said, I encouraged my

---
1 Exodus 34:14, (CEB)
2 Ephesians 1:6, (AMP)

students to ask what the Scriptures say about some of the topics raised by the textbook. This was more than an attempt to integrate faith and learning—we were being challenged to critique the standard psychological theories and interpretations, from a biblical perspective.

Leadership preparation

Later on, when I became the Academic Dean of the undergraduate program, I encouraged an increasing emphasis on what we came to call "Total Student Development"—the integration of students' intellectual, emotional, social, physical, relational and spiritual development—in *all* our academic offerings. This was reflected in a new format we developed for course syllabi. Even more important was our expanding conviction that we were all—students, faculty and staff—becoming, and helping each other to become, all that God intended us to be. We were *all* students; and we were also apprentices and mentors.

I'd obtained my Bachelor and Master of Education degrees, and those opened the door for me to spend a sabbatical at the University of Oregon as a student/apprentice at their Center for Higher Education Administration. There, my family and I flourished. We gained many lifelong friends and colleagues who helped us to gain a larger vision of life, and how we might contribute to it.

And we began to develop an expanded vision for Christian higher education in Canada. My PhD dissertation, *Goal-Setting Using Futuristic Techniques*, would later prove very useful to our planning processes at Trinity Western.

On returning to Winnipeg, I rejoined my colleagues; and in the next year, I was honoured to be asked to serve as Acting President while WBC's President, Dr. Kenneth Hanna, was on a sabbatical in Asia. God had been so good to me and my family; but I was also often reminded that "*to whomsoever much is given, of him shall much be required.*"[1]

Meanwhile, on Canada's West Coast, something very new was beginning to stir.

---

1 Luke 12:48b (ASP)

5

How Trinity Western began

The Trinity Western story is about faith in a God who can bring dreams and visions into reality when His followers are willing to trust him. The vibrant Christian University that Trinity Western is today represents the fulfillment of the dreams of thousands of godly men and women over more than half a century. Great dreams were turned into specific visions. Vision drove planning. Planning gave direction to work. But always the growth was from God, who can do "immeasurably more than all we ask or imagine."[1]

It's important to understand that the Trinity Western dream has always been of an institution whose graduates would be "to the praise of His glory" as they fanned out into careers of contribution, service, and witness to the Gospel of Jesus Christ. Trinity Western's founding President, Calvin Hanson, wrote:

> *"As is so often the case, not until after a project has taken shape and substance is it discovered that there were precursors—the bold dreams of people who saw the vision well before the time was ripe. In the case of Trinity Western College, these first dreamers were Reverend David Enarson and Dr. Robert N. Thompson."*

With coffee and a prayer

In 1952, David Enarson and Bob Thompson were travelling homeward from a conference and stopped at a small coffee shop in Provost, Alberta. Their conversation that day touched on many things; but the main subject was their deep feeling that Canada needed a distinctively different educational institution. They envisioned an institution founded, as the great universities of the past had been, on faith in the God of the Bible—but also a school whose courses would be recognized by provincial universities across Canada. No institution of

Robert N. Thompson

---
1 Ephesians 3:20, (NIV).

David E. Enarson

this kind existed in Canada at that time. If one could be developed, they felt, it would definitely be a dream worth pursuing.

So right there in the coffee shop, they knelt and prayed.

They didn't realize the significance of that day or that prayer until later; but God used it to create the first spark of a great vision. That spark ignited the first real flame five years later, in 1957, when an exploratory committee was established, with a mandate to study the possibility of turning that vision into a reality. Indeed, as they began, it was most likely viewed as a bold vision from one perspective—and an impossible dream from another.

Dave Enarson was a member of the committee; all members of the committee essentially came from a very small church group. Collectively, they had little experience in higher education and an authorized budget of just $500.

Still, with Dave's bold faith and confidence in the vision, it began to grow. In fact, Dave was envisioning a Christian university with up to 2,000 students as early as 1960—two years before Trinity Junior College was actually established. Further, Dave had no doubts about this when he passed this information on to the brother of the Chancellor of the University of British Columbia.

Apart from faith, the idea was, by almost any measure, unreasonable, impractical and maybe even unachievable. The path to success was unknown. The obstacles were mountainous. But a small team of believers had begun to gather around this dream; and in their faith, they were convinced that God could make possible things far beyond their own resources and abilities.

As a result, they began to plan, even as the vision was still emerging. To them, the plans were clear enough to inspire effort and motivate action. Obstacles were seen as encouragements to prayer. Limitations were simply challenges to greater effort.

As founding President Calvin Hanson later wrote, Trinity Western was birthed and grew "*On The Raw Edge of Faith.*" But it was faith with a plan!

The President, the Chairman of the Board, and the dairy farm

Members of that exploratory committee were visionaries, men of prayer and faith. They were not academics; but they recognized that they required people with solid academic credentials to achieve even their start-up goals.

Their unanimous choice for the school's first President was Dr. Calvin Hanson, an Evangelical Free Church missionary to Japan. In the years immediately following World War II, General Douglas MacArthur had decided the only way to plant democracy in Japan was to fertilize the soil with the Christian principles that had nourished democracy in Britain, the United States, Europe, Australia—and, of course, Canada. To accomplish this goal, General MacArthur had appealed to American churches to send missionaries to Japan, and the Hanson family eagerly responded through their denomination, the Evangelical Free Church of America (EFCA).

They had considerable success there until, as sometimes happens, God used an unusual circumstance to bring the Hansons back to the United States. Cal returned home one day to face the devastating reality that carbon monoxide from a flawed Japanese space heater had created serious physical damage to his family, and especially to his wife, Muriel. Suddenly, it was necessary for the family to return to the United States to receive extended medical treatment.

That near-catastrophe had, in God's grace, opened the door to a new chapter in their lives. Just as the fledgling Christian junior college in Canada was searching for its first President, the Hanson family returned to North America in search of God's new calling for them.

Calvin B. Hanson

Dr. Hanson served as President of Trinity Junior College, later Trinity Western College, until 1974. He then pastored a church in Langley, and often graciously returned to tell Trinity Western students how God had brought him and his family from Japan. The whole miracle-filled story is recounted in detail in Dr. Hanson's book, *On the Raw Edge of Faith*.

David Enarson, a bold visionary and a man of great faith, was named as the first Chairman of the Board of Trinity Junior College. He was a great storyteller, and was frequently a welcome guest speaker at Trinity Western chapel services, where he spoke with enthusiasm and conviction about what God had done to bring Trinity Western into being. He would tell students that this wasn't a situation that could be expected to move people to commit themselves and their families to what some others thought was a "hare-brained-idea" (in David's words). But rather, he said, it was very clear that God was working on their behalf. Over a period of time, he and his colleagues experienced many "coincidental" meetings, offers of provisions at just the right time, and even unexpected exercise of influence when it was most needed.

As just one example, it was David who carried the responsibility of searching out an appropriate property for the school. Two or three others joined him as they traversed B.C.'s Lower Mainland, looking for just the right place. There was no Highway One leading into Vancouver in those days, so the committee looked at places with easy access to and from the Fraser Highway, which was at that time the principal thoroughfare serving the Fraser Valley's growing population.

Some excitement was raised when an organization offered the committee 11 acres that seemed to have possibilities for a college campus. But Dave quickly realized that it would require at least three signs to get people to the campus. He tersely said, "If we're going to need three directional signs, we really ought to have the campus where the signs are." Furthermore, he was convinced that 11 acres wasn't nearly enough for the campus; so he counseled the group to take the donation, then "sell the property and use the money to buy what we need."

One piece of property that caught their attention was a dairy farm in northern Langley Municipality, between the City of Langley and the historic town of Fort Langley, British Columbia's first capital. They were drawn to it more than once; and on one occasion they ventured into the pasture for a better look.

I recall once, when David was telling this story, he pointed to a spot not far from the campus Chapel, where he had looked back to see Pastor Walter Cahill removing his shoes.

Dave had laughed and said, "That's not a smart thing to do, out here in the middle of a cow pasture!" But Pastor Cahill came back with a very serious response: "Brethren, I think we ought to be taking our shoes off. I believe we're walking on holy ground."

The Pastor meant what he said. So they all removed their shoes.

On that farm, the men liked what they saw. But the property wasn't even listed for sale, so this was going to be difficult. They prayed the next time they drove to the Seal-Kap Dairy Farm, all the way up to the large barn near the entrance. The dairyman came out of the barn and, as Dave recalled, it was hard to get the conversation started after they introduced themselves. But they finally told the owner their idea of starting a unique kind of college; a Christian liberal arts college.

Dave could cast a vision more passionately than just about anyone I knew. He talked about the values the college would impart, and the notion of whole-person development, and the value it would bring to the whole Lower Mainland, as well as much more! Then he asked the farmer if he would be willing to sell his farm for such a great cause.

The answer was polite, but curt: "Your project sounds interesting. But sell? Never in my life-time!" There was no room for discussion.

So the search continued, as the committee continued to present the vision to churches, politicians, business owners and land owners. It took time, energy and confidence—but David Enarson had all three in abundance! Relationships were built with those in B.C.'s educational establishment; and church leaders, congregations and their young people were challenged to consider the cause.

Just a few months later, the news came that Langley had lost a respected, long-time citizen: the owner of Seal-Kap Dairy Farm had a serious a heart attack and died, just outside the barn where he had been working. This was a sobering reminder of the brevity of life and the inevitability of death. An apparently healthy and hard-working man, actively involved in life, was here one day—and gone the next.

It was some time before the search committee even mentioned Seal-Kap Dairy Farm again. They hadn't forgotten it; but they wanted to be considerate of the widow who had so recently lost her husband. After several weeks, they decided to inquire about the property. They found out the widow had already sold it to two dairymen who wanted to protect and preserve it as valuable farmland.

David said later he knew he was "'way out of my league" in doing business deals, but two respected businessmen from the property search committee accompanied him to the appointment they arranged with the new owners. They were kept waiting until they were received finally with an unusual welcome, as one dairyman said to Henry Friesen: "I think I should know you."

"Well, you should," Henry replied. "As a boy, I used to milk cows on your farm."

The tone of the meeting changed instantly, as Henry's former boss jovially asked if he was going to "get smart, stop selling cars and get into the dairy business?"

Obviously, Henry was on a different mission, and as he introduced his friends, he asked Dave Enarson to share his ideas with the two dairymen. That was all it took to get Dave sharing the vision he so confidently articulated: in his mind, it was a carefully-developed plan that was going to be implemented, one way or another.

Dave spoke with great conviction; and the plan became more and more clear with the telling. At the same time, it seemed as if those who were hearing it began to wonder if there was some way that they, too, could participate.

Before Dave could finish the story, one of the partners asked if the three men would mind leaving while he talked with his partner.

I am certain that David and the others were praying that God would move the dairymen to partner with Trinity Western in some way.

When they gathered together again, the dairymen agreed that they would sell the property to Trinity Western for the very same price that they had paid for it: $150,000. Unknown to the dairymen, this was the exact amount that had been approved for the purchase of property! I know that news alone would have been sufficient to cause Dave Enarson to smack his fist into his palm with a hearty, "Praise the Lord!" But there was more.

In addition, the two dairymen would each write a $5,000 cheque to Trinity Western, as a gift. I can only imagine how Dave and his colleagues responded; if nothing else, I'm sure a chorus of praise and thanksgiving ascended to the Sovereign Lord who had so graciously provided, and done so in such a way that the glory was His alone.

This is not the whole story, of course. Although they now had $10,000 towards buying the property, they needed another $140,000. That left plenty of room for God to continue providing what we needed, and we knew that his provision, whatever it would be, would be "*to the praise of His glory.*"

ROBSON HALL—New junior residence providing housing for ninety-two third-year students, opened in August 1995. It was officially named Robson Hall on January 15, 1996, in honour of John and Ebenezer Robson, brothers who came to B.C. from Ontario in 1859. Between them they devoted seventy years of leadership to the province.

John Robson was an active and committed Presbyterian layman, a journalist, legislator, a "Father of Confederation". He became premier of B.C. in 1971. John developed a reputation for honesty and was known as "Honest John."

Ebenezer Robson served among First Nations people, and preached to gold miners and road builders. He played a leading part in reform movements of the day, and was twice elected to the position of President of the B.C. Conference of the Methodist Church.

TWU Archives

PART II

Casting a fresh vision

Tennyson wrote in The Passing of Arthur: *"The old order changeth, yielding place to new… lest one good custom should corrupt the world." When tasked with building on what someone else has created, we must be guided by a God-given vision. Often, however, that vision is unclear; as the Scripture says: "For now we see in a mirror, dimly…"* [1]

The prophet Daniel wrote that in the last days, "…many will go back and forth, and knowledge will increase." [2] *Today, the sum of human knowledge doubles every 12 months and IBM predicts that will soon be every 12 hours! In such a raging flood, it's important to remember that data are not information, information is not knowledge, and knowledge is not wisdom. Those who teach must steer the ship of education past Secularism and Materialism, to avoid shipwreck. People like historian Dr. Ken Davis helped all of us at Trinity Western to "…ask for the ancient paths, where the good way is, and walk in it;"* [3]

—editor

---

[1] I Corinthians 13:12 (NASB)
[2] Daniel 12:4 (NASB)
[3] Jeremiah 6:16 (NASB)

6

My first visits to Trinity Western College

I first saw Trinity Western College in January of 1974. My host was Rev. Kenneth Lawrence, the Chairman of the Board, a pivotal player in the history of Trinity Western—and, above all else, a great man of God. As I walked onto the campus for the first time, I was surprised by the beauty of the setting, the number of buildings—and the obvious potential for it to be so much more.

I had travelled to Vancouver for a conference, and it had been suggested to Ken Lawrence that he should try to meet with me while I was there. Naturally, I accepted his kind invitation to sit down and talk, not realizing that I would be meeting the Board of Governors.

Although I had never been to the campus, I was already very much aware of Trinity Western and its unique goals. In 1958, I'd spent my Christmas break from Briercrest Bible College with my parents in Vancouver. During that time, I had the opportunity to speak with Pastor David Enarson, a long-time family friend as well as respected Christian leader.

While attending a seminary in the United States, he'd been struck by the high cost of tuition for Canadians, and the near-total disconnect that existed in terms of what was being taught and its application to Canada. So when he returned to Canada, he had a "fire in his belly" to create institutes of higher learning with a biblical foundation. He had shared the seeds of his vision with others, and a preliminary committee had been struck to study the feasibility of creating a two-year Christian junior college.

The committee was only investigating possibilities, yet Dave spoke about it as if it were a certainty. Back then, even before Trinity existed, and while I was just beginning my studies, Dave challenged me to give prayerful consideration to the development of this institution, and the possibility of me joining it at some point in the future.

I told Dave that I would enroll if such a school ever existed, but he encouraged

Rev. Kenneth Lawrence with Neil Snider.

me to get a university degree, saying: "Who knows, God could very well bring you back here some day."

When I met Ken Lawrence in 1974, it was 16 years later—and I hadn't even given a thought to the notion that this could be that very day.

After we got acquainted, Ken Lawrence launched into a much more formal meeting than I had expected. He got down to business quickly, sharing the story of God's goodness in bringing Trinity Western to its present stage of development, which included many miraculous interventions that could be attributed only to God's gracious provision.

This wasn't new language to me. I never doubted the sovereignty of God, nor His willingness to show His grace and power to His children. After all, I'd grown up with parents who had always lived in His Presence.

But the subject soon changed, and Ken began to focus on the future. Dr. Hanson had encouraged the Board to look to the future, as he felt that he had fulfilled his founder's role at Trinity Western.

Having explained that, Ken started off by posing a significant question: "Dr. Snider, we know that you're not interested in joining Trinity Western. You've made that pretty clear. But if you were working to develop a thoroughly Christian university in Canada, what kind of institution would you want it to be?"

I hadn't expected such a clear and definitive question. Just two years earlier, I had completed my doctoral studies, specializing in higher education management and the sociology of complex organizations. During that time, I'd often thought that many of our Christian colleges in Canada would benefit from exactly the kind of work we were doing at the University of Oregon.

At the same time, I also was aware that the dominant perspective in the Canadian education establishment was that private universities did not and probably should not exist in Canada. Post-secondary institutions in Canada were all government-funded, and controlled in many ways by the Association of Universities and Colleges of Canada (AUCC, now called "Universities Canada") where academic freedom, the most important of the AUCC's criteria, trumped all expressions of religious freedom.

Although these comments clarified the challenges confronting Trinity Western, Ken urged me to continue, and to share my thoughts for the future.

I didn't realize that God had been shaping a vision of Christian education through my own experiences and education. But that night, I began to express a passionate desire to see something that didn't, at that time, exist in Canada.

I've always been grateful for the Bible college movement, and what has been accomplished by it through the years. They focus on discipling their students through the Scriptures, and mentoring them to know God intimately: to love Him, and to serve Him by serving others, as a life-long goal. Their stated purpose—their mission—is primarily to prepare people to become pastors and missionaries. Students have also been trained there to serve as directors of Christian education and music.

I'd been part of such communities for many years—not only as a student, but as Director of Music, Professor of Social Sciences, Dean of Students, and Dean of Faculty. I was at that time also serving as Acting President at Winnipeg Bible College, while Dr. Ken Hanna was on a sabbatical, teaching at the Asian Theological Seminary. We were working to increase the number of liberal arts courses for which we could transfer credits from WBC to the University of Winnipeg. If students planned their course choices carefully, they could receive as much as two years of transferable credit for studies at WBC.

Still, there were major concerns. A high percentage of those attending Bible colleges weren't opting for Christian service or ministry. Students who chose to become physicians, nurses, teachers or engineers, for example, would have to start vocational preparation all over again. On the other hand, if Christian students decided to skip Bible college and go directly into a public university, they'd miss the discipling process that could enrich their lives and service—although they could still benefit greatly, even on a secular campus, as I had done, from ministries like Inter-Varsity Christian Fellowship.

With all this in mind, I tried to address the specific question Ken Lawrence had put to me:

"I'd like to see a fully Christian university in Canada," I said. "One that would put God first. Its charter should boldly state the university's faith foundation, and it should include a holistic student development program. I'd want it to have highly-qualified faculty, who would not only model the Christian life, but would also each have the ability to speak from their own foundation of faith, while honestly and fairly presenting varied views of the data.

"Secular universities are as committed to their worldview as Christians are to theirs. So it's important to recognize that the observable data of science and history are the same for both worldviews; it's their worldview that determines how each interprets the data.

"Above all, such a Christian university should have a reputation for excellence—for nothing we do in Christ's name should ever be second-rate!"

Having just returned from Washington DC, where I'd met a judge and a number of other Christian professionals—all of them Wheaton graduates—I added, "Like Wheaton College, which not only has graduates in high places, but also many serving people around the world in all walks of life.

"At the same time, I'd like it to be an institution that bears the characteristics of our most effective Bible colleges—where a warm spirit of fellowship exists, and a strong emphasis is placed on disciple-making and building up one another. In other words, it should have a reputation for being engaged in both the Great Commission and the Great Commandments."

While I'd never visited Wheaton College or Biola University, I knew them by reputation, and I named both of these as desirable models for a Christian university in Canada.

Ken Lawrence then led a lively discussion; as I later learned, it was an aspect of leadership in which he excelled. In the end, we all went away praising the Lord for the freedom to discuss things so openly. It had been a long evening, but we all left with a new vision of what might happen at Trinity Western College in the days to come.

A second look

Having given words to my vision for Christian education, I later wondered how we at Winnipeg Bible College (today called "Providence College"), might move closer to the vision that I had just shared at Trinity Western. As Acting President at WBC, I'd seen many changes that had been in the making for months. It was a great community, and positive expectations for the future were gaining momentum. We were in a new and recently acquired campus; student numbers were growing; and significant curricular additions and restructuring aroused excitement about the future. Several young, well-qualified professors had been attracted, with hope for a long-term commitment to the programs and people at WBC. We were on the move!

A few weeks later, I received a letter from Ken Lawrence—and I could hardly believe what it said: Apparently our conversation had stimulated a great deal of interest, as well as a unanimous decision to ask me to prayerfully consider becoming the second president of Trinity Western College!

I responded almost immediately… by declining. I was grateful for the opportunity and would continue to pray about this, but Marlie and I were committed to WBC for the long term, I said.

At that time, I had my hands full. There was a pending WBC Board meeting and a special lectureship featuring Dr. Jack MacArthur, a pastor and radio Bible teacher from Eugene, Oregon, who also happened to be the father of the well-known author, John MacArthur. Dr. Jack had been our pastor when we lived in Eugene, and I considered him to be a personal mentor. The night that we hosted him for dinner was the first real opportunity we had to share our prayers about leadership at Trinity Western College.

Dr. Jack hadn't heard of Trinity Western, but he listened with rapt attention as I shared the glowing picture that I had gained from my visit. He responded with sincere excitement by saying, "That sounds like a fantastic opportunity! It's very possible that you could be at the ground level of a movement that would change the face of education for a whole nation!"

He then suggested that we really should consider David's thirty-seventh Psalm, *"Delight yourself in the Lord, and He will give you the desires of your heart."*[1]

My reflex response was that I really had no desire to move from a place to which God had so clearly called us. I was pretty sure Marlie agreed. But once again, my mentor offered a strong word of wisdom, saying, "God often has mysterious ways of *changing* our desires."

It seemed as though God was telling us, through Dr. Jack, to think again. So we did. But there were frustrations. We had been asked to pray about the offer, yet word somehow slipped out from British Columbia that we were already considering a move in that direction. Friends and curious acquaintances tried to help us

---

[1] Psalm 37:4 (NASB)

in our decision, yet it seemed that we'd hardly had time to consider it, let alone to do so quietly and prayerfully.

I decided to call my long-time friend, Dr. Kenneth Hanna, WBC's president, who was still on sabbatical leave at the Asian Theological Seminary. To my surprise, he was already shaken by inaccurate news that had reached him, even though no decision had been made. He clearly wanted me to stay with WBC.

I had to make a decision.

That night Marlie and I prayed earnestly! We finally concluded that we were willing to visit Trinity Western if invited, even though we had not yet seen any statement of an official search, nor indications about what expectations were attached to the position.

Looking again

It wasn't long before communication began to flow back and forth from west to east and back again. I learned more of the history and challenges of Trinity Western and ultimately received an invitation to visit the Langley campus again. I agreed to meet the search committee in March, and soon began to anticipate (with some trepidation) meeting the whole college community. Marlie and I had resolved that whatever happened, we would delight ourselves in the Lord. After all, we wanted to do His will and, as in the past, we could expect to receive from Him the desire of our hearts.

We just did not know what that desire would be.

I had a very different feeling about my second visit to the campus. The temperatures in Winnipeg for the whole month of February had never risen above ten degrees below zero, so the green grass and majestic mountains were a welcome sight! Everyone was gracious as I met with various committees and responded to their questions. I learned, for the first time officially, that there *was* a search committee and that they had a list of four key qualifications for the second president of Trinity Western College. According to that list, the candidate should, preferably:

1. have an earned doctorate (in a relevant field);
2. have academic administrative experience;
3. be a member of the Evangelical Free Church; and
4. be a Canadian.

There was no specific discussion of these criteria, but as I reflected on them, I found it amusing to reflect that I was probably the *only* person who met all four!

As I attempted to discern God's will, I thought back to the first day that I had been at Trinity Western. Now, Dr. Cal Hanson, my current host, was gracious and encouraging as he introduced me to various people, and I had thought to myself, "How could I ever fill the large cowboy boots of this godly and divinely-chosen founder of Trinity Western?"

There was only one possible answer for both then and now: If I were to be chosen, I would just have to be myself and trust God for the outcome!

There was to be one more visit, this time to bring my family to visit the campus; and then I was expected to make a decision. But uncertainties still remained. On returning to Winnipeg, we placed the matter of housing before the Lord by listing our home for sale.

Our Realtor came on Friday evening and recommended a selling price that he acknowledged was high for the market, but could still be obtained over time. Considering that housing in the Vancouver area was considerably higher-priced than in Winnipeg, we agreed. On Monday morning someone came to see the house, and by that evening we had an offer that was $4,000 *above* our asking price!

At that point, we finally felt assured that God Himself was calling us to Trinity Western College.

7

Arriving on campus

It was an exhilarating trip—across the Prairies, through majestic mountains, and past scenic lakes and rivers. Travelling this time in our trusty tent trailer, rather than by rail, added to the adventure, as did the sightings of various animals in the province that was to become our new home.

We arrived on campus in early July of 1974. But the furniture movers did not. In fact, we soon learned that we would be waiting at least three weeks for our furnishings and other chattels. So another "first" was established as friendly staff began to set up sleeping arrangements for our whole family in the student residences. Our orientation to the Trinity Western campus was about to begin.

Meeting the people

It was a pleasure, on arrival, to meet President Hanson and Dr. Robert Thompson once more. Board Chairman Kenneth Lawrence and his wife were quick to offer any help we might need, as did Dr. Leland Asa and his wife, Alice, who had already become our accommodating Realtor.

Leland Asa

Most important on this occasion was our meeting with the people who had become members of this first-of-a-kind community in Canada. Those who were nearby during this summer break had prepared a wonderful welcoming party. Whole families came to a picnic in a nearby park, where children could play and adults began to get acquainted. There seemed to be a spirit of anticipation, probably on the basis of God's miraculous provisions for the community in the past.

At the same time, on this informal occasion there was an element of regret. Goodbyes were being said among members within the College family—friends who had been called by God to this unique educational ministry. Now, some were retiring; others were moving on to new positions elsewhere.

Among the long-serving leaders who were leaving was Benno Friesen, who'd just been elected as the Member of Parliament representing White Rock, a beautiful coastal city next to the 49th parallel in the southern part of Metro Vancouver. He and his wife, Marge, were among TWC's original founding "family" as professors of English and Music; and he had also served tirelessly in public relations, student recruitment, student life, and much more. Now they were to become the first to lead TWC people into politics.

Dr. Leland Asa (called "Lee" by his friends), the College's respected Academic Dean, was to become Professor of Psychology at Westmont College in California. He planned to stay on for the fall semester at TWC; but his departure would leave a vacuum in the leadership team; and his wife, Alice, would also be missed as a member of the faculty.

One other strategic administrator had already left a few months earlier. He had left a lengthy and carefully tape-recorded message, which Dr. Hanson quietly left for me in his desk drawer. This former Finance Director had told Dr. Hanson that, for all practical purposes, Trinity Western College was already bankrupt! His recommendation was that the College should be shut down for a couple of years, in order to expand its financial base, and re-establish its credibility.

An unwelcome challenge

But even before the official installation of its second president, Trinity Western College was alerted by the denominational conference of a major and utterly unexpected challenge to its Canadian School. Our sister college, Trinity College in Deerfield, Illinois (today Trinity International University) was bringing to the conference a recommendation that posed a serious problem for TWC. I was asked to join Trinity Western's leaders on campus to meet the American consultants—who had, until then, neglected to consult TWC about the implications of their report.

Trinity College in Illinois was asking to become independent of the denomination, on the assumption that a broader financial base could then be developed. But fearing that churches in the denomination might then redirect their financial support to TWC, they had added a recommendation that TWC should also be expected to become independent. That move could have brought the history of the young Canadian college to an early and untimely end!

In fairness to the president-elect, the TWC Board asked for my opinion. We had to produce a counter-proposal—or at least request more time to respond.

Comparatively, our potential student numbers were few; our churches were small; and Canadian higher education organizations had neither the time nor the desire to even consider, let alone endorse, any kind of private university or liberal arts college—especially when the government of B.C. was at that time beginning to pour money into a chain of new taxpayer-funded community colleges across the province. This was definitely *not* the time for the denomination to abandon this aspiring and unique Canadian college, which God had so miraculously brought into being! Furthermore, who ever heard of a consultant's report including—without apparent research or an on-site visit—recommendations that could so significantly alter the future of another college, in another country… solely on the basis of their findings about a four-year college in the United States?

It all seemed rather odd; in June 1974, at the same conference that had ratified the appointment of a second president for Trinity Western College, the decision was made to allow the Canadian school time to respond to the Deerfield college's recommendation. TWC could now move on to establish its own direction—and ultimately, its God-ordained destiny.

We were grateful for a statement by Dr. Cal Hanson, who was greatly respected in the EFCA, that made it clear that any proposal to cut Trinity Western off from the founding denomination was unworkable.

Taking stock

Here we were, still in our first weeks on campus, and it was already time to take stock. The people were committed; but the challenges seemed to grow by the day. TWC had only received a temporary reprieve from the threat of losing our position as a member of our founding (and funding) denomination. The three-person Cabinet was now composed of a Dean (who would be leaving soon), a voluntary Business Manager (who was primarily our Personnel Director), and the newly-elected President.

There was also an undercurrent of concern about the financial situation. Dr. Hanson said TWC's payroll had always been met; but special arrangements were now apparently being made with our bank to cover expenses for the coming month (August). There were still vacant faculty and staff positions, and every day, prayers were being lifted for an increased number of students—and for Student Life staff to work with them.

There was no question about it: The people of Trinity Western College were indeed living "On the Raw Edge of Faith", to quote the title of President Hanson's book about the College's founding. Now, an altogether new reality had begun to set in. We were facing a daunting challenge. How could we best "get moving" together?

A welcome visit from Ken Lawrence, Chairman of the TWC Board, brought some relief. It helped to re-focus our vision on what God was going to be doing in the days ahead. Ken had come specifically with the message that the Board hoped the new President and his family would take time to visit constituents along the West Coast and in Southern California, from where many students had always come, and where a large number of supporting churches were situated. Not only could we get to know these people, but perhaps we might learn more about what God had in mind for TWC.

Visiting some constituents

We looked forward to meeting some of our American constituents. They were waiting to meet us, and we enjoyed fellowship with all these new acquaintances—many of whom would become long-time friends, and faithful College supporters. This was a welcome opportunity.

Pastors and church leaders, alumni and their friends arranged for us to visit in their homes. They took us to family camps, where our children could spend time with children their own age. On many occasions, our hosts listened to the stories of this Canadian family called by God to serve in their unique Christian college. It didn't seem at all like a hardship to stay in beautiful cottages and have opportunity to water-ski and surf. Still, we all knew we were here for a much more significant purpose. We sang together as a family in churches, and we were honoured in knowing that God had called us to be part of Canada's first evangelical Christian liberal arts college in the 20th century.

On our last such visit that summer, we began to see what God might have in mind for Trinity Western. Speaking at the Evangelical Free Church in Fresno, I not only had the opportunity of meeting a number of alumni and several supportive constituents, but also the sheer joy of sharing our emerging vision for Trinity Western College.

The message wasn't particularly profound; but the passion we shared for developing godly Christians in Canada seemed contagious. What we envisioned was preparing not only those who would go into vocational Christian ministry, but also those who would find themselves called by God into the wider vocational world, where the evangelical community in Canada was not yet intentionally making much contribution. Yet in our emerging vision, every occupation was potentially a Christian calling, if the person in it was adequately prepared and grounded in the faith.

The response to this presentation was positive. One man in particular seemed to understand the notion of God's calling to serve the Kingdom in a secular vocation; and he asked whether Trinity Western had a business program: "I'd be happy to have my son attend a school like yours, but I really want him to go into business with me. Does your college offer a business program?"

He may have guessed my answer; for in the early '70s, liberal arts colleges didn't usually include vocational programs of any kind. But it had occurred to me that Canada didn't even have liberal arts colleges, apart from university affiliates. In B.C., tax-supported community colleges—which by definition included vocational programs—were beginning to be strategically located across the province. But Trinity Western was unique. It had been established after the pattern of American junior colleges in the purest liberal arts tradition. In Canada it might have been called a "university-college".

It was then that I began thinking more about our future. Certainly, many people in our constituency were entrepreneurial business and professional men and women. Many of them came from farming communities. They desired to give their children Bible studies; but Bible colleges and institutes at that time could guarantee little or no transfer credit to Canadian universities. To have graduates start all over again for a degree relevant to a business career seemed much too time-consuming and costly.

This was a dilemma I understood well. After three years of Bible college, I'd received no credits I could transfer to the University of Winnipeg; so it took three more full years for me to earn a Bachelor of Arts degree, and another two for a Bachelor of Education. Although I was already teaching, two more years were necessary to complete a Master's degree. Could Trinity Western meet this kind of special need? Why not consider adding business courses to our undergraduate curriculum? Amazing! Without realizing it, we were beginning to raise our eyes to "the various market places of life", as our still-to-be-developed Mission Statement would one day express it.

It was a joy to meet Ted Smith again when I visited Fresno the next summer. I wanted him to know that we *were* introducing a business program, and had already brought the new leader and his family to campus. He was indeed pleased. But then he added, "My son is only seven years old! So you'll have to wait a few years for him to attend." Ted Smith, a successful business leader, came to our campus several years later and spoke to the Business School. He also established a significant student scholarship.

A first cabinet meeting

Returning to campus, we could soon realized that the rate of activity had increased immensely; our family had to move into our new home, and I was quickly pulled into the new year's activities.

Fortunately, it had been arranged that our founding president, Dr. Calvin Hanson, would remain on staff until the end of August, 1974. He'd graciously vacated his office to accommodate his successor, and stayed accessible during the leadership transition. His knowledge of the College's history, and of the people who had shaped it—along with his confidence that the whole project was God's doing—made his continuing assistance of great value. He was also pleased to have recently welcomed two experienced senior leaders who would become God's answer to the need for a renewed administrative structure: the two Bobs—Bob Swanson and Bob Thompson.

Bob Swanson was an experienced businessman, who with his wife Melba had recently moved to British Columbia from California, where he'd been the Mayor of Burbank. His specialty was organizational and personnel management. Dr. Hanson had challenged a number of such early retirees to serve the Lord at Trinity Western as "dollar-a-year" volunteers who could make a considerable contribution to this growing venture. Bob jokingly demanded his lone dollar in each of the next three years—a total of $3 for 36 months' hard work!—and with his expertise in the areas of personnel and direction, we were able to restructure the President's Cabinet and to provide considerable structural improvement.

Academic Dean Dr. Lee Asa asked for an immediate President's Cabinet meeting. It was a much smaller group than I expected.

At its first meeting of the Fall semester, the Board was to learn that a "structuralist" administrative philosophy would be employed. This management philosophy suggests that having good people is not enough for the administration to work well. It must also be structured so that those people can work together in the most effective manner. The senior administrators were doing their very best to analyze TWC, and to decide how it might best be structured to get done the work that so obviously needed doing.

One of the changes was to expand the Administrative Committee, formerly known as the Cabinet; it would now include, in addition to the Dean and Business Manager, the Director of Student Services, the Librarian, the Director of Athletics, and also the President of the Student Council—an innovative departure in academe.

The fourth member joining us at this very important meeting was Dr. Robert Thompson, Director of Development, who reported on the distressing financial situation with our bank, among other things. It was a lot of challenging information for a new leadership team to absorb. The agenda was like a forecast of cloudy weather—and perhaps with heavy rains to come. A very welcome time of prayer together initiated our working relationship; the responsibilities were heavy, but everyone was intent on having the mind of Christ in every situation.

There was definitely some good news, too. The Registrar's report indicated that enrollment applications were up from the previous year, and more were still coming in, even at that late date. The impact of this on the financial report offered some relief, at least during the waiting time for the next inflow of tuition. And the concern and prayer about needed staff for the new school year produced a series of stories of God's provision of the needed people to our campus. Maybe there wasn't a lot to shout about, but the spirit of optimism was obvious. Many had learned from experience, "Little is much when God is in it."

Student Life staff

The response to the need for trained staff was almost unbelievable. A number of student leaders from Winnipeg Bible College had begun to pray, several months earlier, about the decision that the Snider family had to make. They actually felt like active participants in the process of discerning God's call for us and for Trinity Western. As they learned more about the vision of TWC, several of them also began praying about whether God might be calling *them* to offer their developing leadership skills to this young and growing institution.

Among these were Allan Kotanen and Dwight Johnson, two young men who had been active student leaders together at WBC and in seminary. It began when Dr. Robert Thompson visited Winnipeg Bible College and shared the stories of God's miraculous establishment and development of a unique Christian liberal arts College called Trinity Western. When challenged, Allan and Dwight began to pray about it. But both were anticipating marriage, and of course had to confer with their fiancées; the timing didn't seem quite right for a move west and a new job. However, when I was asked to take a return trip to Trinity Western in June for a quick meeting about the serious challenge that TWC was facing from Trinity College in Illinois, both Allan and Dwight asked if they might accompany me, to learn more. In short, both were very interested in Trinity; interested enough to pay their own way to visit the campus.

It was on the return flight that Allan talked seriously to me. He had completed college and the first two years of the seminary program, but he sensed the call of the Lord quite clearly. His problem though, was that he and Sylvia, who was also a student, were committed to being married, probably the next summer (although he hadn't yet asked for her parents' blessing). He knew that they would sorely miss each other and their vision of being in ministry together. But that was not a 'stopper' for him. He'd already decided that if God called him, he would certainly come to Trinity Western now, regardless. On the other hand, knowing the pressures on Student Life staff, he wondered if a year later might be better. He had worked with me for more than four years at WBC; and really, he was, without actually asking, seeking my advice.

It wasn't like me to be so directive, but for some reason I was moved to respond to my friend frankly: "I think that if you're really serious about joining Trinity Western at this critical stage, you ought to consider getting married first. I know Sylvia and her family well, and I know Sylvia could be a great help to you. However, the Lord can sustain you, one way or the other."

The follow-up of this conversation was that Allan, upon his return to Winnipeg, set up an appointment with Sylvia's missionary parents. For them, as for Trinity, this was a matter for serious prayer. As much as they would have liked to see Sylvia complete her program, they could see that this seemed to be a definite call from the Lord.

Five years later Sylvia's parents, Jackson and Ella McAllister, also decided to join the Trinity Western team.

Both couples, Allan and Sylvia Kotanen and Dwight and Joanne Johnson, were married during the summer, in time to be in Langley to welcome incoming students. At the last minute, Allan was asked to accept a vacant major role: to serve as the Director of Student Services. David Kuehl, from southern Manitoba, became the senior counselor for men. Linda Bergen, from northern Manitoba, became the senior counselor for women students. Dwight took on the role of Church Relations and fundraising, and eventually also taught a business course for several years. In total, twelve experienced student leaders joined our ranks, working in the business office, the print shop, the library, and with food services and as secretaries, as well as serving in Student Services.

Without question, the timing was critical. The need was crucial. Once again, as He had provided so often in the past, God sent the kind of winsome young people who would make a lasting imprint on the life of Trinity Western College. They were remarkable leaders: mentors and disciple-makers who were willing

Bruce Traub, Tom Bulick, and Jackson McAllister (right).

to be servant-leaders for the long haul. Dwight, for example, stayed the course for thirty-eight years.

Recently Allan Kotanen publicly affirmed that there was a very deep sense of calling from God among this group: "I can clearly remember the first faculty/staff gathering in August, 1974. We met in the student lounge, and I recall sharing with this group that I was absolutely confident in God's leading to TWC. Maybe it was a bit naïve, given the challenges that lay ahead; but it was an honest affirmation about the specific leading of a loving Father. Now, 40 years later, His faithful leading remains constant." Allan is presently the longest-serving employee at Trinity Western University.

The members of the original group that came at the beginning of the New Era were, in practical terms, the second president's first "interns". Included were Linda Bergen, Freda and Clyde Bostrom, Edlyn Hebert, Joanne and Dwight Johnson, Sylvia and Allan Kotanen, David Kuehl, and Linda and Paul Schmidt. Clyde Bostrom was the artist who drafted the Trinity Western College logo that was prominent for several years prior to the miraculous achievement of reaching university status. Who would have guessed that these people would be able to set the whole tone of the school as it became a full-fledged Christian University?

8

Facing the future as a Christian college

Change is never easy, but thinking of it as "transition" makes it somewhat easier. But even then, there are two ways to go. Preferably, people will think fondly of the "good old days" as the basis for even brighter and more rewarding accomplishments. Fortunately, there was great respect for Trinity Western's founders, who had always put God first, and gave Him full credit for the remarkable things that had happened. On that foundation, the local community and the constituency in general anticipated great things to come.

A number of new young leaders brought a swell of positive expectations concerning where we might go next. Though neither the new President nor the burgeoning staff had any major discussion about a four-year program, we all discerned, upon arriving, that thought already had been given to the idea. The Fall Convocation announced that the second president would address the topic "*Facing The Future As A Christian College.*"

"This evening," the Board spokesman said, "has been set aside to mark a highlight in the history of Trinity Western College—the beginning of its second major stage of development."

The new President's installation

R. Neil Snider

service was held October 4, 1974. It was a great honour to present a growing vision to such a wide range of people. Government representatives, leaders from other universities and colleges, as well as churchmen, parents and alumni came to wish Trinity success, and to catch whatever vision might be cast.

It was exciting to review what God had done in the first twelve years, and then to suggest that we ask ourselves, as a college community: "What must we do to realize our hopes for the second stage of the development of Trinity Western College?"

Casting a fresh vision

Without question, and above all else, we must retain our distinctive purposes. That appeared obvious; but we knew many schools hadn't given it much creative thought. So in my installation message, I noted that a 1969 study by Ralph Keeton and Conrad Hillberry, *Struggle and Promise: A Future for Colleges*, reached the conclusion that "to be unique is to be strong." The finest colleges, they said, "are those that stand for something, and know they so stand." Three of the finest colleges examined closely, of which two were Christian colleges, including Wheaton—were "noted for devotion to the conservative, Bible-based approach to knowledge, even in the sciences." (Our first President, Dr. Cal Hanson, and Dr. Dean Enoch Mattson, were both graduates of Wheaton, and had on occasion labeled TWC as the developing "Wheaton of Canada"—*i.e.*, a desirable model.) Unfortunately, the study concluded that most church colleges, (and colleges in general, for that matter) had no such centrality of mission. However, this was our opportunity to publicly state that Trinity Western College would indeed continue to develop a distinctive mission.

Ultimately, several summary statements were included:

- **TWC consistently affirms the absolute sovereignty of God.**
  That is, in fact, the most relevant thing a church-related college can do. It has traditionally provided a clarion call to both social and personal wholeness. The integrating idea of the individual determines the character and direction of the community.

- **TWC has answers to the societal and personal** *search for meaning in life.*
  It's important to let the world know that Trinity Western encourages everyone in the community to know Jesus Christ personally, and to become a Christ-follower. The rhetoric may be challenged; but it's impossible to refute the example of those who live consistent lives characterized by deep-seated joy and peace, even in the face of adversity.

- **TWC fosters a concern for *academic excellence.***
   From its earliest days, TWC has upheld tenets outlined in the *Harvard Report of General Education in a Free Society*: "To think effectively; to communicate thought; to make relevant judgments; to accept certain value commitments, including intellectual commitments of respect for learning and tolerance for conflicting ideas of knowledge." Furthermore, we maintain that nothing we do should be second-rate, because we're committed to Jesus Christ, and we also represent Him in and to the world.

- **Finally, *TWC embraces the concept of "Total Student Development".***
   More and more secular and Christian educators emphasise the importance of preparing people to adapt to the rapidly-changing world into which they must graduate. Now, in addition to the academic thrust, we actually state that our philosophy *centres* on "personal development"—a concept that refers to a process to be lived, rather than a quality to attain. We intend to be an academic community living in an environment which will facilitate growth, to maximize each student's full potential.

Facing the challenges

There was no question: we would face major challenges in the days ahead. Intentional action would be necessary to experience the qualitative developments we anticipated. On this occasion, we could mention only a few:

1. For positive developments to take place, a climate receptive to change must be created in each element of our college community. There could be no place for blind loyalty to the status quo. In its place, we must have open examination and honest evaluation of the job being done. Changes in structure, programs, teaching methods, and administrative operations may be necessary. A spirit of experimentation and innovation must prevail.

2. If "to be unique is to be strong", we must consider and realize distinctive curricula, in addition to TWC's current traditional transfer-credits program. Recent discussions had pointed out the need for a strong, distinctive Christian education program; a more developed music major; and a program to help young people prepare for business careers—to mention only a few.

3. Interdisciplinary studies, continuing education and both on- and off-campus studies must be examined, and carefully integrated into the total educational program.

4. We must continue to recruit the most highly-qualified faculty. This refers, of course, to academic qualifications; but much more is involved. We must also look for those who have a commitment to Jesus Christ; who are good teachers; who are person-centred in outlook; and who can relate to the students in all aspects of their total round of living. In fact, we must recruit mentors—*disciple-makers*.

5. We must resist the tendency to treat students as though they were all alike in aptitude and aspirations. As we grow, Trinity Western must call for personalized and perhaps even *individualized* programming, affirming the unique individuality of each student.

6. We must view all members of the college community as being in the process of growth toward maturity. Not even the oldest or best-educated can be considered as "having already attained or were already perfect."[1] Furthermore, individuals may be less mature in one dimension than in other dimensions of development. All should be "living on the growing edge" of their experience.

7. Finally, we must realize that excellence also presumes accountability—to God, to our supporting constituencies, and to each other as members of the campus community.

There was much more to the installation service. Greetings came from unexpected places and from long-time supporters. Parents and potential students attended, as did grandparents and those who were simply curious. For those who had worked so hard to bring in a large gymnasium-full of people, and to provide a beautiful reception for a diverse crowd, it was another great opportunity to praise God for His goodness through the years, and for His promised provision for the days ahead.

Developing a mindset for growth

Casting the vision before the public was an important step. Now it was time to create and act on the new agenda we proposed. The development of a mindset for intentional growth would take time. The administrative team would have to

---
1 Philippians 3:12 (NASB)

engage the whole community in moving forward. We had affirmed our confidence in the Sovereign God, Who had brought Trinity Western this far; now we must look forward, to perceive what He intended to do in the future. We would have to sharpen our focus, and add the distinct and integrated set of provisions that would become our yet-to-be developed Mission Statement.

There was also a series of external relations issues that we had to face. Some people wondered what stance the new President might take. I had publicly stated: "We need to strengthen our ties with the church."

The organized church was then being severely criticized from nearly every quarter. Rather than siding with those who were down on the church, we at Trinity Western saw ourselves as churchmen. Not to say that we were always content with what we saw in the organized church; but emphatically, we are part of that organism—or in biblical terms, the Body of Jesus Christ. As such, we share concern for growth and development of the church of Jesus Christ, in a day when many were openly attempting to quiet its message of salvation, which has rung clear since the days of Jesus Christ Himself.

But a positive attitude toward the church wouldn't be enough. We'd have to be actively engaged in the process of education *for* the church. In the future, Trinity Western might even provide leadership, training, and helpful research.

Handled effectively, external relations would help to shape a positive mindset for development of the new era. Goals would be set for the action plans of the next semester. In this new era we agreed that we needed to:

- strengthen our ties to other universities and colleges;
- strengthen our ties to the local community; and
- strengthen our ties with our supporting agencies and constituencies.

9

Curriculum expansion takes flight

The new President's 1974 convocation address had set before the campus community TWC's seven momentous challenges. They were:

1. We had to create a climate receptive to change in each element of our college community. A spirit of experimentation and innovation must prevail.
2. We had to adopt distinctive curricula, in addition to TWC's current traditional transfer-credits program.
3. Interdisciplinary studies, continuing education and both on- and off-campus studies had to be examined, and integrated into the total program.
4. We had to continue to recruit the most highly-qualified faculty who, in addition to academic credentials, were mentors—and *disciple-makers*.
5. Trinity Western must call for personalized and perhaps even *individualized* programming, affirming the unique individuality of each student.
6. We must view all members of the college community as being in the process of growth toward maturity.
7. Finally, we must realize that excellence also presumes accountability—to God, to supporting constituencies, and to each other as members of the campus community.

Obviously, we were speaking to inform our guests; but also to challenge ourselves—faculty, staff and students—as a complete campus community.

An era of tremendous change and growth was about to unfold for Trinity Western. It was fortunate that none of us had any idea of the enormity of the transformations that were about to ensue, as we would have been utterly overwhelmed by all that God had in store for our College. At this point, all we knew was that God was in charge, and we were all willing servants.

With his expertise in the areas of personnel and direction, Bob Swanson was able to lead us in restructuring the President's Cabinet and the administration of the College.

The other member of the "two Bobs" was Dr. Robert Thompson. He and his family had served as missionaries in Ethiopia, where he had been a friend of Emperor Haile Selassie and a respected official in the Ethiopian Ministry of Education. Upon returning to Canada, he had entered politics, eventually becoming the Leader of the Official Opposition in our federal Parliament at Ottawa. Now retired, Bob served on at least 10 mission boards and had a reputation as a man of integrity and a Christian statesman. Active with Trinity Western for a number of years, he had recently resigned as Chairman of the TWC Board, and was now a volunteer special assistant to the new President.

"Dr. Bob", as he was known to two generations of students, had a long history at Trinity Western, teaching political science for a time. His biography as Canada's pre-eminent Christian statesman in the 20th century was written by TW student Judi Johnson. After her marriage to Ned Vankevich, who later became a professor of Communications at TWU, Judi established a ministry to elementary school students, teaching the benefits of good manners.

Through the process of many meetings and consultations, it had become clear that major changes were needed, and Trinity Western could only thrive if it expanded its student enrollment. The number of Canadian students hadn't met expectations, and while 'Camp Trinity', as some called it, signified fun and fellowship, it didn't reflect the serious outcomes desired. Furthermore, back then, 70 percent of those enrolled stayed for only one year. After careful consideration, there was agreement that in order to expand the student base, we would have to first expand our curriculum.

At that same time, Dr. Lee Asa (whose services we still had for few months) and Bob Thompson shared a vision for a unique addition to our courses—aviation.

As a former missionary, Bob Thompson was acutely aware of the pressing need for an aviation school in Canada. He had been advocating an aviation program, based on a growing need that he was aware of through being a member of the Board for the Missionary Aviation Fellowship (MAF). His idea had also gained the interest of Jungle Aviation And Radio Service (JAARS), an arm of Wycliffe Bible Translators. Christian aviation programs were available in the United States, but there were many Canadians who wished to have this skill as they enlisted to serve as missionaries in remote areas of the world, or to gain entry into the world of commercial aviation.

Lee Asa not only shared this vision, but was also an avid flier who had earned his commercial pilot's license at the nearby Langley Flying School. Lee's relationship with its teachers certainly didn't hurt our efforts to gain their support; nor did his unique ability to share the vision of Trinity Western with potential partners, by offering them an aerial view of the campus and its spectacular surroundings.

Together, Lee and Bob sensed that this was providential timing and they put forth a set of convincing arguments to gain support of the Board and other faculty:

- There was a definite need to serve outlying areas of northern Canada, as well as in many other remote parts of the world;
- Trinity Western had the basic core curriculum to support such a program;
- it met the terms of Trinity Western's mission and ethos;
- it would be the first aviation program of its kind in Canada;
- experienced instructors and teacher/aviators were already available; and
- the local airport in Langley had a reputable flight school with whom we could partner

Another unanticipated benefit would be making it clear to all that Trinity Western really did have a heart for missions, and was developing students to become missionaries.

Both the Faculty and the Boards gave a positive response to the idea; the needs and benefits had been well researched, it would fit in with efforts to expand the student population, and numerous constituents had offered their encouragement and support.

The search for a Director of the Aviation Institute began and, once again, we learned that God had gone before us to prepare the right person to undertake this task and be a builder of this program: Terry Norr responded almost immediately to our search.

At the young age of 27, Terry was a Marine Corps-trained pilot with an instructor's rating. He had spent time in Africa with the Sudan Interior Mission and World Vision, participating in a SIMAR (Sudan Interior Mission Aviation and Radio) project to address the

Terry Norr (right)

famine in Africa. Beyond all that, he had a Master's Degree in Economics and Political Science.

Terry took charge and with the help of Lee and Bob, the Aviation Institute began developing a program and making arrangements with the Langley Flight School. The new program would not simply be an "add-on" program; every student who enrolled for Aviation first had to be accepted into Trinity Western and undergo two years of integrated college education, along with obtaining his/her aviation certification. Once successfully completed, they would graduate with an Associate of Arts Certificate.

The first brochure to announce Trinity Western's Aviation Program described it as follows:

> "… a two-year training program covering six full semesters. The student will take the usual Science requirements for an Associate of Arts Diploma. This includes two years of transferable university academic courses and subjects such as Physics, Geography, Mathematics and Economics. Also included are Aviation courses in Flight Regulations, Traffic Rules and Procedures, Air Navigation, Aerodynamics, Engines and Air Frames, Meteorology, Radio Navigation and Aircraft Care and Maintenance. Students will acquire their private pilot's license, commercial license and, for those who choose it, a fully approved Department of Transport instrument rating certification.
>
> "The student may choose between two major areas of flight training:
>
> - Bush/Float Pilot Program, or
> - Airline Pilot Program
>
> "Furthermore, within each program, there is enough flexibility to accommodate almost any aviation objective. The program was developed to fulfill the Department of Transport requirements for both single- and multi-engine, instrument flying, lifeline and seaplane endorsement."

The curriculum also included Bible 141—Hebrew History, a three-credit, three-hour Bible course. According to the brochure, this expansion of the scope of the program was necessary "because there is a good prospect of our securing transfer credit of the course to UBC."

Not only was Biblical Studies being expanded and enriched, but the whole program was developed with the counsel of MAF, JAARS, and with representatives of the major airlines. Once more we could say with conviction and satisfaction, "Nothing done in Christ's name should be second-rate."

The brochure concluded:

> "For the flight training and technical aspects of this program, Trinity Western College has entered into a contractual agreement with Skyway Air Services Ltd. This fight training school, located near the college, is the largest and most highly respected in British Columbia. It operates 18 planes, including three multi-engine and two seaplanes. The program utilizes the Langley Municipal Airport, a seaplane base on the Fraser River, and several 'bush' landing strips around Harrison Lake."

Almost as fast as we could have envisioned it, the Aviation Program was ready to soar in the Fall of 1975.

Arne Olson was a graduate of Trinity Junior College, served as the third director of the Aviation program and then went on to serve as a captain with Air Canada. Arne now serves with TATC: Transportation Appeal Tribunal of Canada."

10

If Aviation, why not Business?

As we developed the Aviation Program, there was also a growing sense that just as mission groups needed skilled pilots, the corporate marketplace needed skilled workers who were godly, committed Christians.

Business education programs had become increasingly popular and, as illustrated by my interaction with California businessman Ted Smith (see Chapter 6), there was a high demand among constituents and supporters for Trinity Western to develop a Business Program.

It wasn't difficult to convince the faculty or the Board of the need; but as this area of study was undergoing such intense growth at that particular time, it seemed as though all Canadian universities were advertising for business professors. There was an obvious shortage of teachers, and this shortage was exacerbated by our need for professors who would go beyond teaching and become Christian mentors to their students. We had not met many Canadian Christian business academics; and without such specialized professors, we couldn't mount the program.

Dr. Lee Asa was utterly surprised when, after giving it much thought, I came up with the name of one person whom I knew had a PhD in the discipline of Business. I'd met him while on a sabbatical at the University of Oregon; and, although our families had fellowshipped together in the same church, I had absolutely no idea where he was presently located.

I shouldn't have been surprised at God's leading and provision. He had already done so much to bring the right people to Trinity Western. But as this current situation was clarified and resolved, I couldn't help but be filled with awe and adoration as I saw, once more, how He does all things well.

Dr. Kenley Snyder

It took a lot of searching, but I finally located Dr. Kenley Snyder in California. I wasn't sure what to expect, but as I explained our need and our confidence in God's ability to miraculously take Trinity Western College so much further, Kenley calmly replied: "I think we could be very interested in that."

At the time of my call, I didn't know much about Kenley other than that he was a godly family man; I didn't even know his full academic qualifications. But as we talked, I soon realized how God had gone before us to uniquely prepare Kenley to establish our Business Division.

He had an earned PhD from the University of Oregon, an MBA from the University of Michigan, and a BSc degree from Wheaton College. Along the way, he had gained experience in sales, management, consulting and teaching (at both the University of Oregon and the Lewis and Clark College in Portland).

Kenley Snider

Kenley and his wife, Donna, along with their two sons Alex and Tony, arrived just a few months after our first telephone contact. He developed the curriculum for the new Faculty of Business, and it opened in September of 1975, at the same time as the new Institute of Aviation.

It's interesting to note that the Lord often does far more than we could ask or think. Kenley also had unique skills in building and architecture that enabled him to coordinate several major building programs for us.

Kenley Snyder proved to be an effective leader who taught and mentored hundreds of students; he was also a godly and faithful man, who lived "*to the praise of His glory.*" He lived to see the institution that he served so well grow and mature from an enrollment of 400 students to more than 2,000. Sadly, at the age of 57 he was diagnosed with cancer. Kenley Snyder died April 1, 1999.

∽

Sitting in his MBA class at Queen's University in 1970, John Sutherland had no idea that in just eight years he'd become an Assistant Business Professor—and eventually Professor and Dean—in a Christian university in Langley, B.C. Indeed, he'd never heard of Langley, much less Trinity Western University!

Over his years at TWU, all the lessons from John's earlier life found their way into both program development and the approach to individual courses. He structured his courses and plans for the Business major around what he called "the four Cs":

- **Competence** – There's no substitute in the marketplace for competence; therefore, we built considerable rigour into our expectations for students.

- **Calling** – Unique among Canadian schools of business, we emphasized that a business career is no less a calling from God than education, pastoral ministry, or pre-med and nursing programs. And this approach has implications for business objectives and ethical dilemmas.
- **Character** – In conjunction with the liberal arts, the Student Development program, and the chapel program, we emphasised how character, infused with biblical virtues, priorities, values, and goals, is indispensable to living for God in the marketplace.
- **Crisis** – There's nothing like a crisis in business life (and there are crises aplenty!) to test one's competence, sense of calling, and strength of character. Case studies, "real world" research, guest speakers, and so on were used to deal frankly with the problems, temptations, and dilemmas that are part of marketplace realities.

John Sutherland

The Business major soon grew to become the largest single area of study in the University.

"This couldn't have happened without the participation of a host of fellow professors involved in its growth," says John Sutherland.

In 1993 Dr. Kevin Sawatsky believed that God had led him to leave his downtown Vancouver law practice and join TWU's business faculty. But in 2000—with many of his colleagues departing—he began to think that maybe it was time to return to full-time law practice. However, God had other plans. That year, I asked Kevin if he would consider becoming the Dean of the School of Business. Although he was reluctant, because the challenges seemed almost insurmountable, he eventually felt God directing him to accept the position.

The year before Kevin became Dean, we'd identified the need for a revitalized business program. We'd constituted a Board of Governors' Task Force in 2000, chaired by Reg Peterson, to provide a new vision for the Business Program. The Task Force recommended a completely new structure—a School of Business that would be more entrepreneurial in nature, with much stronger connection to the business community. In keeping with

Kevin Sawatsky

that recommendation, the new School of Business opened in 2001. In the years that followed God blessed the new School of Business in many remarkable ways including:

- Almost doubling enrolment (between 2000 and 2005)
- Rebuilding of the faculty team (now thirteen full-time faculty)
- Creation of the Leadership Advisory Council for the School of Business
- Commencement of the BA in Sport and Leisure Management program
- Commencement of the BA in Corporate Communications program
- Commencement of the Certified Financial Planner program
- Development and launch of the MBA program
- Development of strong global business connections (including eventually launching the Great Wall MBA program in Tianjin, China)
- Establishment of exchange programs in Germany, France, Austria and Holland
- Receiving the top rankings of any business school in B.C. in the *Globe and Mail* rankings

These years in the School of Business since 2000 have proved again that even in the middle of a storm, in times of crisis, God is faithful, and the plans He has for us are good.[1]

Each of these contributors has his or her own story of God's preparation in making the Faculty of Business and Economics the success that it became, as one of the most consistently popular programs offered at TWU.

---

[1] Jeremiah 29:11 (NASB)

Don Page and Neil Snider reviewing plans.

TWU Archives

PART III

A period for planning

There's a distinct difference between intentional planning and ordinary planning: intentional planning is always clearly goal-oriented; it has a specific objective in mind, and even if that objective is only a short-term step along the path to the final goal, the end must always be kept in view.

—*editor*

11

Developments in the new era

Undoubtedly the major challenge in the first years of the new era was to recruit people—godly people: experienced leaders, qualified faculty; visionaries who were willing to step out in faith and work towards an uncertain future. That was precisely what the founders had to do. However, as David Enarson would say, "There's nothing uncertain about what God can do—and that's good enough for me!"

As often happens, God had already quietly prepared people to be part of His on-going venture. With the departure of Dr. Leland Asa, filling the position of Academic Dean became a major challenge—or opportunity. Deane Downey, although he'd been with the College for only three semesters and was still completing his doctoral dissertation, really wasn't seeking the task of Academic Dean. Still, his excellent preparation had begun long before; and his recent teaching was very positive and reputable. So for the first while, he became Acting Dean.

Deane had grown up in a godly home. His father was a well-known missionary, preacher, and professor at the Canadian Bible College in Regina. Deane had chosen to attend three of Canada's finest universities: McGill University in Montreal; the University of Toronto; and the University of Alberta in Edmonton, where he would complete his PhD. He was not only a professor of English, but also an accomplished musician. He would go on to write several books, and contribute to many publications.

Deane and Margaret had been married during their student days in Ontario; with their two children, they joined the TWC family in 1973.

Deane Downey

John Van Dyke (right)

Only God could have known that as an experienced teacher, Margaret would later become—in the then not-even-yet-dreamed-of future—a faculty member in Trinity's School of Education.

Trinity Western World's Fall, 1976 magazine was pleased to announce, **"Six Full-time Faculty Join TWC Team."** Recruiting six highly qualified faculty for six different disciplines was an outstanding achievement for Dr. Downey.

Deane and other leaders were intent on hiring the right people for the present—and for the envisioned future; and for highlighting TWC's core values. Certainly we all agreed: nothing done in Christ's name should ever be anything less than excellent! All the new faculty members had graduate degrees, as well as significant research and teaching experience. Three, like Deane and Margaret Downey, would make Trinity Western their place of service until retirement. These included:

- John Van Dyke, PhD, Associate Professor of Physics and Chemistry;
- Elsie Holmes, PhD, Associate Professor of English;
- John Klassen PhD, Assistant Professor of History.

The editor of the *Pillar,* Trinity Western's student yearbook, remarked that the calibre of dedicated, well-trained Christian faculty being attracted to TWC was nothing short of remarkable—particularly as the College was still offering only the first two years of university-level studies, and salary levels were considerably below what instructors at tax-supported post-secondary institutions could earn. Without exception, these new appointees had expressed a sense of enthusiastic anticipation as they were preparing to become involved in the Christian educational experience that is Trinity Western.

In my next Report to the Board of Governors in 1976, I wrote:

Elsie Holmes

"I will mention that my prayer to God earlier in the year was that, because of our busy schedule, I would desire that He should send us the people He would have to be with us, without our going out and looking for them. *It would appear that this is exactly what has happened."*

Building community

Unless carefully planned and communicated to the whole community, annual themes or slogans may have only limited value. But handled properly, they can bring unity. For example, **"15 years to the praise of His glory"** may not immediately seem to speak in much depth to a young student body. But as a means of introducing them to what God has already done, and what we can expect Him to do in the current year and in the future, both for the institution and for them personally, it can make all the difference to the campus community.

John Klassen

Every year, the TW campus became extraordinarily active by mid-August. There were retreats and orientation sessions for faculty and staff, and preparatory sessions for those who had been chosen as student leaders. In the early years, this included only RAs (Resident Assistants), whose responsibility was to help student groups to help one another in the common quest to each become the unique person that God intended, and to learn to build up one another.

The first student leadership retreat in this new era was an RA retreat. It was scheduled for just two days, but it had a very obvious impact on those leaders, who brought sleeping bags, Bibles and notebooks. Allan Kotanen and his colleagues had developed an amazing program to inculcate a basic mindset that would facilitate personal growth, teamwork, and discipleship. The time was filled with learning and laughter—and maybe longing for more sleep! But one thing was certain: everyone got to know everyone else, including the President's family, who had the privilege of hosting the whole crew. It made for close fellowship. The guys had the upper floor and the gals the lower. There was no empty floor space left in the Snider home, and Marlie was kept busy acting as gracious hostess to all that energy!

It didn't take long before student leaders from other parts of the community also began to enjoy the leadership development that was being carefully planned and managed. The Student Council wanted more recognition, as did commuters and student leaders assisting in athletic activities or in library support. The community was coming together. But in three years, only three senior administrative leaders had been added to help that happen.

Dr. Arvid Olson, with his wife, Ruth, and family were Canadians who, after completing their education, had been engaged with the Christian Service Brigade. They had been transferred to Denver, Colorado, where Arvid had been made responsible for overseeing that ministry for all of south-western USA. He had set up a meeting in the Vancouver area with the intent of finding and hiring a prospective associate for his work. Providentially, he also visited Trinity Western College at that time, where he knew several people (including the President, with whom he'd gone to college in earlier years). His vision was to evangelize and then mentor young leaders to become disciples and disciple-makers. He was moved by the challenge he saw in this young institution that was so intent on attracting and grooming potential leaders, highly qualified and willing to become the persons God had created them to be. It made good sense.

Although he was challenged by what he saw, Arvid initially passed up the opportunity to join TWC, in order to remain loyal to his earlier calling. But after returning to Colorado, he and Ruth prayed about the matter; and one day Arvid said that he felt confident that if Dr. Snider called again, it would be God's indication that he ought to accept the challenge at Trinity Western. Shortly after that, I did. And he did. Arvid became the first Vice President for Student Life, and Campus Chaplin.

So the Olsons joined us for the fifteenth year, *"To the praise of His Glory."*

Arvid was a student's man, with a deep commitment to biblical discipleship and leadership training. He began immediately to expand and strengthen those emphases, and to sharpen the focus on Student Development. Arvid often said, "There are two things that will endure forever: human souls, and God's Word. This is an opportunity to invest my life in both."

Still missing, however, was a full-time Academic Dean. When Dr. Deane Downey had so effectively completed his three semesters as Interim Dean, and none of the candidates for the advertised position ultimately accepted, our committed, congenial, and creative Librarian, David Twiest, agreed to carry the responsibility as Faculty

Arvid Olson

Chairman for the 1976/77 academic year. His was then the role of Acting Academic Dean while the college searched for a replacement for Dr. Lee Asa. The continuing miracle of faculty responding to the exciting challenge of this new College was inexplicable. But it certainly provided convincing evidence that it must be of God's doing.

A new residence for women: Fraser Hall

Long before we made 'the decision', we'd begun planning for anticipated increased student numbers. Residences were already near capacity. There was, however, open building space between McMillan Hall and the Gymnasium.

Dave Twiest

In 1978, with more than 500 students enrolled, TW was bursting at the seams. A new women's residence was needed. Fraser Hall was to be named for Simon Fraser, a fur trader and explorer who navigated the river that was later named for him.

But in the first place, this building would have to be financed through a commercial mortgage. There was no other source of funds at that time, but it was deemed feasible. There was however, an immediate hold-up: although we had more than 100 acres, we knew it wasn't wise to tie up the whole campus with one mortgage. But once again, the Lord had a prepared solution. When the major freeway adjacent to our property had been built, a municipal road next to our property had been cut off; and in the process, a new boundary had been established, setting apart about six acres—the very space on which Fraser Hall was to be built; and we could seek a mortgage on only that piece, and the building to be erected on it. More than that, in years to come three 'wings' would be added to the complex, which we might never have anticipated.

There's a lot to be said for strategic planning. There is even more to be said for a miracle-working God! We were certain that He had provided, but we couldn't project very far into the future. We needed to be dependent servants—sometimes simpler said than done.

The mortgage was certainly necessary if we were to expand, and we were convinced it was God's doing. Unfortunately, mortgage rates were high at the time, and we were pressed to take a three-year term. No one could have guessed that the rates would be out of sight by the renewal date! In advance of our deadline, I had one of our regular lunch visits with our branch manager. He'd been the young banker who had carried the request to a senior level of the Royal Bank for the first loan to purchase the Seal-Kap Dairy Farm. On this occasion, he let me know that ¼ percent above prime was the going rate for our kind of 'business'. I wondered if it might be possible to request an adjustment for a privately-funded charitable organization that was bringing so much good will and quality of life, as well as the business it was bringing to the community.

Very few, if any, higher education institutions were then totally privately funded. That's still true today. Our banker agreed it was worth considering, and said he'd take the matter to his Royal Bank superiors. Within a short time he reported back that our rate had dropped to prime, a very good rate at the time. That was a start.

An even greater blessing came in the form of special arrangements with our financial institutions. Knowing that our three-year mortgage might be faced with interest rates that were then rising beyond 20 percent, we knew we needed help. The Royal Bank agreed to replace some of our mortgages with a more favorable bank line-of-credit to fund our capital needs. This arrangement made it possible for Trinity Western to reduce capital debt in the years to come. When the tuition income arrived at the beginning of each semester, our line-of-credit could be substantially reduced, then rise as the months passed, until the next refreshing semester made possible more debt retirement. Not only was the debt being retired, but the high interest rate began to fall consistently through the years, finally dropping to single digit figures, and a retired debt.

Completing a cycle: a President's Report

At the conclusion of the 15th anniversary year—in May of 1977—a President's Report was sent to the Board of Governors, summarizing what God had done, and projecting what might be anticipated in the days ahead. It was exciting—and almost frightening at the same time. Were we moving too quickly? Did we have any choice?

In part, that President's Report said:

> "Once again we have completed a cycle. In fact this year, that is true of both a smaller and a larger cycle. At the conclusion of this school year, we can look back and see again that there has been tremendous progress in many areas. The challenges have been great. But then, the victories

are even greater. We have much for which to praise God because of our present school year."

The growth in student numbers, the influx of highly competent faculty, and the obvious development in the area of Student Life had not been overlooked. And now, an application from a new Academic Dean was reason for great rejoicing. Once again, the Lord had uniquely prepared someone for our academic leadership. Dr. Craig Seaton, with his wife Marsha and their two children, would be joining us in time to prepare for challenges arising in the face of a potential four-year program—and all that might entail.

No firm commitment had yet been made to transition to a four-year program. It just seemed to be "happening". Somehow or other, nearly everyone sensed that this was providential—it would happen in God's timing—perhaps sooner than we thought.

The President's Report continued:

> "In the larger cycle, I'm completing my first three-year term of office. In retrospect, I see that the challenges were even greater than we could have imagined, or than we actually realized as we were facing them. The restructuring of the organization; the procuring of personnel; the relating to our various publics; and the broadening of our support base were among the larger challenges. In addition, the capital expansion—including the print shop, two apartment buildings, and the administration building—have given cause for tension in terms of finances; but satisfaction in view of expanded opportunities in our college ministry.
>
> "I feel greatly honoured in the confidence the Board has given me to assume leadership for another three-year term. Much of the credit for the good things that have been happening goes to my administrative colleagues and assistants, who have served faithfully, joyfully, and almost untiringly, far beyond the normal call of duty, 'as unto the Lord'."[1]

God had been good to Trinity Western! Why wouldn't we respond loudly with joy and satisfaction:

"Fifteen years to the praise of His glory!'

And so a tradition was born. Meanwhile, just as the *Pillar* emerged to be the name of our yearbook—reflecting the pillar of cloud and fire that guided the

---

[1] Ephesians 5:22 (KJV)

Israelites in the wilderness, (and which served as the theme of founding President Cal Hanson's first convocation address)—this tradition leapt into being from the words of the Apostle Paul. These words also formed the first College Seal in 1962: "…to the praise of the glory of His grace."[1]

This theme caught on quickly. Fifteen dynamic years; many miraculous God-interventions, including unexpected academic recognition for Canada's first privately-funded, two-year, faith-based, Christ-centred liberal arts college; shaping a community that was even then beginning to envision its development into a four-year degree-granting university-college. The name "Trinity Junior College" had already been changed to Trinity Western College.

Exuberant expressions of praise and thanksgiving for institutional development are wonderful; but this theme was also to become a stimulus for personal resolve. Surely God's will was—and is—that each of us becomes the person He uniquely created us to be. His work in the life of committed Christ-followers brings Him glory, by renewing our mind, our heart, and our will. This provided a helpful focus; only God knows how many resolved to live to glorify Him in every aspect of their lives.

Awakening to the past

Our annual theme held the possibility not only of memorializing history, but also extending the lessons of that history into the future. Most 1976 students would still have been in preschool when Trinity Junior College began. But wise people learn from the past. The daily Student Chapel became an ideal setting for real, live pioneers to visit and tell their marvelous stories of how God can work in the lives of His people.

Students during that 15th year at Trinity Western and throughout the years have been also encouraged, enriched, and challenged by the lives of the founding families, and by the growing number of deeply committed teachers, mentors, apprentices and followers who were all becoming members of the TW community.

That theme would be repeated another half-dozen times. Every fifth year, we reviewed again, with joy, the significant things God was continuing to do in our lives, in our community, and in our project to establish a school that would graduate godly Christian leaders for the nation.

It's always refreshing to be with people who think and live beyond their self-interest. Christ-centred relationships and meaningful worship are positive indicators of living to the praise of God's glory.

---

1 Ephesians 1:6 (KJV)

12

The practice of planning

King Solomon observed, *"Wise people think before they act… it is pleasant to see plans develop."*[1] Of course, Solomon was experienced in planning, and he also said many advisors, and good listeners who learn from thoughtful criticism and work together in harmony, would see great results. He also reflected that, *"there is nothing better for people than to be happy in their work. That is our lot in life!"*[2]

The 1979-80 years would be very important for Trinity Western College. We needed to plan! There was so much happening, most people wouldn't have begun to understand all that occurred or was under way. Fortunately, I could report to the Board that we were going into these years with the best overall morale among faculty and staff we'd ever experienced.

There were several reasons for this. No doubt the media opposition directed toward us during the 1979 summer months had united our whole community and our supporters behind Trinity Western's general purpose. We'd become a four-year college. Forty-nine Junior students had stepped out in faith, believing their credits would count toward a degree. Seventeen had pre-registered as Seniors. The second class of Juniors was nearly twice as large as the first. There was confident expectation that Trinity Western would be granted the right to offer degrees.

Then too, we'd achieved a focus towards our goals over time. Still, any organizational specialist could tell us that integration of new people takes time; and we were definitely moving through a rapid growth period. We needed to be planning!

But whatever the reasons, we had a very positive spirit on campus. We wanted to make sure this would continue, and it seemed the best way to do this would be to develop clearly defined areas of responsibility and commensurate authority. We were pleased the way our first third-year class carried their temporary role as Seniors so well, a role they'd have the privilege to repeat.

From its beginning, TWC had enjoyed a very positive and supportive

---

[1] Proverbs 13:16 (NLT) & Proverbs 13:19 (TLB)
[2] Ecclesiastes 3:22 (NLT)

relationship with, and from, the Evangelical Free Church of America. The denomination had approved the development of the college, primarily on recommendation of a relatively small number of Canadian leaders who were convinced of the need for such an institution. The EFCA was sensitive to the Canadian higher education environment, and not only encouraged, but expected the Board and Administrators to "make it work" effectively and efficiently. They were vocal in their praise of the remarkable developments that had occurred in such a short time. They, too, would say ***"To the praise of His glory!"***

However, changes had to be made to accommodate growth. The number of elected members to the Board of Governors had been expanded, and members from outside the EFCA had been added.

These members were placed in Board committees on the basis of their commitment and their areas of expertise. Also, an Advisory Council had been created, from which Board members could be drawn, and special advisory groups such as Business and Aviation Committees established.

I believed that it was important for Trinity Western to maintain its relationship to the founding denomination. We were treading a completely uncharted path as a Christian liberal arts institution in Canada. Pressures were on us concerning our doctrinal statement. Suggestions had already been made that we ought to simplify or modify it. There had been suggestions that the statements on eschatology, and even on biblical inerrancy, were "not really relevant" to a liberal arts institution.

I disagreed completely with these sentiments! Our Board and administrative leaders agreed that we must hold firm to our doctrinal position, and also to the lifestyle emphases on biblical piety that mark our evangelical tradition.

We needed to engage in futuristic planning!

Major issues: facing the future

One of the concerns that would probably always be with us centred on the lack of understanding of the differences in organizational structure between public and private institutions like Trinity Western. Since we're unique in Canada, my view was that Trinity Western should use, as a criterion for evaluation or comparison, Christian liberal arts colleges in the United States, rather than taking guidelines from Canadian public (and secular) institutions. There were those in our community who felt that Trinity Western ought to work on a Senate arrangement, similar to public institutions; that hiring ought to be done at the departmental level; and that more organizational direction ought to be given by the faculty than was generally the pattern in any Christian college I knew of. I believed that the present Board and Administration had the challenge of facing this viewpoint, and at the same time utilizing the expertise of our own faculty members in developing policies to be adopted by the Board.

Two unique features of our college needed clarification. First, we are focused on "Total Student Development"; and unlike any Canadian public institution we knew of, the faculty must be seen as part of a larger team of individuals, all working together to foster holistic personal development. Most other colleges and universities look upon everybody but faculty as merely "support staff". We maintained that our student personnel *especially* are an integral part of our professional staff, to enable us to achieve Total Student Development. In fact, *all* staff work directly toward this goal.

A second uniqueness related to our need to be responsive to a specific identifiable constituency. It's important, then, that the Board should see its function as "trustees" responsible to the evangelical Christian community. The administration and the rest of the staff in turn are responsible to the Board, and must be held accountable by them. This is a far different picture than that held by public universities, where the professionals (*i.e.*, the faculty) have all the responsibility for the direction of the program. Our college must remain responsive to the will of the constituency it serves. "To be unique is to be strong" isn't just a slogan; it's a deep conviction. Our vision requires that it must be so.

At the same time, it was quite apparent that Trinity Western is a project almost too big for the EFCA—not to mention the recently emerging Evangelical Free Church of Canada. It seemed essential to continue our policy of expanding our base as widely as possible, while retaining our foundational ties. We'd made good progress in this direction, and now looked forward to the addition of elected and appointed board members from different areas and denominations.

Institutional planning

There was great appreciation for the Four Year Study Commission that had set the stage for our proposed university program. It had also drafted a Core Values document that would ensure that all students would be addressed with our integrated institutional perspective. However, in the fall of 1979, we were faced with a real financial crunch, due to the anticipated lack of students. This didn't change the need for an academic plan; but it may have heightened the need for both program evaluation and future planning.

There were several philosophical questions arising, that we needed to address:

1. Do we still agree with the philosophy verbalized in our catalogue?

2. Do we continue with the development of our outlined program?

3. Do we want to follow through with seeking membership in the Association of Universities and Colleges of Canada?

4. If so, how and when should we follow through?

It seemed to me that essential to all of these issues would be the development of a five-year academic plan. This would have to be closely coordinated with every other area, of course—including enrolment, financial resources, facilities, and personnel. While we'd been working hard at this, the fact was that we didn't yet have the human or financial resources to do it adequately. It might take a major adjustment in our thinking to correct this deficiency.

Early seminary suggestions

I'm sure someone may have asked, "Why on earth would you consider starting a seminary, when you aren't fully set up as a degree-granting University?" The likely answer would have been that it wasn't our idea! Nor did it make sense to us, initially.

However, we'd determined that we would never say "No" before asking God what He might want of us. Trusted friends had confronted us, earnestly asking us to at least listen to what they were thinking. And we had to listen!

Their story wasn't new to us. We knew the Canadian scene very well. Many pastors serving in evangelical churches had graduated from solid Bible institutes or colleges, of which more than 40 existed in Canada at that time. Northwest Bible College and Seminary, situated nearby, was one of the few with a graduate program; but that program was built primarily upon their under-graduate Bible college. They were finding it increasingly difficult financially to sustain the costs of the enterprise.

There was little to report publicly at this early stage; but even before Trinity Western's university status had been attained, conversations had begun at local levels and with Trinity Evangelical Divinity School (TEDS) in Chicago and Bethel Seminary of the Baptist General Conference in Minnesota. Those conversations would soon lead to discussions that might awaken serious possibilities. It would take time. We needed to plan! We also needed to act!

There was a great deal of community optimism, in view of God's provision of the four-year charter and our first class of Seniors. We were also still in the process of becoming a university. There was, understandably, some uncertainty and frustration. The President's 1979 Fall Board Report cited the example of our senior Finance Director, Reg Reimer, as one indication of our need for a balance between "task achievement" and "program maintenance". We were finding that when people left our employment, we were often forced to hire two people to fill their place! Reg sensed an inadequacy to keep up with the general account, and at the same time to give oversight and make the necessary long-range projections. To maintain controls in our financial area required a complicated fund-accounting system with three general ledgers, which were then integrated into one for reporting. Obviously, this surpassed the needs of most normal small businesses at that time; the need for computer services began to seem essential.

The same principle held true in the academic area. Division heads were teaching full loads, and the Dean had all he could do to maintain the regular duties of his office. For that reason, I recommended a special study commission with a full-time director.

But a less costly alternative plan might be to utilize the services of our recently-hired Guy Saffold, who was already giving oversight to planning and operating the Admission functions. We'll meet him in Chapter 14.

13

The decision

There was never a precise time when we began speaking formally about a four-year program. The idea just emerged. The direction seemed increasingly clear. The Aviation Program and the Business Institute had opened the door for what seemed our ultimate destiny. A cohort of highly-qualified faculty had joined the ranks. Dr. Craig Seaton, an experienced administrator, had come on board as the College's Academic Dean, with the implied mandate of researching the four-year option.

It was time for the Board of Governors to formalize the process. Pastor Ken Lawrence was a very able Chairman. He was also a visionary leader, who had unwavering confidence in the sovereign God Who had miraculously brought Trinity Western College into being, and had sustained it in the face of opposition.

We were fortunate to locate data from research into other institutions that had attempted to expand from a two-year to a four-year academic program. There were very few, if any, Canadian institutions in that category, and those that had attempted such a move in the U.S. had mostly experienced a very disappointing result. Indeed, the majority not only failed the change, but soon disappeared. The costs were simply prohibitive.

This was certainly not the message we wanted to report to our Board. With all the expectations that had been building, this seemed like a catastrophe. It was as if we had been following a rabbit trail that led to a bleak ice plain—it led everywhere, but showed nowhere to go!

But that wasn't all. Another report, concerning the financial implications of such a move, was even more depressing. We had only the simplest research tools at the time; but we hoped that we might expect an expanded enrollment, in view of the expanded curriculum we hoped to introduce. Besides, we would be a very unique Canadian institution; one that should prove very attractive to Christian students.

The financial analysis, however, indicated that Trinity Western College could go as much as two million dollars into debt over five years—if we could last that long.

I didn't add the report that had been left for me by an earlier finance director, who said we were already effectively bankrupt, and should close down for a couple of years.

There was a deadly silence in the room. Chairman Ken Lawrence was on the spot. We needed to stop everything and pray! This isn't what's usually done in formal board meetings, but it was normal for Trinity Western. Ken asked that we kneel, and each bring the matter before the Lord before we did anything else. There was a heartfelt response. Surely the God of Creation could handle the matter which presently confronted us!

We began to pray. They were short prayers. What else would we pray about, with the immediate concern that faced us? Everyone joined in. Following the prayers, and true to his nature, Board Chairman Ken Lawrence began to sing a familiar chorus: *"God can do anything, anything, anything! God can do anything but fail!"*

As we all joined in, we rose to our places. Then Ken explained that he'd like us to do something "a little unusual." A little unusual?!? He wanted us, having prayed, to reflect on our own thoughts. He wanted each of us to decide in our own mind what we thought God wanted us to do. We might decide to cancel the whole idea. Or we might postpone our decision. Or we might step out in faith and move ahead, trusting God to provide the means.

Two or three minutes of reflection seemed a very long time. Then Ken began with the person on his left, asking him what he thought; then he asked the whole circle the same question. There seemed to be a Presence of the Lord in the room. We spoke with confidence, as if He were directing our decision. As it turned out, it was unanimous: we resolved, God helping us, to become a four-year institution. That was enough for one day. We would soon have to consider many more issues on this topic. But for today, it was enough to be in agreement, and at peace.

I can't help but remember the words of Eugene Peterson in his book, *Practice Resurrection* (page 154):

> "I bow my knees before the Father.
>
> "The physical act of bowing before the Lord (Ephesians 3:14) is an act of reverence. It is an act of voluntary defenselessness. While on my knees, I cannot run away. I cannot assert myself.
>
> I place myself in a position of willed submission, vulnerable to the will of the Person before whom I am bowing. It is an act of retreating from

the action so that I can perceive what the action is, without being in it, without me taking up space, without me speaking my piece.

"On my knees I am no longer in a position to flex my muscles, strut or cower, hide in the shadows, or show off on stage."

A lawsuit that had nothing to do with us

From the earliest days at Trinity Junior College, there was a clear understanding that, as a Christian college, we would never ask for, nor accept, operational funds from the government. We were very aware (as were many other Christians) that many colleges and universities in Canada had lost their initial Christian mission and vision, once they became dependent on government money. Total secularization inevitably followed.

It was utterly surprising, then, when Dr. Bob Thompson, MP (a former chairman of the Trinity Western Board of Governors and a special advisor when I first arrived at Langley) approached me early in 1975 to state that there was a possibility of federal funding coming to Trinity Western College—with no strings attached!

Dr. Bob had been an elected Member of Parliament since 1962, and was currently very much aware of a growing battle amongst the provinces over the ability of their respective students to afford university. The federal Cabinet was considering the idea of providing "equalization grants" to higher education institutions across Canada to remedy these imbalances. At the same time, such payments could cause constitutional challenges (since, under the Canadian Constitution, education is solely a matter of provincial jurisdiction). But as always, the provinces were quite pleased to receive federal funds; so an independent foundation and a formula were established for distribution of grant monies to the provinces, to redistribute to their post-secondary institutions. The payments were made on the basis of student enrollments, and the overall purpose was to reduce costs to students and allow academic institutions to employ greater numbers of staff and faculty.

Dr. Thompson thought Trinity Western should be qualified to receive these payments; after all, our Registrar, Dr. Enoch Mattson, had been faithfully forwarding our records of eligible student numbers each year to the government. Yet the Social Credit Government of British Columbia did not release any of the funds to us.

Bob Thompson encouraged me to visit Victoria and our recently-elected NDP Premier, Dave Barrett, to request our share of the funds, since our growing College was in need, and had, in our view, clearly met the established criteria. Mr. Barrett proved to be a welcoming and congenial host, who was very much aware of Trinity Western College. He had a particular appreciation for private schools, and spoke warmly of the two private Catholic universities that he had attended in the United States.

When I raised the matter of equalization grants, the Premier deferred to his Minister of Education, Eileen Dailley. He asked her to join us and, when she did, he briefly reviewed the situation for her, reminded her that this was federal money, and that it would be good for the province. After all, Mr. Barrett suggested, it was "no skin off our nose" to pass the grant on to Trinity Western.

Unfortunately, the Education Minister failed to see the situation in the same light and her response was disbelief: "Oh no! When we give money, we want control!"

I cannot remember her saying anything else. With a shrug, the Premier shook my hand. "Well, I guess you have your answer. Good luck."

Some months later, we learned that British Columbia had entered into litigation with the federal government, and the issue centred primarily on the money given to the province for education. British Columbia and Ontario were unlike the other provinces, in that they had a Grade 13. Although it was a part of the high school curriculum, it was the equivalent to first year university in other provinces. Apparently, Ontario had received funding for its Grade 13 program, but British Columbia had not. Further, the province of Quebec had two-year college programs which functioned as the equivalent to Grades 12 and 13; and, like Ontario, it had received funding for these programs. British Columbia considered this to be clearly unfair!

It did not happen immediately; but, eventually, British Columbia won its case.

The media gave high billing to these events, announcing that the B.C. government would receive an extra $81 million from the Federal Government for its Ministries of Education and Health. It would take some time before the distribution of funds would be revealed, although it initially mattered very little to Trinity Western, since the Education Minister had made it clear that we were not to be included. Or were we?

After the lawsuit, a forensic auditor was appointed to organize the distribution of funds and as he 'crunched the numbers', he came to the realization that the British Columbia government had been receiving funding for the students attending Trinity Western for some time, and that money had not been passed on.

Thank the Lord for the actions of Dr. Enoch Mattson, who had continued to submit our student numbers each year, even while we received no funding and had no expectation of receiving funding!

As a result, and out of the blue, we received a telephone call from the independent foundation that was responsible for distributing the education equalization grants. The amount owed to Trinity Western had yet to be determined, but once that amount was finalized, there would be three payments making their way to our Finance Department over the next four years.

A report had projected that Trinity Western could have a deficit of about two million dollars if we went forward with the transition to a four-year university. As it turns out, the provincial government decided we were entitled to a total of almost $1.83 million dollars! The money would come to us in payments over four years.

Equalization grants start to arrive

We had been 'left in the dark' for what seemed a long while, but finally the first equalization grant money arrived—with no strings attached! It was another day of rejoicing! God had blessed our efforts to become a four-year college, and now we were carefully planning and praying that university status would be soon achieved. We hadn't forgotten that many, if not most junior colleges fail in their expansion attempt; nor the projection that we could be as much as $2 million in debt within the next five years.

Fortunately, the Equalization Grant payments were spread over four years. You can't imagine the surprise and excitement when we received the first payment. Typically, it called for a prayer of thanksgiving.

The first payment, $568,000, was probably the largest payment for operations we'd ever had to date. The next year, it was $500,000. Two years later, it was $720,000. And finally, a "clean-up" payment of $38,000 in 1982. Altogether, we received $1,826,000. These funds weren't for capital expenses, such as buildings. They were, in fact, God's provision of operational funds that would enable us to transition from a junior college to a free-standing four-year university-college.

We had hoped and prayed that God would provide in some way. It was not just wishful thinking; but rather there was a "confident expectation" that the Sovereign God Who had brought us miraculously through many unusual tangles of 'impossibilities' would continue to act on our behalf. We just never expected that His way would be through government funding! But the news led to a time of thanksgiving and rejoicing by our entire community. It was a very clear sign that God had ordained our steps for us, long before we knew which direction to go.

Once again it was **to the praise of His glory!**

14

A pastor brings TWC's first computer

When I came to Trinity Western in 1974, the dream hadn't yet reached the goal of the little junior college becoming an internationally recognized, degree-granting institution of academic excellence. That would require yet another team of people, whom God now began to gather. And, just as miraculous as the steps towards the achievement of the goal, was God's preparation of these people to meet the extraordinary needs of the time.

An outstanding example of this was the career of Guy Saffold, who came to Trinity Western in 1978, where he was initially employed to assist the Registrar. In those days, Trinity Western didn't have an Admissions Department; that was just a subordinate function of the Registrar's office. Guy was hired to assist the Registrar in the area of student recruitment.

At various times, during the 28 years we worked together, Guy served TWU as Director of Public Affairs, Vice President for Strategic Planning, Vice President of Advancement, Executive Vice President, Dean of the Trinity Western Seminary, and then as the chief administrator of the Associated Canadian Theological Schools (ACTS), public spokesman for the University during legal challenges, and Professor of Theological Studies—and more! He has taught Linear Algebra, Statistics, and Management Information Systems for the undergrad division, and eventually Leadership for undergrads and for seminary students at ACTS. He led campus planning; and that committee, under his leadership, produced maps that are not much different from the layout of the campus today. His personal motto is:

"Serving Jesus—any time, anywhere, at any cost, to do anything."

Here's Guy's own capsule summary of his early life, and his coming to Trinity Western:

—*Neil Snider*

By Guy Saffold

My mother was an American who had grown up in France during the 1920s and '30s. She spoke French fluently. When concerns over the approach of WWII grew, her family relocated back to Massachusetts.

My father served in the Merchant Marine, dodging submarines while carrying military cargo to England and Russia. He survived, and I was born to the young couple in 1947 in New York City—right in Manhattan. My father was opposed to religious faith, so I grew up in an entirely secular household. But during my last year in high school, in Winnetka, Illinois, I had friends who were part of the Young Life ministry at New Trier High School.

I came to faith in Christ that year, and the following fall (1965) I entered the University of Illinois to pursue a degree in electrical engineering. The age of solid-state electronics was just beginning, so advisors recommended that I enroll in a Physics major. Along the way, however, I became involved in campus evangelism with Inter-Varsity Christian Fellowship, and found my desires changing. In my third year, I changed from Physics and Mathematics to Psychology and Classics, picking up a lot of philosophy and two years of Greek.

Upon graduation, I enrolled at Trinity Evangelical Divinity School in Deerfield, Illinois. I arrived in the fall of 1969 with just enough money for tuition and room and board—only until November, hoping that God would provide the rest. My new room-mate arrived with no money at all. I gave him half of my money, so the two of us now had enough for six weeks of a three-year program. As it developed, God did supply all that was needed. We both graduated three years later—without debt.

There were few women at seminary in those days, just a small number in the whole student body of several hundred men. I was fortunate enough to connect with one of them, Susan Marston from Orange, California. I would later learn that her church youth group leaders were the parents of Shawn Francine, the future wife of Ken Kush, who would one day become Student Life leader at Trinity Western. So even at that point God was weaving threads together.

Sue's father had also been a returning soldier—a ball turret gunner, flying bombing missions over Nazi Germany. Both he and my father had seen so many friends die that they talked very little about their war experiences. It had hardened them to take pain and disaster in stride, and keep on going.

Sue and I were married December 21, 1973. She graduated the following spring, and we went together to the placement office to ask about churches that needed pastors. To our surprise, they recommended a small Evangelical Free Church in North Vancouver, B.C.

Canada? Never in our wildest imagination had we thought about going to Canada! And like many Americans, we knew next to nothing about the country to the north of us.

Nonetheless, we agreed to candidate at the church. As I exited immigration at the Vancouver airport a tall, white-haired bundle of energy named Carl Fosmark met us and swept us off to the church where he was working as Interim Pastor. We were called to that church, and arrived in Canada in the summer of 1974, expecting to be in Canada for perhaps a few years before going back to the United States.

Forty years later, we're still here!

One Sunday, Dr. Snider spoke about Trinity Western College at that North Vancouver church, and met the Pastor—me, Guy Saffold. An elderly woman from my congregation decided to will her small North Van home to Trinity Western. She contacted the development office at the school—and no one responded. She tried again, and was promised that someone would be out to see her one afternoon. She was not well, but she painfully cleaned her home and made tea ready. No one came.

I got quite angry about it all, and called Dr. Snider to say that this was really quite unbelievable. Her home was almost all she owned and she wanted to donate it to the College, but apparently no one could be bothered to visit her—and even after setting up an appointment, didn't keep it! Neil stepped in and put all this straight; and some years later, upon her death, the home was sold with the funds going to TW.

One day, I saw an opportunity to combine my scientific and theological training to teach students biblical languages. As part of my physics major, I'd worked a lot with computers at the University of Illinois. Computers, in those days, were large, warehouse-sized monsters! But in the fall of 1977, while driving down Rupert Street in Vancouver I saw a store advertising "micro computers." That sounded quite interesting, so I walked into the store. I didn't know it then, but I was about to discover the early world of personal computers.

As I sat in the store and experimented with what was a rather primitive but functional machine I thought, "This could be a great tool for helping students learn Greek and Hebrew!" After some research, I bought an Imsai PCS 80/30 personal computer. This machine had a video board that could be re-engineered to display Greek and Hebrew characters, which no other computer at the time could do. It cost about $4,000 back then—the equivalent of much more today—which was a huge expense for a young family; but we managed it. I was able to re-program the video display card to provide Greek and Hebrew characters. I wrote several software programs to display biblical languages, and to implement vocabulary-learning and grammar-teaching systems.

It occurred to me that this might be useful at Trinity Western. So I called President Snider, who invited me out to the Langley campus. The screen on the Imsai was only 4 inches wide, so I borrowed a larger screen and headed out to the campus. I arrived at the appointed time only to discover that that Neil's office had cancelled the appointment! I thought, "This kind of experience is familiar to me," and I was little inclined to ever try working with TW again. However, Neil called me, graciously apologized, and asked that I come again, which I did.

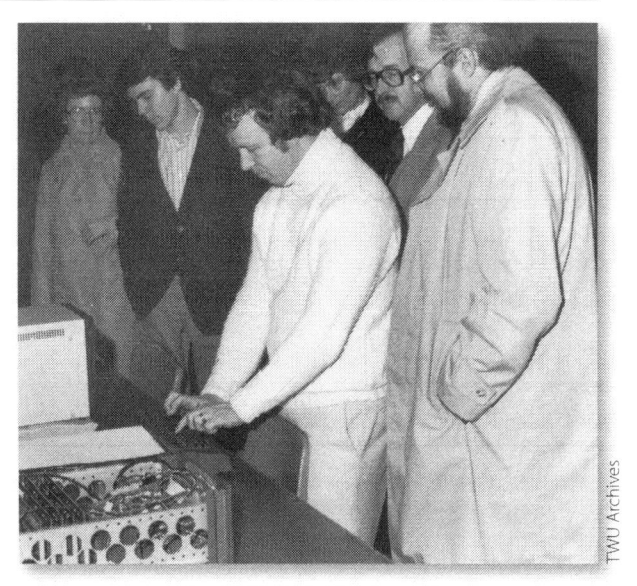

Guy Saffold (at keyboard)

At that point TW didn't teach Greek or Hebrew; so once more, there seemed to be little point in further connection. However, not long afterward, Arvid Olson called, said that the college wanted to expand, and asked if I could come to help recruit students. After much prayer and discussion, Sue and I agreed; so I began a new job in the area of student recruitment in the fall of 1978.

As with our original move to Canada four years earlier, it still seemed likely that my time at Trinity Western would be short term—only a couple of years before we returned to the U.S. Once again, I couldn't have been more wrong!

15

Amending our two-year charter

The decision to become a four-year college would have many implications. Obviously, the cost would be great. Furthermore, the *Trinity Western College Charter*, with its provision to offer a two-year Liberal Arts program in British Columbia, would have to be amended. This posed a tremendous challenge to our young privately-funded Christian institution. There was no hope that any political party would even consider bringing forward such history-making legislation. It would require a Private Member's Bill that would be evaluated by an all-party committee. Rarely does such a Bill ever reach the floor of the Legislature.

Dr. Robert Thompson was asked to work with John Cherrington, who had served for many years as legal advisor for Trinity Western. Their responsibility was to locate a friendly Member of the Legislative Assembly (MLA) who would approve a draft and accept the responsibility of presenting an amending bill to the Legislature. Burnaby MLA Elwood Veitch agreed.

It was the spring of 1977 when The British Columbia Legislative Assembly received the Private Member's Bill seeking to amend Trinity's existing Charter to allow for the development of a four-year academic program and the granting of bachelor's degrees. There was little response in the days before the scheduled meeting of the Private Bills Committee. The day before, however, we received an important alert: Dr. Pat McGeer, the Minister of Education, informed us that we were to meet with him that very day, one day before the day the Private Bills Committee would meet. It didn't take long before John Cherrington, Dr. Thompson and I were on our way to Victoria. We had no idea what was to come, so we just enjoyed the beauty of God's creation as we crossed on the ferry to Vancouver Island.

We arrived in mid-afternoon—only to learn that Dr. McGeer wouldn't be available until after 7 o'clock that evening. This gave us more time to review the bill, and to meet a few friends—who also had no idea why we'd been called. At nearly 9 p.m., after Dr. McGeer's regular evening workout, we were invited into his office.

The Minister was courteous, but he soon let us know of his concerns. We were quite sure that with his busy schedule, he hadn't taken the time to really understand what we were asking of him. Now he felt he had to inform us that he wouldn't support our Bill. We knew immediately there was no way we could proceed without the Minister's support.

We didn't give up easily, however. We listened intently as Dr. McGeer pointed out that there was no precedent for such a privately-funded college in Canada. Once, a religious institution had attempted something like it; but it couldn't be sustained—Notre Dame College in Nelson, BC, where he said the faculty weren't able or willing to work for "unmanageable" salaries. That college eventually had pressed the government to bail them out—only to realize, after a couple of years, it would still have to close. Even after trying to be helpful, the government had ended up with "egg all over its face"—and he had no intention of letting that happen again!

By way of response, we spoke about all that had happened in Trinity's short history; how we had, from the beginning, no intention whatsoever to ever ask for government money to fund operations; and that we planned to follow the pattern of successful private institutions in the USA. With deep conviction, I shared the vision of our Total Student Development philosophy, which was already producing the kind of people who would make a difference: positive, goal-oriented leaders.

Finally Dr. McGeer responded: "I cannot support this bill," he said. "However, if you agree to remove the clause that makes it possible for Trinity to offer degrees, I won't oppose it." That meant we'd have to remove that clause before the bill went to the committee—the very next day.

That called for a pertinent question that had to be addressed: What value is a four-year college, if students who graduate don't receive a degree?

Quick responses indicated that thought had been given to this question. The idea of adding other, less academic courses didn't even warrant a response. The possibility of working out a degree-granting mechanism with Simon Fraser University, or even with UBC, was suggested. Finally, a promise was made that the Ministry would work out some kind of arrangement within the next year. I'm sure we didn't express any confidence in these suggestions; but we knew that the meeting had come to a close.

We thanked him for listening, and he expressed appreciation for what we were trying to do. But that was all he was prepared to do.

It was amazing! We looked at each other and agreed: there was no way we could back down! In fact, we agreed that we ought to move forward and get what we could from this bill—and that meant that we had to get to work. We made the necessary changes to the bill, deleting only the clause about granting degrees, and in just a few hours we had the new draft printed and waiting for the opportunity to share the next step we believed God had made possible.

The Minister agreed that although he would not support the bill, he would not oppose it; and he did promise to work out another path to becoming a university-college.

The Trinity Western proposal was first on the agenda Tuesday morning. I was asked to explain the purpose of the bill, and why it was important to have the government approve this Charter change. I considered it a privilege, and I warmed up to painting the vision we'd been following. I then had to report that there'd been a change from the original document we had disseminated. I explained, as simply as possible, that we'd chosen to delete the clause referring to the degree-granting issue… for the time being.

Immediately, there were questions: "Why?"

A leading member of the Opposition asked directly if the Minister of Education had asked us to delete that clause.

I did my best to avoid embarrassing the Minister by saying that the timing didn't seem right; but I'm quite certain that my answer was less than convincing. As it happened, the discussion took a sudden turn, and the Opposition began to speak supportively of our good intentions. Apparently, if the Minister was not supportive, the Opposition didn't mind supporting the Bill. Politics! The Private Bills Committee voted to approve the Bill, and we were one step further toward our goal.

Some weeks later, the Bill came to the floor of the Legislature. There were very few questions about the Bill, and it was approved with little opposition. We were now a four-year college!

It remained unclear what the Minister's objection had been; perhaps it was an attempt to force us into an affiliation with one of British Columbia's public universities. They would then be responsible for granting the degrees. But in such an arrangement, the public university would also be in a position to control both curricular and faculty decisions.

The question of authority to grant degrees would need early resolution before a new university program could be fully implemented.

16

Seeking the right to grant degrees

There had been great relief at the coming of Dr. Craig Seaton, not only on the part of Deane Downey and David Twiest—who had both had to carry double loads, as Professor and Librarian respectively, while also acting as Dean. The whole community seemed to recognize that ours was a major challenge, as well as a spiritual battle. Once again, God had prepared a senior leader to challenge and encourage our academic and student development programs in this time of major change.

Craig Seaton was offered the challenge of developing Trinity Western into a university-college when he accepted the position of Academic Dean in September 1977. His experience in higher education had included time as a student, faculty member and administrator in public, private and Christian Higher Education. At the time when he was selected to serve as our Dean, he was on the staff of the California Post-Secondary Education Commission.

Several major steps toward becoming a university had already been taken, and programs such as Business and Aviation had already moved us beyond the traditional liberal arts and sciences curriculum. Furthermore, a rich core curriculum had been developed, that was required for all Trinity Western students, to provide them all with a broad spectrum of arts and sciences,

Craig Seaton

and selected professional studies with Christian perspectives as the bases for integrating faith and learning, including first-year English; Arts, Media and Culture; History; Human Kinetics; Interdisciplinary Studies; Natural Sciences; Philosophy; Religious Studies; Society and Culture; and a unit called 'My TW'.

Craig was fully aware of, and in agreement with, TWC's plans to become a four-year Christian college. In a very short period of time, we'd already seen the Charter of our two-year junior college legally changed to a four-year Christian college. But a major challenge remained: the right to offer degrees to our students had not yet been obtained.

Dr. Seaton was well-prepared for the task. His education had been at three different universities, ultimately receiving his PhD from the University of Southern California. His working experience appeared to have been carefully laid out as a preparation for what he would be doing at TWC. He'd served as a social worker, and as chief of training at the California State Department of Social Welfare. He'd been a naval officer for three years; he was a licensed marriage, family and child counsellor; and also a policy researcher, charged with planning for state-wide higher education. He'd also been a professor and administrator at Biola University, and then at Simpson College. He'd taught Sociology, Psychology, Management, and Human Services. And yet with all that experience, he still looked very young!

17

Playing politics

Craig and Marsha Seaton were confident that God had called them to join the Trinity Western College community. The Board of Governors of Trinity Western approved his appointment as Academic Dean in October of 1977, at almost the same time they appointed a Four-Year Study Commission. That commission was charged with designing an academic program that would lead to the awarding of baccalaureate degrees.

The very ambitious timeline required an interim report for the Board by the first week of December, 1977; and outlines of new academic programs for the January, 1978 Board meeting. The Commission included: David Twiest (Librarian), and faculty members Dr. Deane Downey, Mr. Elmer Dyck, and Dr. Jack Van Dyke. Craig chaired the commission, and I served in an *ex-officio* capacity. The Board framed its charge to the Commission with a very specific philosophy it wanted to see reflected in the new four-year program:

> "The central purpose in the establishment of Trinity Western College is to provide for persons of any race, colour, or creed, a university education in the arts and sciences, with an underlying philosophy and viewpoint that is Christian."
>
> —*(Page 2 from the Guidelines for the Four-Year Study Commission)*

This central purpose statement was very significant, particularly in light of the misunderstanding by some of the public and media, who frequently viewed Trinity as being narrowly parochial. The guidelines also called for "training in communication and critical thought to foster the acquisition of such qualities as poise, tolerance and cooperativeness in social relationships." (*ibid.*)

The basic design of the new four-year degree program was approved by the Board of Governors at their meeting in January of 1978. The implementation schedule was to be:

1. 1977-1978 academic year (construct program, hire additional faculty for 1978);
2. 1978-1979 academic year (begin third-year studies, acquire authority to grant degrees through an amendment to the *Trinity Western College Act*, hire more faculty);
3. 1979-1980 academic year (begin fourth-year studies and award first degrees).

In the fall of 1978, we had 25 third-year students among the 504 enrolled. This was reminiscent of the 17 who, in 1962, had stepped out in faith, believing God had led them to Canada's first Christian junior college. To move into the third year now, without assurance that their courses might ever be accredited, may have required even *more* faith: there was more to lose. The campus community at large was confident about the quality of the programs, and also of the ability of God to expand and enrich our community. The first graduating class would expect to receive their degrees in 1980.

One of Craig's first political meetings at Victoria in 1979 was with the Leader of the Opposition, former NDP Premier Dave Barrett. He was quite candid. He said that while he wasn't personally opposed to our amendment, his party would use the amendment as a vehicle to do as much political damage to the Social Credit government as possible.

Craig had extensive contact with politicians during spring and early summer, trying to give them a clear picture of why Trinity Western was qualified to award degrees, and why it was important to amend the *Trinity Western College Act* during the current session.

Bill Ritchie, the new MLA from Central Fraser Valley, was the sponsor of a new Private Member's Bill that would amend the existing Act. July 11, 1979, Craig testified before a Legislative committee to argue the case for degree-granting authority. Dr. Neil Perry, a representative from the Universities Council of B.C., and Dr. Walter Hardwick, from the Ministry of Education, also testified before that Committee. Dr. Perry said giving Trinity Western degree-granting power would be a major policy change. However, he didn't oppose the amendment. Dr. Hardwick said Trinity Western had a legal right to seek degree-conferring status through a Private Member's Bill. The NDP members of the Committee were respectful, if not supportive.

None of the NDP members voted in favour of recommending approval to the full Legislature. All members of the Social Credit Party voted to send the proposed amendment of the *Trinity Western College Act* on to the full Legislature. Peter Hyndman, MLA from Vancouver South, was a particularly strong advocate for the amendment.

Two days later, the chairman of the Universities Council of B.C. was quoted as opposing the private member's bill. Council Chairman Bill Gibson said the College had no right to apply to the government for such status before consulting Council members. "We really don't need a fourth degree-granting university in this province," he said. Gibson was also worried about the type of education being taught at a religious college. "What kind of biology will they be teaching?" (July 13, 1979 *The Province*) Stories appeared in the press daily from July 11 until early August about Trinity's attempt to gain degree-granting authority. Gibson's opposition was misinterpreted in later news stories to have also taken place at the July 11 Legislative Committee meeting, so there was an outpouring of negative headlines and stories.

It seemed a show-down would happen at the very end of the session. It was understood that the week of July 23 would likely be the last week the Assembly would sit. If the Trinity Western private member's bill were not heard, the process would have to start all over in 1980. Various special-interest groups were lobbying against the bill, and there were rumours circulating that the bill would not be brought forward in this session. When Craig spoke with government members, a good number seemed non-committal.

Craig prepared a news release to answer all the arguments being put forward by opponents of the bill. He placed the release into the Legislative mail system to be delivered to all members Wednesday morning (July 26). That release made the following arguments:

> "We ask that both Social Credit and New Democratic Party MLAs ignore the pressures of special-interest groups, and allow the *Trinity Western College Act* amendment to be brought before the Legislature…
>
> "The bill (sponsored by Bill Ritchie, SC-Central Fraser Valley), passed Committee on July 11, but has not come up for second reading, and it seems clear that the session will end shortly. The next session will probably not convene until early next year. The amendment makes explicit the degree-granting powers of the College, which was previously given authority to provide a university program, by legislative action in 1977. Those who oppose the idea of an independent degree-granting

institution should have made their case during the debate preceding that legislation.

"Students entered third-year studies last September. Out of the 504 students enrolled last year, about 25 were third-year students. They will complete their respective programs this coming April. In this coming year, more than 600 students will enter the College, and about 60 will be in third-year studies.

Opposition arguments are faulty

Financial

"It is clear that we are in an era in which universities across Canada are concerned about enrolments that are leveling off, and in some cases falling. This has potentially damaging effects on the financial health of some universities. However, to oppose degree-granting status on a basis related to financing and/or enrolment is unsound for at least several reasons:

"First, the College does not seek provincial tax dollars that are or will be going to support education.

"Second, the College seeks to provide an opportunity for university-level education on a smaller, more personal scale than B.C.'s public universities. Development plans project an ultimate enrolment of only 1,200.

"Third, for every B.C. resident who elects to pursue post-secondary studies at TWC, there is a savings to the taxpayer. The cost to the provincial taxpayer per full-time student at the three public universities ranges from $5,000 to more than $6,000 per year. (This does not include capital costs for facilities and equipment.) Last year, 307 of our students who were from B.C. provided for substantial savings to the Province.

Academic Standards

"… The performance of TWC students going on to other institutions in the province and elsewhere demonstrates notable success. In the five-year period from 1973 to 1978, data compiled by the independent educational research organization, B.C. Research, showed that students who had completed one or two years at TWC, and … continued on at the University of British Columbia, had a significantly higher Grade-Point

Average than students from B.C.'s other two-year colleges. And in addition, TWC students also had a higher Grade-Point Average than those students who had taken studies only at UBC. It was also found that TWC students attained the highest average grade from any B.C. college in the faculties of Arts, Commerce, Agricultural Science and Applied Science. TWC [transfer] students achieved the second-highest average grade in the [UBC] Faculty of Science.

Consultation with government authorities

"Prior to enactment of the 1977 legislation, the College presented briefs to both the Universities Council and the Ministry of Education. Since that time, the flow of information has continued on a regular basis. In August of 1978, I met with Universities Council Chairman, William Gibson, in his office.

"On November 24, 1978 I (Craig Seaton) wrote to Chairman Gibson and outlined our plans for the 1978-1979 academic year, and invited him to come to our campus. Contact with the Ministry of Education has been considerably more extensive…

Pressure groups

"In the past ten days, lobbying of MLAs from both parties has been intense, as some who oppose the idea of an independent degree-granting institution in the province have sought to prevent the bill from receiving a fair hearing on the floor of the Legislature. In one such effort, the president of the alumni association of one of the provincial universities sent telegrams to all MLAs, opposing the bill. This was done without consulting the membership of that alumni association.

"I call upon all MLAs to honour the principle and the process of the Legislative Assembly, and to bring the bill forward for debate and a vote. Those who oppose the bill should be willing to publicly vote against it, just as those who support it should be given the opportunity to vote for it, and to state their reasons for doing so."

Reaction to the press release

Craig was watching from the public gallery when MLAs began to go through their mail before the session began July 26. Our release had a red border, so it was easy to identify as they began to read it. Bill Ritchie, sponsor of our bill, read the release and then looked up at Craig and gave him the "thumbs up" sign. He also received other encouraging feedback from MLAs about the news release; but the bill was not put on the agenda for that day.

Later that day, an MLA asked Craig if Trinity Western could wait until next year. Craig explained why that wasn't feasible because of the students who had already entered, and those who would be coming in September.

Craig spent the next day in the public gallery, waiting. The bill wasn't introduced that day, but it was announced that the Legislative Session would continue into the next week.

The final day of the Legislative Session was July 31. The late afternoon finally included the introduction of Trinity's private member's bill, in a very colourful way by George Mussallem, MLA.

The political climate of the day was best reflected in these newspaper headlines:

College's statement of faith condemns non-believers to hell
(July 28. 1979 *The Province*); and,

Trinity run around Universities Council raises academic ire
(July 31, 1979 *The Province*).

In the story accompanying the "statement of faith" headline, the author wrote:

> "University academics are raising Cain over a statement of faith Trinity Western College instructors are required to sign which condemns non-believers in their faith to hell and damnation. The question raised by university officials is how college instructors, who vow to follow the doctrines of evangelical Christian doctrine, can objectively teach…"

Another article said:

> "University pundits also say they are afraid BC may become a mail-order degree province and lose its academic reputation by granting degree status to institutions without first examining their credentials.
>
> "The bill before the house was still awaiting passage on Monday and observers thought it was unlikely it would now be enacted before adjournment."
(July 30, 1979 *The Province*)

But not all newspaper accounts were so negative:

"Taking his first walk through the legislative forest, Bill Ritchie has unexpectedly kicked over a hornets' nest... 'Frankly speaking, I did not expect that I was stirring up a little storm which could become a hurricane... but I feel confident... (my) first piece of legislation will be successful.' "

(July 25, 1979 *Abbotsford, Sumas and Matsqui News*)

Debate on the bill

The Opposition NDP opposed the bill—principally, they said, due to a lack of a comprehensive analysis by either the Ministry of Education or by the Universities Council. (Although on this occasion, like several others, they misspoke about information they'd received.)

Their assertion that the Universities Council had provided a negative report was rightly challenged by MLA Peter Hyndman, who was also a member of the same Committee. He quoted from the testimony of Dr. Perry of the Universities Council that "Trinity Western certainly has been performing superbly, as far as we know. We've always had a favourable report on both the performance of the students after they leave Trinity Western, and on the substantive content of the courses offered by Trinity Western." (*HANSARD*, the official record of the proceedings of Parliament, page 1139)

Much of the criticism of Trinity's attempt to gain degree-granting status was based on utilizing a Private Member's Bill instead of one offered by the government. However, Opposition NDP MLA Ernie Hall indicated that "I find no objection whatsoever in the fact that the petitioners came by way of a private bill. According to the testimony in front of us, that was the only way in which the petitioner could find his way into the Legislature." (*HANSARD* page 1139)

Eileen Dailly, who had been the Minister of Education in the former NDP government, argued, "We're opening a Pandora's box... Any group in B.C. who wants to have degree-granting status can simply come before the Private Bills Committee, talk to enough Social Credit members and get degree-granting status without any input whatsoever." (*HANSARD* page 1139)

Dailly also raised a concern that eventually Trinity "would be seeking public money."

Education Minister Pat McGeer responded to the criticisms from the NDP by:

1. rejecting the idea that the Universities Council had jurisdiction over a private institution; and

2. arguing that if Canada were ever to develop an élite institution—like Harvard, Princeton, Columbia or Cal. Tech—such an institution would develop from private funding, and would have to prove itself in the marketplace: "Trinity Western will prove itself credible in the marketplace or it will fail; either way, it will be no financial burden to the taxpayer."

After more acrimony, at the end of the afternoon a vote was taken, and the amendment passed 30-17. All Social Credit members voted in favour, while 9 NDP members, including Leader Dave Barrett did not vote. He didn't attend the debate.

Media response

On August 1, 1979 *The Province* newspaper summarized what had happened in Victoria:

> "The controversial Trinity Western College in Langley was given four-year degree-granting status Tuesday over charges from the NDP that the government had railroaded the legislation through the House.
>
> "During debate on Mussallem's motion Ernie Hall (NDP-Surrey) condemned the government and Education Minister Pat McGeer for bypassing the Universities Council of BC, which opposed the proposal before the private members committee (a mistake consistently made in the media).
>
> "Former NDP Education Minister Eileen Dailly (Burnaby-North) said the issue is not one of complaint against degree status; but that a committee was asked to make up its mind in one day without any public inquiry.
>
> "Ironically, the same request to give Trinity Western degree status went through the private bills committee two years ago, with little opposition by the NDP and some NDP members even approving. It never got through the house, being withdrawn at the last minute by McGeer."

Headlines on this date included:

TWC bill squeaks through legislature

(Langley Advance),

Socreds vote degree status to trinity [sic] **college
& NDP protests bill railroaded**

(The Province),

Marketplace to test wisdom of Trinity degree-granting law

(Vancouver Sun)

Allan Fotheringham's column in the *Vancouver Sun* on August 2, 1979 said:

> "You don't have to be too bright (or even a graduate of Trinity Western College) to figure out that McGeer, as education minister of the province, is using the example of this jumped-up fundamentalist factory—with an enrollment lower than most Vancouver high schools—to get even with a few enemies."

In September, another *Sun* columnist, Marjorie Nichols, offered a more insightful observation about the coverage Trinity Western had received in the news media over the last number of weeks:

> "The recent spate of sniggering commentaries about Trinity Western College, BC's newest degree-granting institution, raises some interesting questions concerning academic and religious tolerance in this province."

(September 11, 1979 Vancouver Sun)

Craig's brief reflection on the experience of participation in the process

Craig later said that when he arrived at Trinity, he had no idea that so much of his time as Dean would be occupied with external relations and lobbying politicians. He didn't anticipate the negative and unfair press accounts about Trinity Western, and our Evangelical faith position. However, he said, "I *did* anticipate that God could and would use this institution to change and to mould lives. And I *did* believe that Trinity had the potential to make a difference, not only in Canada, but elsewhere across the world."

18

Developing 'Management by Objectives'

We had gained the legal right to grant degrees—a great way to start a new academic year; but it also greatly increased the need for futuristic planning. Student numbers had also increased, and for the first time since my coming to Trinity Western, we had a full complement of administrative colleagues at the top level. The addition of Craig Seaton as Academic Dean was timely, and Arvid Olson was providing significant leadership for our "Total Student Development" emphasis. He was a strong asset: sensitive to student needs, and capable of motivating all of our community to a student-centred outlook.

One administrative policy of the Board was that a supervisor would not hire a person until his (or her) own immediate superior had been consulted on the matter. To be consistent, this meant that the President would consult with the Board on each major administrative appointment. It was to be a cohesive practice that strengthened confidence in the values and vision of the community. This practice was also extended to Faculty and Student Life personnel, as well as to the Advisory Council.

Barry Palfreyman, Neil Snider, and Doug Harris.

Three gifted leaders

Three more young but experienced administrators moved in to share senior leadership responsibilities. Director of Public Affairs Barry Palfreyman, a goal-setter and an extremely hard worker, was already outlining goals in his area for the current year. In coming years, he would become President of the General Conference Baptist Seminary, one of our partnering seminaries in the Associated Canadian Theological Seminaries (ACTS).

During the recent period of rapid change, and particularly with the introduction of fund accounting, Trinity Western had come near to a disaster a couple of years before. We were more than two months behind in our bookkeeping, and it took a person like Reg Reimer to pull us out of that position. He was obviously God's man for the job! The auditors emphasized, again and again, that Reg had done a remarkable job. He was growing in his ability to take leadership, and we were relying heavily on him for the whole budgeting process. In a real sense, he was the controller of controllers. Each major administrator was responsible to control the funds designated for his area; but it was Reg's responsibility to ensure that it was actually happening.

Reg Reimer

A third miracle worker was Business Manager Doug Sneath—who, like Reg, had come from Steinbach, Manitoba, where they'd been students together. The best word to describe Doug Sneath's work was "outstanding". I had received only enthusiastic recommendations from department heads working under him. He was goal-oriented, energetic, willing to take initiative; and unafraid to make difficult decisions. In his first report to the Board, Doug stated:

> "A major concern of mine, after being at the College only three months, is the general condition and upkeep of the older buildings on campus. With reference to our gymnasium, we have learned that nearly $25,000 would be required in the immediate future to avoid having the building shut down. I believe we have an obligation to make our campus more fire safe; and quite frankly, I am thankful that we are being forced to take a closer look at this area. I share this with you because of the unforeseen costs involved."

Doug Sneath

In addition to giving oversight to the print shop, snack bar and bookstore, Doug had to evaluate and reshape food services, and also to support the maintenance and custodial staff. Perhaps his greatest achievement was as our building superintendent. Five major multi-million dollar construction projects, with the help of only one competent assistant, were completed in time to accommodate the rapidly-growing Trinity Western community. The owners of the construction companies, who also generously supported the projects, were pleased to have Doug Sneath work with them.

As I reflected on God's gracious gift of godly, competent leaders to join Trinity Western in its time of expansion, I couldn't help expressing gratitude to God and to those who gave of themselves so willingly. At the same time, I cringed at the realization that Reg and Doug stayed only a few over-worked years, during which we should have given them more support. After making such a great contribution, each of them chose to move on with their beautiful families, rather than to risk burn-out under the unrelenting pressure. Still, as He often does, God has enriched their lives as He has ours. They stand tall in our memories!

Guarding the vision

As the vision for a four-year college became more and more clear, the sense of responsibility on the part of all leaders became more acute. *"… if any man aspires to the office of overseer, it is a fine work he desires to do,"* wrote the Apostle Paul.[1] In a very real sense, the task of serving on the Board of a Christian college like TWC required the willingness and the qualifications of a biblical "overseer". These requirements also held true for administrators, faculty, professional staff—for all employees, as had always been the case.

We knew that it would take time to develop criteria for hiring, and to develop

---
[1] First Timothy 3:1 (NASB)

administrative processes that would effectively shape the values and expected outcomes of a God-honouring college community. We believed that the most effective process to accomplish that endeavour would be to clarify and develop goals that would unite the whole community, focused around TW's soon-to-be-developed Mission Statement.

Probably the first and most important place to start, when developing a goal-oriented approach to management, is with a description of the parts of the organizational structure. Typically, reference is made to job descriptions. But I preferred to think, in the first place, of each position in terms of the job *specifications* that include all activities under the umbrella of each particular position.

The second step would be to match a particular person to those job specifications. A very personalized job description could then be drawn from the job specifications, since different people go about their tasks in slightly (or even significantly) different ways. It was most rewarding to look over the organization and see that most positions had not only job specifications, but personalized job descriptions as well.

The final step in the process was to establish criteria against which the degree of success could be measured. This could be a difficult task, and constant review and refinement would have to become a way of life. With regard to internal management, one of my chief goals was to ensure that such refinement took place, so that this system would become more and more the total pattern of operation for TWC.

Envisioning goals for 1977-78

The practice of goal-setting had been established in the 1974/75 school year. It took time for people to appreciate what could be accomplished if we set goals, then developed strategies describing how those goals might be achieved. It made good sense for the President to set out a number of goals for 1977 and 1978 that would facilitate laying the groundwork for becoming a university. Abridged, they might sound simple enough; but they would call for focused action:

1. To strengthen TWC's reputation as a leader in Christian higher education in Canada. This could be strategically planned to focus on key centres across Canada;

2. To implement our Board's expansion. The original nine-member Board, which at one point included seven pastors, could hardly provide the kind of representation that a college Board required;

3. To see our four-year program clarified and introduced for the Fall of

1978. A study commission would have to be implemented, and the Board needed to bring in outside consultants to assist in the implementation of this program;

4. To press for the development of continuing education programs, including conferences led and directed by TWC personnel;

5. To continue the development of staff and faculty personnel policies, which were in dire need of updating;

6. To get a direct-mail plan developed and operational, implementing then-still-new computer technologies;

7. To complete plans for the Robert Thompson Centre, and start construction;

8. To establish a commission to develop a new constitution for our student organizations, in keeping with our new four-year status.

But this was only one set of goals. Each of the divisions would also establish its own work agendas, in the form of goals. These goals would each encompass a large domain, and would call for a tremendous output of energy and coordinated effort on the part of all of us. I expressed to the Board my sense of inadequacy for the task before us. At the same time, I was confident that God had brought each and every one of us into the Administration, and onto the Board of TWC, for this exciting part of our history.

I believed that as we worked together, we were going to see the continuing miracle of TWC unfold before us. In just the fourth year of the new era, the vision of a four-year institution was beginning to emerge, as goals set in faith were being realized.

19

'A great door for effective service!'

A spirit of confidence began to grow as we saw applications come in for our first class of third-year students. There could be no question that we had made progress. Who would have guessed that a privately-funded Christian college would ever see the light of day in British Columbia? It seemed like an opportune moment for the President to focus the attention of our Board and Advisory Council on a significant desired future: the Apostle Paul once wrote that *"… a great door for effective service has opened to me, and there are many who oppose me."*[1]

As I looked back over a most exciting year and thought of all that God had done for us as individuals, and as a College, I began to identify with the Great Apostle as he wrote to the Corinthians from Ephesus. There was a strong sense of optimism. A series of more obvious miracles was fresh in the minds of our College people, our friends, and in the broader constituency. Still, history and personal experience had been teaching us that whenever God is at work in unusual ways, it doesn't take long before attempts will be made to hinder His work.

One of the reasons we had such a great opportunity for effective service centred on our uniqueness as a college. I was convinced that "to be unique is to be strong." I wanted to review with our leaders once again some of our unique features.

Unique distinctives

While no single distinctive may render a college unique, a group of factors surely distinguishes Trinity Western from all other colleges in Canada. Consider these distinctives:

- Fully Christian, in the biblical sense of the word;
- Total Student Development philosophy;
- University-level programs;

---
[1] I Corinthians 16:9 (NIV)

- Wide acceptance in academic circles;
- A breadth of programs which includes not only general education, but which also has an emphasis on vocational preparation in several areas;
- A broad spectrum of participants at every level: students, staff, faculty, Board and supporters; people of different ages; representatives from many differing geographical, ethnic and denominational backgrounds; and
- Limited competition on the Canadian scene.

Unique opportunities

The unique distinctives speak for themselves to describe the opportunities that exist. Stated separately, some of the more obvious opportunities might be as follows:

- To be a leader in Canadian Christian higher education;
- To be a beacon of hope in a generally despondent academic world;
- To provide a voice of assurance based on authority, in contrast to a purely relativistic mindset;
- To provide stability and grounding in God's Word for young Christian students;
- To provide a meaningful alternative for the heart-thirst of the non-Christian student;
- To assemble groups of Christian scholars, intent on bringing the Christian perspective to their own disciplines; and
- To unite people from various denominations and backgrounds in a common effort.

Unique Challenges

While each of these opportunities presents a challenge to us, several other concerns also come to mind immediately. I referred to these needs, among others:

- To establish our unique identity as a college;
- To recruit and retain good faculty and staff;
- To improve salaries and benefits;
- To recruit students;

- To expand bursary and scholarship funds;
- To select and establish programs to meet the public's felt needs;
- To broaden the support base, exercise tight fiscal controls, and manage as good stewards;
- To involve more churches in our total program;
- To expand our mailing list; and
- To maintain our concern to serve, to minister, and to complement other ministries of the church.

This was more than a handful, but it also indicated that we were in dead earnest. It seemed reasonable, then, in view of our unique position at this time in history, that we should give ourselves to careful planning for the future. It was my hope and prayer that all of us would be able to contribute to both the process of planning and to the implementation that makes up the development process.

20

Expanding the vision for Student Life

In 1978 there were still many challenges before us. While it was exciting to think about the developing four-year curriculum, it would be necessary to update policies and procedures, and to establish a comprehensive plan for faculty and staff development that would include integration of a biblical worldview in all the various disciplines. But it was imperative that we also focus on the outcomes of our students' lives. We needed to be intentional in encouraging our students to godly living and serving. And one of the ways of moving more intentionally was to create a strong core of Student Development personnel. In 1976, when Arvid Olson joined the department as Dean of Student Development, we did this in several key areas.

Director of Student Services: Initially joining me in 1974 was a solid core of Student Development staff. Allan Kotanen came as Director of Student Services to coordinate the whole department, working with students. Joining him were Linda Bergen and Bob Payne as women's and men's Resident Counselors, respectively.

Two years after my coming, a major conceptual development took place in the expansion of the Student Life Department with a fresh perspective, as we saw the Department as a whole community. Nancy Johnson and Dale Heide also joined the staff as Assistant Resident Counselors; and then a year later Ardie Vance replaced Nancy Johnson.

Allan Kotanen

Ken Kush joined out staff as Director of Community Life, and proved very gifted in helping us visualize Student Life as a community working together to help one another become more of what the Lord intended us to become. Also joining us at this time, not only to help us bolster the community life concept, but also to help us develop a Career Development Department, to help provide assistance to students seeking guidance in regards to their future, was Gary Thuveson.

Just as the Lord had prepared other leaders whom He brought to TWC, so He prepared all these people and others for their ministry on campus.

Ken Kush

Dean of Student Development: Like other senior administrators, Arvid Olson was laying the groundwork for an expanded student body. His concern wasn't just about the number of students, although there were more than 500 by this time, but about shaping staff of professional educators—mentors and disciple-makers, counselors and coaches—people who were called and prepared, and able to encourage the personal development we envisioned. Once more, we were amazed how God had prepared people ahead of time for the unique kind of education that was to be at the heart of Trinity Western.

Director of Community Life: After spending his early life in Burlington, Ontario, Ken Kush began his undergraduate degree at Ontario Bible College. Entering into a one-year special program, he was able to finish a Bachelor of Religious Education before going to Wheaton College, where he completed the MA with a double major in Church Ministry and Counseling. It was there that Ken developed a philosophy of ministry that provided him with the answers to the "why" and the "what" of ministry. Three areas—educational theory, counseling psychology and organizational management—based on scriptural presuppositions concerning people and their relationship to God, helped him understand the notion of whole person development, and our responsibilities within the community. Coming to Trinity Western, first as a Resident Director and then as Director of Community Life, enabled him to flesh out this ministry to the individual, in the framework of the whole college community.

Ken was enthusiastic about TW's Total Student Development" concept, which he agreed was the "plus value" element for graduates of a Christian university-college. He stayed at TW until 1984, when he enrolled at UBC to complete his PhD in Counseling Psychology, and later joined UBC's Student Service staff.

Director of Career Education: Gary Thuveson was a native of the Greater Vancouver area, and a member of the Evangelical Free Church; he'd heard about Trinity Western College during his high school years. After he graduated from high school, he decided to attend TWC (1970-72). It was here that Gary realized his strong interest in psychology, and his desire to work with people. The following year, he attended Moody Bible Institute, and in 1976 graduated with a BA in the pastoral major. During his studies at MBI he served as a Resident Assistant on one of his men's residence floors. This sparked an interest to work in the area of Student Life, and in 1976 Gary enrolled at Azusa Pacific College in California, in their MA program of Social Sciences, with an emphasis in Student Development. Then the Lord opened the door for Gary to join us at TWC.

Special-interest student groups: Because of the increasing number of students living on campus, as well as a larger number of commuters attending, there was a concern to be more responsive to their individual and group needs. As a result, the Student Affairs leadership appointed one of the Resident Directors, Ardie Vance, to focus specifically on the needs of international students, "MKs" (missionary kids) and commuters.

Some of the international students had been in Canada for a year or more; others had come more recently. Their needs were as many and as varied as each individual. Generally though, they worked hard and long at their studies, because of the need to use English. Socially, they needed times to be together, other times to share with Canadians and Americans, and the experiences of travel and sight-seeing in the local area. Spiritually, there was a great concern among the Christians in their group that other international students also have the opportunity to come to know Christ. Those who weren't Christians were reasonably open talking about spiritual things. At least one student from Indonesia had accepted Christ through the witness of her roommate.

So an International Student Coordinator had been appointed, and an International Club, inclusive of American and Canadian students, had been formed. The leadership came from the students themselves, with the International Student Coordinator as an advisor. Host families among the faculty, staff and local churches were sought to "adopt" international students and build relationships with those students by inviting them to their homes, or on outings. A further need that was being looked into was for an International Student Centre on campus, where students could socialize and relax. Another special interest group was "MKs", or missionaries' kids. They had certain common-only-to-one-another experiences which drew them together. Their times of meeting allowed them to share common frustrations and joys involved with being the children of missionaries. Some of these seemed to need considerable attention, while many were proving to be strong student leaders.

A third special interest group was the commuter students. It was hard to call them a group, because of their varying degrees of interest in campus involvement. There was a Commuting Committee as part of Student Council, which had already led one chapel, and was planning future activities for commuters. It would seem that a major change might be just around the corner. How could we expect commuters to benefit from our central thrust of Total Student Development, when many just dropped in for classes and failed to become integrated into the campus family?

There was no unusual frenzy about what was happening. Nor was there any doubt that God knew what He was doing. We were gearing up to be an unquestionably Christian four-year university-college. As part of TW's emphasis on planning and five-year goal-setting, the Student Affairs staff were also asked to develop five-year goals for their areas. Here are some of the objectives they set for the 1978-79 academic year

Primary Student Life objectives for 1978-79

1. To put into writing our philosophy of Total Student Development and community.

2. To create an atmosphere of concern and warmth for students on the part of the Student Affairs Department.

3. To develop a program of in-service training for the Student Affairs staff.

4. To unify the student body leadership—*i.e.*, the Student Council and the Resident Assistants—by working very closely with them and planning joint activities.

5. To create a climate conducive to spiritual growth; this was to include more Bible teaching series in chapel, a new believers' Bible study group, a strong emphasis on student ministries, a greater use of the Spiritual Life Committee, and more emphasis on student prayer time.

6. To increase the emphasis on and opportunity for short-term missions, as well as to provide more financial resources to assist students to go on such missions.

7. To develop greater consistency in dealing with the inevitable discipline problems.

8. To further develop the part-time Career Resource Centre, enabling it to help students make career choices, find part-time work now, and receive assistance in locating and applying for jobs upon graduating.

9. To help commuters feel more a part of the campus community.

David Thompson turning the sod for the Robert Thompson Building, with Neil Snider and Robert Thompson looking on. David, one of Dr. Bob's five sons, was a very popular personality on campus working on the grounds crew.

21

New growth, new pressures: 1979-80

It was the middle of summer. Being disseminated across the country was a stunning announcement: Trinity Western College had achieved university status! Canada's first privately-funded, distinctly Christian liberal arts and sciences university-college had arrived! Great news for some of us. Serious concerns for others.

Three things were most obvious:

- We needed several **major facilities**;
- We needed **more students** to make the program feasible; and
- We needed **key leaders and faculty** to manage the expansion. All of these required finances—which we didn't have. We were facing the greatest expansion yet in any single year.

We weren't really surprised about the concerns that existed. Canada's highly-respected universities were all government-funded. Academic communities were primarily secular in perspective, while holding a high standard of academic freedom for all participants. Questions of academic freedom—seen as determining quality in the classroom, or in research, or in publishing—were sure to arise concerning a fledgling university-college that had not yet proven itself.

But we had not suggested that we had arrived. In fact, we were intent on proving that we would do everything with the highest quality, the kind that should and would be expected by the Association of Universities and Colleges of Canada (AUCC). We had already set the goal for our becoming a member of that organization. We were not shy in saying that we, as a Christian college, would not want to do anything in Christ's name that would be second-rate.

Having welcomed our first fourth-year class, who would become recipients of our first degrees, we settled down to consider the major challenges before us in this coming year.

Facilities: The Robert Thompson Building

Dr. Robert Thompson, in addition to his many other talents, was an unusual visionary. There was no question: we needed more classrooms, and it occurred to "Dr. Bob" that many donors who were particularly pleased with the early addition of Business and Aviation, might be encouraged to finance a building to house them. Space needs were far beyond the needs of only those popular and highly-visible programs, however; so it became clear that many of the core curricular courses should be included. Dr. Thompson carried the responsibility for the fund-raising.

RNT Nelson Centre.

The "RNT" (Robert N. Thompson) Building may have been our first on-campus building to be named before it was actually built! It had attracted friends from areas where the deserving Robert Thompson had lived and served in earlier times. Some of his friends offered to organize a series of banquets honouring Dr. Thompson, with a view to raising funds for what would be the "Business Building". There was a hugely positive response. Many of Dr. Bob's friends learned with excitement about our Christian college, and particularly about the Business and Aviation additions. We'd gained many new friends. We'd also created many opportunities for both new and long-time friends to commit financially to the development of the appropriately-named Robert N. Thompson Building, that would one day be called affectionately "the RNT Building".

A stumbling block

Our 1979 Fall Board meeting was planned for mid-October. It proved to be a time of great rejoicing, but also a time for careful reconsideration. Many things were going well; but some challenges were of great magnitude. It had been decided that we would not begin construction on any further facilities until we had the required funds, either firmly promised or actually in-hand.

On this occasion, the issue centred on the RNT Building. Unlike residence buildings, that could produce their own revenue stream, administrative and teaching facilities like the RNT Building must account for the major cost in advance. The amount that had been raised was encouraging, especially from the many new friends. Still, we were short of our goal by approximately $400,000. That may not sound like a large amount now; but although we'd been raising capital for several years, we still had a small (though growing) constituency.

It was a difficult time for both administrators and board members. Here was a glaring need. We were already crowded. The contractors needed to begin by late January if the building were to be completed before the start of the next school year. We considered several possible but unconvincing solutions.

We were accustomed to stopping to pray, most often to ask for wisdom; but also sometimes daring to ask for such specific resources as the clearly-needed Robert N. Thompson Building. Someone's prayer added the unquestionably overcrowded Chapel, that needed renovation and expansion. There was no hint of demanding. Just fervent prayer that God would provide once again, in His time and in His way—to the praise of His glory.

At the conclusion of our time for prayer, it occurred to me that—with the Chairman's consent—I might pass along what I had learned just the day before. It was not usual for me, but early on that Sunday morning I had watched a few minutes of the Crystal Cathedral telecast. Dr. Schuller was thinking positively about how one might determine whether an envisioned project might or might not actually be in line with God's will. That immediately caught my attention. As I recall, he suggested four questions should be asked:

1. Is the project really needed?
2. Is it something you possibly could do?
3. Is it in line with your mission statement?
4. Is anyone else already doing it?

He might also have wondered (with us) if God was giving us His peace about proceeding. Regardless, I was encouraged and stimulated to consider more fully any and all ideas that might have come to us in our visionary community at Trinity Western, God helping us.

All of this was an interesting "aside". It was easy to see that each of these questions when answered would say, "Yes, move forward! Accept the challenge!" And finally, "Go ahead! No one else in Canada is doing it!"

I soon realized that this might not make life any easier for me, nor for my colleagues. One of our Board members suggested, almost apologetically, that perhaps it would be a good idea for the President to set aside many of his regular duties for the next month, and give his full attention to raising the funds that would enable us to proceed with the building.

There was a short period of silence; but others soon joined in softly, suggesting it could be a good idea—if for only one month, and if the President agreed—and if his senior colleagues would agree to share some of his other responsibilities during this period.

There seemed to be a growing sense of relief once we had come to agreement. No one wanted to see the building postponed for another year, although we had agreed that that would be God's answer if the funds didn't materialize. Our Board members and regular donors had also stepped up to the plate, and welcomed others to share the "over and above" challenge we were facing. It was a difficult time to raise money; facing a possible recession, many businesses were struggling.

In His time

It was about 9 a.m. on the day when the Executive Committee of the Board would call to receive the final report. I received a phone call from new friends whom Marlie and I had recently visited in their home. This was a welcome call. The kind message simply informed me that our friends had decided to give their first-ever gift to Trinity Western; and it was in the amount of $20,000. They didn't know that their gift was exactly the amount still needed to reach our goal! In one sense, and in view of the crucial date, this was a most important gift—one that may have changed the course of history! We all knew, however, that the whole process was definitely of God's doing.

The archives much later recorded that the Robert N. Thompson Building was completed in the summer of 1980, and was dedicated September 14, 1980. This facility provided space for classrooms and administrative offices, and initially housed both the Aviation and Business Divisions. The Stanley Nelson Centre, added in 1982, was a memorial graciously donated by the deeply committed Ray Nelson family. It provided half again that needed space. In 2004, the space of the

Robert N. Thompson Building was doubled, and in 2015 its was refurbished, and again slightly expanded, to extend and continue to fulfill the mission that God had directed to be envisioned back in 1980.

Facilities: the Calvin B. Hanson Chapel

It was David Enarson, once again, who accepted the 1980 challenge to expand and refurbish the Chapel. Since its doors first opened, students had always referred to the building at the heart of the campus simply as "the Chapel". The campus centre for worship and fellowship, among many other things, had been planned to seat 250 (under pressure). The old church pews that had served well, now refused satisfactory reshaping into a classroom setting. Like several facilities, this first multipurpose building had also served as the first library, as extra classrooms, as choir and small music practice rooms—and even as a chemistry lab! Now, before graduating our first senior class, we had to ask how we could maintain, expand, and improve this major centre, because the campus population had reached 500 students—not counting faculty and staff, many of whom also often attended daily Chapel.

At a time when many plans were being laid, and operating funds were scarce, David had his hands full with this extra project. It was not so much what David did, but who he was. His confidence in what God could do liberated his energetic, creative and motivating abilities to draw up plans, to recruit competent volunteers, to locate needed materials—new or used—and to complete on time what he had started. The chapel expansion was finally completed, and on March 20, 1980, it was officially named after the founding President, Dr. Calvin B. Hanson.

David Enarson just couldn't stay away from Trinity Western! This dynamic Founding Father often visited the campus, even though he had become the District Superintendent of the Evangelical Free Church in Washington State. It was not a surprise that he would consider returning to British Columbia. After all, he never talked about retirement; he would say "Retire? No way. ***Refire!***"

Still, he often left his "formal" work and talked with me about assisting in our public relations. Both he and his wife, Eileen, were very capable relationship-builders. Eileen had been the President of the Women's Missionary Society of the Evangelical Free Church, and for the second time that group had raised significant funds to build, and now to expand the Calvin Hanson Chapel at Trinity Western.

Facilities: New residences for men

Dave Enarson had jumped to the opportunity of developing needed facilities in 1980; but it wasn't the first time. He often recounted the fascinating story of how, in 1962, God had enabled him to reclaim a cluster of portable buildings that would provide Trinity Western's men's residences for the first 18 years.

That had happened in part because David was always right at home with the entrepreneurial friends who would help him to discover and purchase the dairy farm that became the Trinity campus. It was Pete Friesen, the building mover, who first learned in 1962 that the Mannix Company, which had just completed construction of a $30 million hydro-electric installation on the Cheakamus River 90 miles north of Vancouver, wanted the camp dismantled and moved out—a three-week job.

Pete explained to the School-for-Canada Committee: "All the buildings needed for working and living are on that site… all prefabricated. Let's get a work crew together to do the dismantling. I'll supply the crew to supervise and trucks to move it."

It was agreed, and Friesen went to Mannix with a proposal: "We'll dismantle your buildings and haul them away, in return for half the prefab materials." The Company, however, thought it could do better, and approached several other movers. But all the major building movers in the area were Christians; and Pete had already gone to them and explained the lofty purpose and pressing need. The other companies agreed to back out of negotiations; however, the Mannix administrators were still not ready to agree to Friesen's proposal.

The summer wore on. On Labour Day, Pete phoned Dave Enarson and said, "I have another appointment with Mannix tomorrow. Will you go with me?" David agreed, but added: "I don't know what good it will do."

"You can never tell," was Pete's rejoinder.

In their plush corporate offices Pete introduced David to the senior Mannix executive. The man looked at him questioningly: "Enarson… that's an interesting name, but not very common."

"It should be common at Mannix," David responded. "My Dad worked for Mannix after he and his brother Gus sold their construction business to you. My uncle Ivor, cousin Ernest, and three of my brothers all worked for Mannix. Uncle Gus worked here practically all his life."

Without saying another word the executive went to a cabinet and pulled out the company publication for the month Gus had passed away. His picture was on the front page with the caption: ***"A Tribute to the Faith of Gus Enarson."***

He looked at Dave again. "Why in the world do you want this material?" Quick as a flash, Dave replied, "We want to continue to propagate Uncle Gus' faith." (Later Dave said, "If ever I was inspired, it was then!")

I'm sure Dave gave further explanation; and within a short time the deal was completed, and the date set for dismantling the camp. I'm just as sure that Pete and Dave went on their way thanking and praising the Lord for his obvious provision!

In less than a month, they organized a work crew of some 50 pastors and laypeople. Pete had all the cranes and equipment needed for the dismantling; and another Christian mover, Henry Nichol, brought in his equipment and crew. Included was a cook car: a fully equipped mobile kitchen—and the ladies to run it! It was one happy extended (if hard-working) picnic!

There were ten buildings to dismantle, but it didn't take these dedicated crews the projected three weeks. Indeed, by the fifth day, the last building was taken down, the site swept clear of all debris, and the work crew were on their way back home over the treacherous mountain roads! They arrived triumphant, exhausted—but with mission completed; and without injury. Everything was ready to reassemble on cement foundations that would be laid on the new campus.

Four housing units were ultimately assembled from those materials saved from the builders' village. They were anything but fancy; but then, what kind of adventurous young men would be looking for something fancy? These were, after all, only intended to be short-term residences. So by their eighteenth year, they were more than ready for retirement.

That had happened back in 1962; but now, in 1980, planning for a new men's residence was once again under way. It would require a major gift before we could begin to build to accommodate the growing student population. A major corporate gift, which we received from our deeply-committed friends at Reimer Express Lines, actually arrived for the 1982 school year, and we were pleased to be able to dedicate Douglas Hall. The young men were more than pleased with their new accommodations; if asked where they were staying, they would often respond, "At the Hilton!"

—to the praise of His glory!

When we write about a vision, all too often we ascribe it to just one person, whom we term 'the visionary'; but in developing a complex institution like a university, the vision must be shared by many of the participants—ideally, by a majority. In building a new Christian university, the most vulnerable visionaries—and therefore the ones to whom the most credit should be given—are the students: all university students, of course, enroll without knowing whether they will succeed; but in Trinity Western's case, the first students also enrolled without knowing whether there would be a degree waiting for them after four years, no matter how diligently they worked. And much credit must go as well to the faculty and staff, whose careers were also at stake while the dream was being realized.

—Neil Snider

22

Our first four-year graduates

Looking back over the fulfillment of all those plans, 1980 had been a pivotal year for Trinity Western: it was the year we awarded degrees to our first class of four-year graduates—ten men and six women who had, by faith, enrolled in the first class of our four-year programs at a time when there was no assurance that there would be a degree waiting for them after four years of study. In many ways they were linked in spirit and faith to Trinity Western's very first students, the 17 courageous souls who had enrolled in 1962, trusting that God would reward their studies with credits they would be able to transfer to university.

Similar faith was shown by the students who had enrolled in 1978 as third-year students, not knowing whether they'd get credit for their studies.

A special graduation speaker

At our 1980 graduation ceremonies, with Dr. Will Norton, a former Dean of Trinity Evangelical Divinity School (TEDS) as the principal speaker, we also gave time on the platform to a respected academic from Ontario, who had come to Langley to negotiate an arrangement for students of Richmond College in Toronto to transfer their credits to Trinity Western. That plan didn't work out, and a few years later Richmond College closed its doors—but it had provided the very first exposure to Trinity Western for Dr. Ken Davis, who would soon become Trinity Western's Vice-President and Academic Dean.

When Craig Seaton resigned as Academic Dean to go back to his first love, teaching—still with TWU—our first task as a new University was to search for another Academic Dean, still someone with intellectual weight and spiritual warmth; but also one who knew and could articulate the mission of the University within the unique context of Canadian higher education. As one Board member would later say, it was surely the hand of God that brought Kenneth Davis, PhD to Trinity Western to become Vice-President and Dean of Academic Affairs in 1980—an appointment that he almost refused!—not for lack of enthusiasm for

TWU; but when we first offered him the appointment, he had already made another commitment.

A published scholar, and director of a graduate doctoral program in the History Department at the University of Waterloo, Dr. Davis was also an ordained Baptist minister, who donated one evening each week to teaching at Richmond College in Toronto. He, too, had long held a vision for a Christian university-college in Canada. As far back as the 1960s, Ken Davis was concerned, like other Evangelicals, about the fact that the church in Canada was losing so many well-educated young people. If they wanted to transfer their Bible college credits to university, they had to go to the United States—and most never returned to Canada. Ken Davis had previously been involved in two unsuccessful attempts to establish an accredited, degree-granting evangelical Christian university-college in Canada, before coming to Trinity Western.

Just before being invited to come to TWC, Dr. Davis had accepted another year's contract at the University of Waterloo. "God will have to do two things for me," he said. "Both would be miracles. It's not good ethics, after having accepted a new post, to back out. God will have to provide a way. And also, we can't afford to come unless we find a buyer for our house in Ontario. Nevertheless, I leave myself in God's hands."

When Dr. Davis returned to Ontario, he laid the situation before the Dean of the University of Waterloo, as I had recommended. The Dean said, "Trinity Western? That's a challenging opportunity—and exactly right for you!" And so Ken was gracefully released from his contract (but with an agreement to also accept an appointment as Adjunct Professor, to complete the mentoring of some of his PhD candidates).

The second miracle—the sale of the Davis' house—didn't come until the last day before the deadline for their purchase of a home in Langley!

Dr. Davis brought to Trinity Western a spiritual depth and academic expertise that were remarkable. Over time, he made strides in unifying faculty and structuring academic programs in light of our stated mission. He stressed disciple-making, and insisted on integrating faith with learning; his conviction was—and remains—that everything, including scholarship, must come under the lordship of Christ; and that excellence must always be the standard of anything done in Christ's name.

Dr. Davis admits he had no wish to leave teaching, his first love, to take on an administrative post. "But I realized Trinity Western is more than a university. It's a vision of the highest order. I came here because God called and prepared me for it."

Our first four-year graduates

Cheryl Bergman, Diane Bremner, Kathleen Jo Carter, Carmen Daniels, Diane George, Nels Hawkinson, Ernest Hollenbeak, Paul Huesken, Deborah Jones, Ron Knoller, Ellis Kurniawan, Scott Nelson, Stanley Ng, Robin Smith, Daniel Splinter, and Cliff Underwood

23

Crafting our Mission Statement

One of the most important projects in the history of Trinity Western University was creating its Mission Statement. The task was undertaken initially by Dr. Guy Saffold, Dr. Howard Anderson, staff writer Lori Michener, and me; but it ultimately involved the whole campus community.

On July 31, 1979, the B.C. Legislature had extended its authorization for Trinity Western to grant a baccalaureate degree, and with that, the most significant hurdle in the plan to become a four-year university had been cleared. We could now enroll our first graduating class for their final year; they were on their way to greater things and, so it seemed, was Trinity Western. What had seemed impossible only a few years ago now seemed within reach, if we continued with faith in God, and did our work well.

"History shows that one of the largest risks for a… Christian university is that, over time, other elements of the educational process may supersede, and even replace, the spiritual objectives for which the university was originally founded."

We all sensed the significance of this step. Our two-year junior college was now on its way to eventually becoming Canada's largest Christian university. An especially critical element of the work ahead was to establish a razor-sharp focus on the purposes for which God had brought Trinity Western to this point, and His purposes for the years ahead. Although there were many immediate needs, challenges and pressures, ensuring a clear purpose seemed one of the most important long-term choices, and one that could not be delayed.

During my doctoral studies in goal-setting at the University of Oregon, I had read the innovative work of Philip Selznick of the University of California at Berkeley. Selznick's work was then still fresh, and generating wide-spread comment. In fact, so ground-breaking was his work that his book, *Leadership in Administration*, first published in 1957, is still in print today, 60 years later. It is an almost unheard-of record for a book in the otherwise continuously transforming field of organizational leadership.

One of Selznick's key insights was that unless an exceptionally clear sense of purpose is set in place *and continually emphasized*, organizations are likely, over time, to drift away from their original purposes. Running organizations such as universities—and perhaps especially universities, which are, by nature, broad-based enterprises—requires a relentless focus on many intensely consuming processes. Doing these processes with excellence is one of the hallmarks of high-quality university education. However, the intensity of effort required to pursue and sustain excellence can also be a trap, as Selznick's research had clearly identified. Pursuing excellence in *methods* can lead to a curious form of "disorientation" in which organizations can lose their way:

> *The tendency to emphasize* **methods** *rather than* **goals** *is an important source of disorientation in all organizations. It has the value of stimulating full development of these methods, but it risks loss of adaptability and sometimes results in a radical substitution of means for ends. Leaders may feel more secure when they emphasize the exploitation of technical potentialities, but the difficult task of defining goals and adapting methods to them may be unfulfilled.*[1]

History shows that one of the largest risks for a specifically Christian university is that over time, other elements of the educational process may supersede—and all too often even replace—the spiritual objectives for which the university was originally founded. We were determined that, so far as it depended on our efforts, we would do all we could to lay foundations that would keep Trinity Western pursuing both excellence as a university, but also high aspirations for Christian mission and outcomes.

In Selznick's terms, this required that we define the clearest possible statement of Trinity Western's purpose as a Christian institution of higher education. To do so would, Selznik pointed out, be a critical foundation for the identity and character of the institution, as well as a primary point of contribution to its longer-term continuity and effectiveness:

> *When institutional continuity and identity are at stake, a definition of mission is required that will take account of the organization's distinctive character, including present and prospective capabilities.*[2]

With these concepts deeply on our minds, we set out to define a Mission Statement for our soon-to-become University.

---

1 Selznick, [at location 571 of the digital edition]
2 ibid., [at location 2679 of the digital edition]

In the fall of 1979, I received the Board's encouragement to move ahead with the process. The first task was to develop an initial draft. It wouldn't be the final document; but the draft would define some of the key concepts that would likely become part of the finished result.

One morning, the four of us went off-campus to the library of the Langley Evangelical Free Church. Along with Guy Saffold and me were Dr. Howard Anderson and one of our staff writers, Lori Mitchener. Dr. Anderson, a New Testament scholar who was then serving as President of Northwest Baptist Theological College, had become a good friend of TW. He brought to the process the scholarly insight shaped by his PhD studies in Britain. Moreover, as President of the next-largest Christian institution of higher education in British Columbia at that time, he also understood the issues facing our developing university.

That off-campus meeting proved to be pivotal. As we exchanged and debated possible elements of purpose and mission, God led us increasingly to focus on a core of key concepts:

- Trinity Western had to be be understood as one element in the larger plan and mission of God for His church. TWC had been birthed by initiative from within a specific church denomination, the Evangelical Free Church; but it was clear to us that its purpose had to embrace the entire Body of Christ, and to remain closely linked to it in spirit and mission.
- The church, we maintained, is a mission-focused enterprise to take the Gospel to the world. Evangelicals typically refer to this central purpose as "The Great Commission" after the words of Jesus in Matthew 28:19-20:

    "Go therefore and make disciples of all nations, baptizing them in the name of the Father and of the Son and of the Holy Spirit, teaching them to observe all that I have commanded you. And behold, I am with you always, to the end of the age."

This conclusion was, of course, open to challenge, and soon would be challenged, on the grounds that the Great Commission is the *religious* mission of the church and not the educational mission of a Christian university. But we were convinced that Trinity Western had to build this world-embracing outcome into its sense of purpose. After all, Jesus said, *"For whoever would save his life will lose it, but whoever loses his life for my sake and the Gospel's will save it."*[1] This central focus on the Gospel as a key element in the mission of Trinity Western could not be diminished!

---

1 Mark 8:35

The primary "outcome" of our mission would not be the institution itself, as if simply being a Christian university were the goal. Instead, the essential outcome of our efforts (and therefore the focus of our mission) had to be the students who would graduate from this University. We envisioned class after class of students graduating from TWU who would have a positive mindset, eager to pursue large goals, and capable of working toward them with faithfulness, intelligence and from the perspective of a Christian worldview. This implied diligent effort to cultivate the intellect, and a corresponding effort to anchor that development to biblical values.

Our discussion had brought us this far, but we still realized that defining our mission absolutely required distinguishing Trinity Western from the ministry-preparation task of Canada's many Bible colleges. Although we had no thought that our graduates shouldn't become pastors or missionaries (and many, over the years, have done exactly that), we were an institution of the liberal arts and sciences, aspiring to become an authentic and biblically Christian Canadian university—a very different *kind* of institution. As we talked this over, we became increasingly drawn to two concepts.

The first was development of a Christian mind as the intellectual goal of our university. "Mind" meant just that: an intellect that is well-trained, disciplined, informed and capable of thinking at university level.

But it must also be a "*Christian* mind," operating on the principle that "all truth is God's truth" and therefore ready to engage the intellectual challenge in any direction God might call, whether to the study of literature, the arts, science, or indeed any of the multiple academic disciplines within a modern university.

The second concept was preparing of students to engage with the full range of careers and enterprises that make up the Canadian (or world) societies into which graduates might enter. To capture this concept, we hit upon the phrase "the various marketplaces of life." By this we didn't mean solely commercial enterprises, but rather the "marketplace", broadly understood as those arenas that shape the life and culture of a nation. Christian faith was not, in our view, to be sheltered in a cloister; but rather to be carried boldly and unapologetically into the hustle and bustle of society and life.

Over the next weeks, with the help and input of many others, an initial draft was developed and slowly refined. It read as follows:

> *The mission of Trinity Western College is to glorify God in building His church and in fulfilling the Great Commission of Jesus Christ by producing university graduates with thoroughly Christian minds, shaped by biblical*

values and characterized by a positive, goal-oriented commitment to serve God and man in all the varied marketplaces of life.

It was good to have an initial draft. But wide input is both expected and necessary in a university community. The draft was put into a campus-wide message, inviting feedback from all members of the campus community, with written responses requested by March 17, 1980. Many members of the campus community sent in thoughtful responses, and a second draft was developed:

The mission of Trinity Western College, as an arm of the church, is to glorify God in fulfilling the Great Commission by producing positive, goal-oriented university graduates who are maturing disciples of Jesus Christ. Graduates should have acquired the foundational spiritual, emotional, and intellectual abilities needed to integrate Christian faith with learning, to apply biblical values to contemporary living, and to serve God and man in all the varied marketplaces of life.

This draft was again circulated to the entire campus community for comment. Responses continued to come in over the next several months, as the statement was edited and re-edited. One year later, by the Fall of 1980, a final draft was ready and approved by the Board of Governors at their October, 1980 meeting. With the subsequent change of only one word ("serve God and man" became "serve God and people") that statement has endured to the present as the fervently declared purpose and goal of Trinity Western University:

The mission of Trinity Western University, as an arm of the Church, is to develop godly Christian leaders: positive, goal-oriented university graduates with thoroughly Christian minds; growing disciples of Jesus Christ who glorify God through fulfilling the Great Commission, serving God and people in the various marketplaces of life.

From this point forward, the Mission Statement became a primary tool for guiding all the affairs of the university. Its emphasis on the "various marketplaces of life" moved us toward academic programs that could have strategic impact on those marketplaces. Every Trinity Western University program had the capacity to affect society in important ways, and all were asked to use the Mission Statement as a guide in the development of curriculum and new academic programs. We began to envision programs in high-impact areas such as health care, leading eventually to the establishment of a School of Nursing; and education, which became first a faculty, and later the School of Education.

Drawing on the direction embedded in the Mission Statement, we developed a vision to prepare graduates who would serve with distinction in public service. This led, in 2001, to establishment in Ottawa of Trinity Western University's first remote campus, the Laurentian Leadership Centre, where Junior and Senior students could spend a full semester living in Ottawa, and gaining practical internship experience in parliamentary and similar public service offices, including non-profit and ministry service.

The new Mission Statement made it imperative for TWU to develop a holistic understanding of curriculum as inclusive of both formal studies and the many campus experiences outside of class called "Student Life". We developed one of the strongest Student Life programs of any Christian institution in North America, and constantly laboured to integrate Student Life and academic studies for the fulfillment of our mission. This led eventually to establishment of a unique set of collegia for commuter and graduate students, to provide these groups with an anchor to campus activities, events and social life similar to that which residential students more naturally experience.

Mission-based planning became our goal, as the Mission Statement was used in overall strategic planning for the University's future, and also in annual budget development. Especially where choices had to be made among alternatives (as is always the case in budget building), consideration was given to which alternatives would most effectively support the mission.

In the area of personnel, the Mission Statement became a primary criterion for hiring in all staff areas. It was clear that faculty hiring should be done with a view to implementation of the mission; but we also introduced the concept of mission fulfillment into evaluation of all potential hires. It turns out that the custodial staff in the residence may see students as much as, or even more than the faculty in the classroom. The roles were different: faculty provided instruction, and other staff met other needs; but we believe that all these interactions are important in reaching our mission-focused goals; and so all staff needed to 'own' the University's mission as their personal responsibility.

The Mission Statement became an invaluable tool in student recruitment, as it enabled us to share a life-transforming vision with each prospective student. The students we wanted would be drawn to the Mission Statement, whereas those who did not identify with it were more likely to consider other choices for their education. Many students who enrolled with little idea about their future plans were influenced over time to shape their plans around the values of the Mission Statement, and then to live it out as a personal objective after they graduated.

"Where leadership is required," Selznik had written, "the problem is always to choose key values and to create a social structure that embodies them." It is, he said, a matter of joining "immediate practical goals to ultimate values." For us at TWU, the Mission Statement became the guide for joining practical business goals to the ultimate values for which we believed God had raised up Trinity Western University. Its importance to the creation and on-going development of the University's plans, purposes and operation can hardly be overstated.

In the end, however, the Mission Statement became far more than a guiding policy and planning tool. Its ultimate significance went far deeper than that. It is exemplified by the following story:

Ten years after his graduation, an alumnus was being interviewed about what had developed in his life over the years. He made a comment that we found was echoed in one form or another by many: "When I was on campus," he said, "I kept hearing the Mission Statement over and over again. It was used so often, that I became tired of hearing it. But, you know, somehow, that statement stuck with me.

"Now, it has become the description of the kind of person I want to be."

24

TW's 'paragon of planners'

The three needs we had identified in 1979-80 were for **facilities**, **senior leaders**, and **students**. Now having the facilities in hand, our second major requirement was the need for more students; that brings us back to the early years in Guy Saffold's 28-year-long history with TWU.

By 1982, Guy had been working with good success in student recruitment for several years. Instead of returning south, it was beginning to look as if he was going to stay at Trinity Western.

Recognizing the importance to Trinity Western of the academic qualifications of its leaders, Arvid Olson had gone to Seattle University (SU) to earn his doctorate; and he very helpfully encouraged Guy Saffold in that direction, also. Guy enrolled in the SU doctoral program in 1983 and completed his studies in 1988 with an ED in Educational Leadership. Guy's doctoral dissertation concerned organizational culture's shaping influence on the personal identity of organization members—and vice-versa. He used a variety of multi-variate tools for factor analysis and cluster analysis, to show how this played out at TW, where he had gathered the data for his thesis.

Although Guy was new to our senior administrative team, where he would make his greatest contributions, the innovator in him was already coming to the fore; assigned to revise our admissions procedures, Guy began to use the small personal computer he had built at home to streamline the process of handling enquiries and promoting enrolment, and we sent musical teams across the country to perform in churches and tell their young people about TW.

Guy continues his own recollections of the story:

> "I knew nothing whatsoever about marketing. Craig Seaton had become my supervisor, and he sent me to several admissions marketing conferences in the U.S. Fortunately for me, at least, Trinity Western's recruitment processes were at that time underdeveloped—so it was possible for an

untrained person to make good improvements simply by applying some common sense and what I had learned from those seminars.

"When students would write in to the Registrar's office for admission, their names would be written on a file card and stored in a large bank of metal boxes. I asked, 'What happens next?' The response was something like: 'What do you mean, "what happens next?"'

"I wanted to know: 'Do you ever follow up on those inquiries?' There were thousands of cards in those metal boxes, but it seemed like an overwhelming task to follow up on so many cards by hand. Instead, if a student chose to write back, the card would be removed from the file and a tick-mark made. Perhaps another letter would be sent. And then the card went back into the file until the student wrote in again. There was more to it than this. The Registrar's staff were doing the best they could with manual processes, but there was so much more that could be done with a little bit of automation. So I took the small computer I'd programmed to teach biblical languages, and repurposed it to do mailing lists."

Guy hired an assistant to type the information from those thousands of cards into the computer; and that began a data-based admissions follow-up program, with the computer keeping track of addresses, information available and needed, and the next steps in follow-up. We bought a letter printer (for the then-huge cost of $2,000) and began to send letters. This, along with all the other promotion going on, was successful, and Trinity Western's enrolment began to rise rapidly.

1978 was the period when we were working to get the necessary bills passed in the B.C. Legislature to enable TW to become a four-year institution. One important part of this process was to analyze the historical data about enrolment and retention at B.C.'s two-year colleges, and then make projections to give some idea of what might happen in a four-year model. Guy compiled about 40 pages of graphs, charts, and tables, showing what might occur under various assumptions. The projections showed that if the underlying assumptions held true, the enrolment forecast, although initially slow, might escalate rapidly.

A few years later, when we were attempting to deal with a second bill—the one that would give TWU degree-granting capacity—an important question was whether TWU students would be able to compete academically at the provincial universities. The implicit question was: "Is the Trinity Western program of sufficiently high academic standard?"

As it happened, in 1978 an organization located on the campus of UBC, called B.C. Research, had been studying the performance of B.C. students who transferred from community colleges to the provincial universities. The data had been shared with all two-year schools, so we had a shelf full of thick binders containing printouts of the raw data from these studies. There were thousands of pages of data, organized by student ID number at the provincial universities—one line for every student, in each semester. The entire set took about eight to ten feet of shelf space—billions of numbers! A few volumes were missing. Guy called B.C. Research to see if we could get the missing information. A very helpful project manager there, Glen Forrester (who would later join the staff at TWU himself), invited Guy to visit B.C. Research, where he was warmly welcomed and given the data to complete his set of information.

B.C. Research had run averages for all the publicly funded community colleges, to see how their students fared after transferring to UBC. However, although they had also collected the same information for Trinity Western students, and printed the raw data in those huge volumes, they hadn't provided any summary statistics for us. But the information was all there, if some way could be found to compile it. If done by hand it would have been an overwhelming task, but once again Guy's small home-built computer held the solution.

He hired a student to go through the books line by line, to pick out the TW student data. This time, Guy wrote programs to enable the little machine to develop the missing summary statistics. He loaded that data into the machine, and the results—based on B.C. Research's own data—tumbled out.

It turned out that TW students fared very well indeed when transferring to the provincial universities! In fact, it showed that students who did their first two years at Trinity Western, and then completed years 3 and 4 at UBC, had higher average GPAs (Grade-Point Averages) than students who began their first two years at UBC!

That information was very helpful in some key places in the later campaign for the bill to give TWU degree-granting status!

Many years later, Glen Forrester told Guy that one of the principal researchers on the study of transfer students was really quite annoyed that his own data had been used to support Trinity Western's case. The data han't been gathered for that purpose, he said; but unable to fault the data source, he said instead that the better GPAs of TW students were most likely an indication that TW started with "better" students. He gave no credence to the possibility that the learning environment engendered by TWs Community Standards enabled students to learn better.

But really, it hardly mattered; because the fact was that it proved there was absolutely no academic deficit among TW students—quite the opposite, explain it as you may.

And so we were helped on our way to becoming a university by a stark and undeniable mathematical reality—unearthed with a homebuilt computer!

Sod turning for the new Reimer Student Centre, December 1, 1995, which was named in honour of Delbert Reimer, a founding and long-time member of the Board of Governors.

25

Dreams, visions and plans

Someone has written: "The key to success is to plan your work, then work your plan." The team at Trinity Western was blessed with people who knew well how to plan; but they also had the determination and commitment to work their plans. And that has made all the difference! Scripture has many stories of dreamers and visionaries—but God granted success to those who acted! Here Dr. Guy Saffold summarizes TWU's planning experience.

—*Neil Snider*

By Dr. Guy Saffold

'Expect great things from God. Attempt great things for God.'

—*William Carey*

The Trinity Western story is about faith in a God who can bring dreams and visions into reality when His followers are willing to trust Him. The vibrant Christian University that Trinity Western is today represents the fulfillment of the dreams of thousands of godly men and women over more than half a century. Great dreams were turned into specific visions. Vision drove planning. Planning gave direction to work. But always the growth was from God, who can "do immeasurably more than all we ask or imagine."[1]

By today's measures, those early plans may seem small and overly simple, and the vision still emerging; but it was a bright vision nonetheless, and the plans were clear enough to inspire effort and motivate action. Obstacles were seen as

---
1 Ephesians 3:20 (NIV)

encouragements to prayer. Limitations were simply challenges to greater effort. And like all worthwhile visions, it also inspired sacrifice.

A local pastor and his wife had worked to save the large sum—in 1950s dollars—of $100 to buy a washing machine, so the daily load of children's diapers would no longer have to be washed by hand in a tub. They prayed together, and agreed that the Trinity Western vision was more important. A washing machine could wait. The plan for Trinity Western could not. Others made similar decisions to give sacrificially according to or even beyond their capacity, and the dream began to move toward reality. As founding President Calvin Hanson wrote, Trinity Western was birthed and grew *"On the Raw Edge of Faith."* But it was faith with a plan!

Trinity Western College and The Four-Year Plan

By 1976, the dream had birthed a vision for two-year Trinity Junior College to offer baccalaureate degrees. President Snider and the Board commissioned a Four-Year Plan to see the two-year school mature into a four-year, degree-granting college. This vision wasn't just an enormous step of faith; it was an intensive exercise in planning. An institution that was currently offering two years of very general courses, within a period of twenty-four months would have to offer four years of courses, with the additions being the more advanced courses necessary to offering a credible bachelor's degree. Who would teach these courses? A plan for faculty, including recruitment, salaries and tenure had to be developed. Where would they be taught? A plan for classrooms was needed. Where would the students come from? A plan for student recruitment. Where would they live? A plan for residences. And so it went, through every area of operations.

Not least was the question of how all this expansion could be paid for. A careful plan was developed that showed how much it would all cost—but there were no sufficient answers to where the money would come from. Committing to this step of growth was going to require a very large element of faith! But such is always the case with vision. Vision just naturally stretches the limits of what seems possible. In many ways, this became the model for all the plans that followed: study what needed to be done, define the critical factors for success, set out a clear plan of action, and resolve to work the plan, trusting the rest to God.

Guy Saffold

The four-year plan was approved and set in motion. God miraculously provided the funds through arrangements that He had set in place years earlier, but were unknown to us at the time of decision. *"Before they call, I will answer,"*[1] Scripture promises; and so it was in the case of the little junior college stepping up to become a four-year institution.

By 1982, Trinity Western had navigated the shift to four years, and had two years of graduating classes under its belt. Execution of past plans continued, but a new phase of future visioning was launched, called the "Comprehensive Plan". The most significant need of the moment was planning how to accommodate the rapid rise in enrolment. How many students could Trinity Western actually manage on its campus? A number of focused study groups formed and were tasked with bringing recommendations on science laboratories, drama facilities, music facilities, and library. But the growing campus had other needs as well, including housing and food services, and the unglamorous but essential issue of sewage, since at this stage the campus hadn't yet been connected to the municipal system.

The Comprehensive Plan studies recommended that the current enrolment of 808 students could be allowed to expand by 10 percent over the next two years. Optimum enrolment for Trinity Western's current facilities was 885 students by September of 1984. Enrolment at that date was a little less; but by fall of 1985 had surged to 963 students.

It was a difficult balancing act! More students meant more revenue from tuition, and that would help to manage growth and pay for urgent projects. Besides, it hardly seemed wise to turn away qualified students when Trinity Western was hoping to grow in the longer term. At the same time, growth always put more pressure on facilities and services that were already strained to their limits. We were delighted with the growth, but quite frankly struggled very hard to keep up.

Over Christmas in 1982 I was encouraged by an observation from the great American theologian, Jonathan Edwards. He'd been part of the astonishing revival movements of the mid-eighteenth century that today we call the "Great Awakening". Thousands of people poured into churches throughout the American colonies; and that movement provided a major impetus to the founding of institutions of higher learning that today are among the most widely-known and respected, including Brown, Dartmouth, and Rutgers. Edwards himself would later become the President of one of these institutions, that we know today as Princeton University. Reflecting on those days of enthusiasm and growth, Edwards wrote these words:

---
1 Isaiah 65:24 (NASB)

"When God took the work in His own hands, there was done in a day or two as much as men, with all the endeavors they can use, will accomplish in a year. And with what blessing it was done!"

There could be no question that God had taken this work in hand with blessing. At one point Harvey Ouellette, Trinity Western's Comptroller, was heard to say, "I feel as if we're running to catch up with our shoes!" And perhaps that was true. Trinity Western's "shoes" were running ahead faster than we had imagined—but the shoes were on God's feet, so we buckled down, planning and working as fast as we could.

The extensive capacity studies done as part of the Comprehensive Plan helped us manage Trinity Western's needs for the short-term; but as part of the process, it had become clear that much longer-range planning was needed. Once again we pored over our projections and estimates, and began to draw the outline for another major advance.

Part of the reason was simple necessity. More first-year students quickly become second-, third- and fourth-year students, swelling the overall enrolment. And there were more first-year students each year, as well as others transferring in from other institutions because they wanted to complete their studies here, and earn a Trinity Western degree. One answer to the pressures would have been to cap growth—and this suggestion was made often and considered seriously. But capping growth would cap income, and capping income would severely limit TWU's opportunity to expand its programs, grow its faculty, and build quality. The better answer, it became clear to us, was once again to establish the vision and plans that would lead us forward.

Harvey Ouelette

No merely human plan: '1300 by 30'

In April of 1983, President Snider recommended to the Board of Governors that TWU commit itself to a plan we called "1300 by 30"—which stood for reaching an enrolment of 1,300 students by September 1992, TWU's thirtieth anniversary. It's worth quoting at length from his President's Report in April of that year:

> *Before Trinity Western stands an open door to a ministry of national, strategic importance unparalleled anywhere on the Canadian scene. I believe the time has now come, as an expression of our belief that Trinity Western can*

become the greatest Christian university in Canada and one of the finest in North America, to commit ourselves to this specific, long-range objective:

THIRTEEN HUNDRED BY THIRTY

BY 1992, Trinity Western's thirtieth anniversary, to have

1,200 undergraduate AND 100 graduate

students in Langley studying on a modern

fully equipped, debt-free campus.

With remarkably little variation, enrolment projections from the early 1970s onward have pointed to an enrolment of 1,200 students by 1990. Trinity Western's actual growth corresponds rather closely with these projections, as God has consistently brought dreams into reality. I believe this is a cause in the name of Jesus Christ, of the highest order. It is worth everything we can give to it: our prayer, dedication and sacrificial commitment.

In the academic year that this goal was announced, TWU's fall enrolment had reached only 808 students. Growing to 1,300 students would require a 61 percent increase—not only in student enrolment, but in everything necessary to serve those 1,300 students with the quality that they would expect, and that we so very much wanted to deliver. Moreover, the plan called for expansion into graduate education as well, with all the attendant requirements for even higher, and more extensive resources.

Impossible as it might seem, if this goal could be achieved, it would be a true fulfillment of the original TWU dream. President Snider continued:

No merely human plan, I am convinced that this is the vision God would have us adopt: the open door for effective ministry He has provided. Its realization will be the culmination of the dreams and prayers of thousands of men and women who, over the years, have believed in the strategic ministry of Trinity Western as a unique Canadian ministry of higher education.

The Board of Governors, in a step of faith as large as (and perhaps larger than) the commitment to become a four-year institution, concurred with this sense of vision, and approved the goal. It was time to begin the planning in detail; but it would be a very extensive process!

BIGGER AND BETTER—TWU's new permanent two-lane bridge was officially opened on Monday, October 23, 1989.

TWU Archives

PART IV

Trinity Western becomes a university

As we laboured to have Trinity Western admitted as a full member to the Association of Universities and Colleges of Canada (AUCC, now called "Universities Canada"), I know that there were a few among us who perceived the AUCC as a barrier to be breached; but my own experience wasn't like that: I met these colleagues as guardians of a national tradition of academic excellence, and I respected them for it. What we had to do was prove that the same kind of excellence was also our objective. And that took some doing!

As you've just read, Trinity Western's distinctive identity as a junior college was determined long ago by the vision of its founders; but with its development towards becoming a full university-college, it became necessary to clarify and develop that identity more fully. We needed to expand that vision much further to prepare for acceptance into the Canadian academic milieu. Dr. Ken Davis here elucidates that expanded vision—and the reasons for its necessity, very articulately:

—*Neil Snider*

26

Our academic and spiritual roots

By Dr. Kenneth R. Davis

In spite of having some fine Bible colleges spread across our country, evangelicalism grew much more slowly in the 20th century in Canada than it did in the United States. Why?

A key reason is that the United States has scores of fully-accredited and ideologically Bible-believing university-colleges and universities, capable of training dedicated laypersons to become leaders who could articulate evangelical Christian alternatives and perspectives within the major professions.

In contrast, for most of the 20th century, Canadians had no evangelically-oriented university. Christians who were capable, and who desired distinctly Christian university-level training in order to become functional professionals, went instead to Christian colleges in the United States. Sadly, most never returned. Those who remained in Canada were trained in secular institutions and, often unknowingly, developed and articulated secular viewpoints. As a result, evangelicalism made very little impact on the key structures in Canadian society, such as education, law, the media, business, government and social services.

This deficiency brought serious limitations to Canadian evangelicalism, such as a failure to effect social change, or even to discuss issues from the vantage point of biblically Christian principles. As a result, Canada has become a predominantly secular nation.

Kenneth Davis

Clearly, a distinctively Christian university-college was needed; and Trinity Western College expanded to meet this need. But there were so many models of "Christian" university-colleges in the United States, it was difficult to determine which model Trinity Western should emulate. Its essential character had been already spelled out by the founders of Trinity Western and by its supporting denomination, the Evangelical Free Churches of Canada and America. In the College's Statement of Faith, it was referred to as a conservative, orthodox, believers'-church-based "evangelical Christian" university-college.

This was the spiritual identity of the four-year university-college that would eventually be approved by the British Columbia Government in 1977, and authorized in 1979 to grant its first Baccalaureate degrees in 1980. It was consistently reaffirmed by those involved in its expansion, as well as by many in the founding and supporting constituencies. Finally, it was made ultimately clear in the college's student calendar, which stated concisely: "Trinity Western College's program is shaped by a view which is openly and unapologetically Christian."

This identity was first expanded and clarified by a Community Standards Covenant that promoted a biblically disciplined, others-sensitive, holiness-pursuing community of scholars; and, second, by the development of its Mission Statement, which would guide future development.

Let me quote briefly from my address to students, faculty and staff at a chapel service in March, 1983, while the campus community was awaiting the response of the Association of Universities and Colleges of Canada (AUCC) to our application for admission. Entitled "Sharing the Vision," it added important details about our philosophy of education:

> "Trinity Western, by dedicated design, is committed to be more than a university; it is a *biblically Christian* university, without apology! We take seriously I Corinthians 10:31: …'to do all to the glory of God;' and we believe that 'all' includes university-level education. Indeed, failure at this point to give God glory in who we are and what we do… would surely bring God's displeasure upon us!
>
> One only needs to read Romans 1:21 to discover that God gave people up to ruin and destruction because 'when they knew Him they glorified Him not as God.' Moreover, Revelation 16:9 adds that the vials of God's wrath were poured out on mankind because 'they repented not to give Him glory.' **God's glory must be the Number One objective**—that

which counts above anything and everything else in this undertaking. It must count even more than our desire for academic recognition.

"We must also take seriously Colossians 1:18, which says Jesus Christ, our Saviour, rose from the dead 'that in all things He might have the pre-eminence'—even in academic freedom and academic inquiry. 'All things' means that every discipline, and our whole educational process, is under the lordship of Christ... again without apology, because Colossians 2:3,4 teaches that 'in Him (Christ) are hid *all* the treasures of wisdom and knowledge....'

"Trinity Western is to be a biblically Christian university which—let us always be honest about it—has opted for certain interpretations or understandings of what is meant by 'biblically Christian'."

From 1980 to 1983, I was TW's Academic Dean and worked to define and articulate an historically acceptable identity for a Christian institution, a detailed philosophy of Christian education, rooted in academic history. I knew this would be critical for Trinity Western's approval by the AUCC. But I also sought to achieve acceptance and understanding, especially by our faculty, of the need for a philosophy of education that was both compatible with the founders' vision, and acceptable to AUCC as educationally valid and socially constructive.

In several major addresses to students, staff and faculty, I summarized this philosophy by pointing out that the humanities in Western Civilization began with the ancient Greeks and Romans, seeking to build a "good" society:

"Their assumption was they could know, discover, and teach (by philosophy) what human values define the "good" (*e.g.,* Socrates and Plato).

"This failed; so they then sought to encourage people by rhetoric, literature, history, poetry, music … and even by a civic humanism (Cicero). But this, too, was ineffective, so they tried to promote "the good" by emphasizing the power of beauty (Plotinus).

"It is important to understand that the liberal arts' educational goal, originally and throughout Western education, has always been to maximize both individual capabilities and good citizenship.

"In the third to fifth centuries AD, Christian scholars promoted an integrated Christian humanism: it had a similar educational goal, but found motivation and responsibility in God—His will, purposes, and values—with the added provision of redemption in Christ; and also advocating an inner spiritual renewal by adding Jesus' emphasis on, and modeling of, the Christian virtues of unselfishness, love (even for one's enemy), forgiveness, and justice tempered with mercy.

"But educationally, apart from the Celtic Christians, Christian humanism largely died (as did the universities) through the early Middle Ages in Western Europe.

"Graeco-Roman educational humanism was renewed in the West during the Renaissance of the 13th to 15th centuries; and then, in the 16th century, Christian Humanism was also revived, especially in northern Europe during the Protestant Reformation, and Loyola's Jesuit education (*e.g.,* Thomas More, Erasmus, and making available the Greek New Testament).

"The revival of universities in the West was largely a product of the philosophical integration of Christian faith and reason (*e.g.,* Aquinas); then later adding the Christian humanities (at Paris, Oxford, Cambridge, etc.) The pattern continued in America with the Christian foundations of Harvard, Yale, Princeton, Wheaton College, *etc.*; and in Canada with Waterloo Lutheran, McMaster, and Acadia university-colleges. As late as 1948, it was still required of all freshmen to study at the university of Toronto Newman's writings on the nature of the university, in which he emphasized both the educational importance of the humanities, and their Christian integration 'for an ideal university education.'"

The Christian heritage of integration, and Trinity Western's identity

This awareness of an extensive and respected "Christian university" heritage, and a respected historical pattern for the integration of faith and reason, was further impressed upon us at Trinity Western in 1983 when an eminent Christian scholar, author and statesman, Dr. Charles Habib Malik, visited our campus. As a philosophy professor at Harvard University, and former President of the United Nations, he emphasized the importance—indeed, the *necessity*—of restoring faith and spirituality (especially Christian) to university education, if we are ever to see real social progress in world civilization.

As a follow-up to Dr. Malik's visit, we brought Dr. Arthur F. Holmes, an esteemed philosophy professor and author at Wheaton College, to provide a week of lectures to the whole university (plus faculty seminars) on relating faith and reason, in the context of achieving a biblically Christian worldview. His taped lectures later became the basis for a Christian worldview course, which (under the guidance of Professor Dr. Deane Downey) became for several years the capstone integration course for all graduates of Trinity Western College and, later, Trinity Western University. Eventually, it led many Trinity Western faculty to publish scholarly studies relating each and every discipline to a Christian worldview.

The distinctive faith component to our identity

While the distinctive faith identity in this process was clearly understood to be historic biblical Christian orthodoxy (i.e. the evangelical world- and life-view), its implications for articulating a university-level philosophy of education and instruction were initially far from understood or consistently developed, even by our faculty. How we educate must be consistent with our beliefs and faith standards, to be genuinely and biblically Christian. Here, in summary, is how we described some of the key elements:

1. A Christian philosophy of education is not secular; it is faith-affirming because we believe something. We begin with the premise that God *is;* this fundamental truth colours everything else. To reject ultimate intelligent design is to call into question order, rationality, and even the ability to know anything; which leads, ultimately, to skepticism. But if God *is,* then Truth is knowable, and education is much more than just the accumulation of knowledge; it has purpose and a basic unity.

2. A Christian philosophy of education emphasizes God in Christ as the source, the model, and the centre of our faith. It also stresses the importance of a life-changing relationship by the Spirit with Him as Lord of Life, of all wisdom and knowledge.

3. It affirms the need to carefully rethink and critique the presuppositions of every secularly-developed discipline—and then to reconstruct them Christianly.

4. It affirms both the power to change, and human responsibility for one's actions, (rather than the power of fate over our actions).

5. It affirms a liberal arts education that promotes a holistic approach to education, developing the whole person and the unity of personality. This means that the intellectual and academic cannot be divorced from the emotional and spiritual dimensions of life.

6. It is oriented to whole-person growth in the academic setting. It also emphasizes the broad development of general intellectual skills, rather than emphasizing extensive knowledge of one discipline only, or preparation for only a specific task or vocation.

7. It affirms a unified Christian worldview of education (rather than any other system, *e.g.,* Marxist, Secularist, etc.). It affirms that the best education is first to get one respected historic pattern straight, thus having something with which to evaluate all other philosophies; and thus to be able to make legitimate choices.

The so-called "educational pluralism" of many universities today often leads to receiving a profusion of unrelated data—even contradictions—or to becoming an unknowing receptacle for others' hidden convictions.

These seven criteria would all be activated by Trinity Western University's Mission Statement (described in Chapter 23).

TWU's philosophy of instruction

The essence of this aspect of our identity is derived from a major evaluation of the educational role and contribution to society by some 800 private Christian colleges and universities in the USA—an extensive study by the Danforth Foundation. That study isolated three types of institution, and evaluated the educational and social value of each: First, the "church-related" type—most schools studied were only environmentally Christian (e.g., providing moral dormitory rules, a chaplain, a chapel, etc.); but intellectually, academically and instructionally functioning as secular; essentially ideologically identical to public institutions. The Danforth study concluded that this type had minimal value as a "Christian" institution, and contributed nothing unique or distinctive, educationally or socially. They only duplicated the public system, and had little significant *raison d'etre.*

The second type adhered to a strictly "doctrinaire" Christian instructional philosophy (such as the ultra-fundamentalist Bob Jones University, many Bible colleges, or even the 16th century Roman Catholic institutions, with their indices of forbidden books, etc.); being (Danforth said) both educationally limited and limiting; lacking respect for academia in general—and, indeed, providing only a narrow educational preparation, even for Christian witness in a largely secular world. Instructionally, this type was judged by Danforth to be propagandistic, controlling, and protectively exclusive. Without providing their students the opportunity to make informed choices, their convictions tended to be reactionary, and inadequate to enter into meaningful interaction and debate. Indeed, they often reflected almost a commitment to ignorance.

Rather than those options, I chose to present the Danforth Foundation's third and most positive option as the only one fully consistent with TWU's identity, defined as instructionally and institutionally faith-affirming.

Danforth described such institutions as presenting fully, competently and fairly the development and range of human learning in each discipline, and the normal personal developmental objectives of a liberal arts curriculum (as in any public university); but also with faculty able and willing openly and with conviction to affirm their personal faith; intellectually and/or spiritually to articulate and defend a distinctively alternate Christian life perspective; and to academically critique the presuppositions and biases of secular rivals, *and* with integrity to provide an alternative Christian rethinking—in some cases virtually a Christianized "rebirth"—of a discipline, both in class and among peers. This would enable the student to integrate the subject into a Christian world- and life-view. To leave out any of these would render the education inadequate. This pattern alone provides for informed choice by all students, and leads to a reasonable expectation that most will choose positively (but all are free not to—and all must know that by so doing, their graduation is not jeopardized).

In a "faith affirming" institution so defined (as TWU is), these are the primary professional and instructional tasks of every faculty member. Danforth concluded that the exercise of this option *alone* justifies an institution's existence and funding as a private Christian university or college.

As recommended by the Danforth Foundation, this instructional pattern should—and will—elicit respect, and make a significant and valuable contribution to the academy, to a free society, and to the church. This "faith affirming" type of university is who we are at TWU; it is embodied in our many "identity" statements and by our "Academic Freedom" statement.

27

One final step to academic acceptance

After the B.C. government had confirmed Trinity Western's status as a four-year, degree-granting university, there was still one very important step to be taken: seeking membership in the Association of Universities and Colleges of Canada (AUCC). Without that affirmation, TWU would remain an academic "outsider", and the benefit of our degrees to our graduates would have been diminished.

Now the wisdom of God in preparing the people of TWU became even more apparent to us: He had brought to TWU a deeply-committed Christian scholar, an historian whose academic credentials were widely-recognized within Canadian academia: Dr. Kenneth R. Davis, who'd just joined our administrative team as Vice-President and Academic Dean.

Ken Davis is both an ardent Christian, and is recognized as a scholar within Canada's university milieu. One of Ken's first actions was to tell us that Trinity Western wasn't yet properly prepared for admission to AUCC; he withdrew our application for membership, while he guided our work to improve our academic preparedness and qualifications.

In his first address in 1980, entitled *Sustaining a Rich Christian Heritage in University Education*, he carefully elaborated exactly how the whole administrative team envisioned the goals of TWU: "To be a *Christian* college of the Arts and Sciences"; to provide "a privately administered, independent, alternate university education in accord with *both* the highest academic standards *and* the finest biblically Christian ideals, for the glory of God and the benefit of humanity." But also, he said, the goal was to provide this education not only for the Canadian evangelical community at large, but "especially for those in the free or believers' church tradition"; and furthermore, to do so while sharing with the public universities a social responsibility to preserve, pass on, and build on Christian education's "rich heritage of human knowledge and achievement…", at the same time stressing that "it is to be also an education from a thoroughly evangelically Christian perspective—without apology."

The students, faculty and staff hearing his address understood how important it was to spell out our goals in such detail. And we soon understood why it was important to be much better prepared than we were for admission to the AUCC.

To achieve this vision, Ken's primary role would centre on three basic essentials:

1. to build a genuine university-college academic program—one that would be recognized throughout Canadian higher education as having both intellectual quality and academic integrity;

2. to fully sustain, institutionally and academically, our unique identity as a biblically Christian university-college—just as our founders and supporters intended, and rightfully would expect;

3. to unify Trinity Western's faculty and administration around a valid, respected Christian educational heritage and philosophy of education and instruction.

Few people were as qualified for this integration of faith and academic rigour as Ken Davis: as an historian, his field of study equipped him to bring to light how biblical scholarship had laid the foundations for modern academic scholarship.

So Ken withdrew our initial application for membership in AUCC, and set about making TWU more ready for the AUCC examination.

The first step was recognizing that all university instructors are expected to contribute to the advancement of learning, as well as to teach courses. The goal of a Bible college is preparation for ministry, but the goal of a university is the advancement of knowledge. In addition, faculty requirements for a university include PhDs from recognized universities; and pay scales, tenure and promotion standards have to be both academically valid, and just.

It was also essential that TWU have a statement of academic freedom, which Ken Davis, drawing upon extensive resources within his own faculty and from contacts across Canada and the USA, drafted for us. That statement is so important, it's worth quoting it in full now:

"Trinity Western University recognizes that academic freedom, though varyingly defined, is an essential ingredient in an effective university program. Jesus Christ taught the importance of a high regard for integrity, truth, and freedom. Indeed, He saw His role as in part setting people free from bondage to ignorance, fear, evil, and material things while providing the ultimate definition of truth.

"Accordingly, Trinity Western University maintains that arbitrary indoctrination and simplistic, prefabricated answers to questions are incompatible with a Christian respect for truth, a Christian understanding of human dignity and freedom, and quality Christian educational techniques and objectives.

"On the other hand, Trinity Western University rejects as incompatible with human nature and revelational theism a definition of academic freedom which arbitrarily and exclusively requires pluralism without commitment, denies the existence of any fixed points of reference, maximizes the quest for truth to the extent of assuming it is never knowable, and implies an absolute freedom from moral and religious responsibility to its community.

"Rather, for itself, Trinity Western University is committed to academic freedom in teaching and investigation from a stated perspective, *i.e.*, within parameters consistent with the confessional basis of the constituency to which the University is responsible, but practiced in an environment of free inquiry and discussion and of encouragement to integrity in research. Students also have freedom to inquire, right of access to the broad spectrum of representative information in each discipline, and assurance of a reasonable attempt at a fair and balanced presentation and evaluation of all material by their instructors.

"Truth does not fear honest investigation."

This program of strengthening and enhancing the new University's academic programs went on rapidly—both to prepare for AUCC, and to keep pace with rapid growth. To our four divisional and six disciplinary majors in 1979/80 (available for the first baccalaureate degrees), were added by 1983/84, liberal arts majors in Christianity and Culture, Music, Biblical Studies, Geography; a Divisional major in Physical Education; the BSc for a Divisional major in Natural Science; and a major in Applied Math. All majors were strengthened by added PhD-level faculty. Development towards several new majors was also well underway, and by 1983 reached the level of concentrations in Drama, Communications, Biology, Human Services, Computer Science, and Education. Also, 18 of the courses in Business/Accounting had been approved by the Institute of Chartered Accountants.

Several faculty had already prepared and published scholarly articles in their fields. More would do so. There were also significant steps to improve facilities, equipment, and library resources. With all these areas well in hand, at last we felt academically confident to re-open our application for admission to AUCC—and their examination of TWC was scheduled for 1983.

28

Meeting the AUCC in Toronto

We'd worked long and hard to be prepared for this day. The process had begun in 1978, or even earlier. Five years later, having made the decision to become a four-year academic institution, we'd also resolved, God helping us, to attain active membership in the national accrediting agency. We knew that rather than creating accrediting associations for blocks of States, as was the case in the US, Canada had developed a nationally recognized body of academic institutions whose presidents were the active members.

The Association of Universities and Colleges of Canada, (AUCC), doesn't see itself as merely an accrediting body, but much more. The presidents are highly respected leaders, colleagues who not only represent their own institutions, but collegially work to maintain, protect and enrich our national culture through higher education standards, in Canada and abroad.

As I travelled to Toronto, I felt very much alone. The October, 1983 AUCC meeting was to be in conjunction with a large gathering of several hundred North American colleges and universities, focused on "the Liberal Arts in Education". I was an invited guest to only the business session of AUCC, to be held apart from the Conference Friday morning between 10 a.m. and noon. I waited outside the room until the question of TWC membership was to be considered.

In arriving at our spacious hotel, I realized that I knew very few of the presidents entering the room. I guessed that about seventy-five would be present, and I was pleased to greet, as they arrived and welcomed me, the three members of the AUCC committee that had visited TWC to examine our faculty, facilities and students. I'd stayed overnight at the home of my mother-in-law who, like so many others, was praying that our membership would be accepted.

I had time for reflection as I waited. I was here 'wanting' some things. I wanted TWC to be acknowledged for its quality. I wanted the benefits of this membership, *i.e.*, opportunities for our students to move into graduate programs, to receive research grants for faculty, for students to receive scholarships, and other recognitions. And I wanted to see the future open up for us to become so much more in Christ's name.

I began to think further: what, really, should we be bringing to the table? We could share our focus on "holistic student development" as a major thrust to our educational outcomes. In fact, we could easily share the effects of our new Mission Statement: our commitment to developing the kind of leaders whose goal would be to live and work with excellence for God's glory, and for the good of others.

But right now I was waiting to be asked to join the presidents. The Chairman, Dr. Lloyd Barber, President of the University of Saskatchewan at Regina, offered me a warm welcome. We would soon hear from Dr. James Downey, then President of the University of New Brunswick. He was Chairman of the Evaluation Committee that had visited our campus, and would now report openly what had already been reported to the AUCC Executive Committee, and more recently in writing to the entire membership.

I knew what was coming, and smiled to myself as my thoughts flew back to the visit paid to us in May. The three examiners had arrived in Vancouver two weeks after our school year closed. It seemed unfortunate that there'd be few students on campus when they arrived. However, it was a beautiful spring day, and our Aviation leaders were excited about the opportunity to take our guests for a flight over and around our campus. It was breathtaking (as one said), and they couldn't stop talking about the beauty of the Fraser Valley, the surrounding mountains, and the unforgettable city of Vancouver.

They had a routine to follow, however, and we had been pleased to bring in a good number of students, who enjoyed telling of their academic experiences and life at Trinity. The committee met with our faculty and staff members, visited our facilities, and spent time observing, investigating and writing their reports.

Finally, the examining team met with our Academic Vice-President, Dr. Ken Davis and me. The tenor of the group was that their visit had been a "delightful surprise", for they hadn't heard much about our institution in the far west. Dr. Downey had spoken highly of the beautiful setting and facilities, but gave special attention to the impressive students they'd met, and the faculty who related so well to them. Each examiner had spoken conversationally of their area of review, asked a few clarifying questions, made some suggestions, or gave reference to areas that were already in planning or under development—all as positive observations.

At one point I had said I was concerned about our library, although I was proud of the progress we'd made in such a short time. To my surprise, the member who responded had been a librarian and was now a staff member of AUCC. He said he'd given special attention to the library, and although it was limited, as might be expected for a young institution, the selection had been very wisely chosen. He expected we'd continue to build our holdings, and considered the situation as well in hand.

One issue, however, had concerned them: they wondered about whether our Statement of Faith, that faculty signed, might be antithetical to academic freedom. They recognized the similarity of our orthodox statement to those of religious teaching orders or colleges. But they also knew that most Canadian universities didn't have faith statements, and probably few or none required faculty compliance.

Our response had centred on our concern for both religious and academic freedom. No freedom, we pointed out, is ever absolute. We welcome students of any race, colour, or creed. We are not doctrinaire; our faculty attempt to fairly present other perspectives, even though they speak and teach from our biblical perspective.

Ken Davis had also formulated an Academic Freedom Statement that, among other things, "rejects a definition of academic freedom which arbitrarily and exclusively requires pluralism without commitment, and implies an absolute freedom from moral and religious responsibility to its community." Dr. Davis had carefully researched and documented statements from similar discussions by several scholars and accrediting institutions in the USA in the recent past.

The examiners had seemed to appreciate the answers we had given to clarify our position, and the conviction that our students were being challenged about their personal development. At the same time, they were unsure how the Executive Committee or the AUCC membership might respond.

Within a few weeks, we'd heard back from the Executive Committee. They informed us that the Examining Committee had enjoyed their visit, and were very impressed with their findings. They'd reported that TWC met all of the criteria for membership. On that basis, they recommended that TWC be accepted into the AUCC as a full member. They'd also reported on the issue of our Faith Statement.

By mid June, the Executive Committee had informed us that after another thorough review, they'd approved the recommendation of the Committee. At the same time, they wanted us to be aware of an uncertain outcome; the members could well be divided over the issues of academic freedom and our faith statement. However, the Executive Committee advised us that they would be recommending our membership—and I, as President, was invited to attend the October General meeting as an observer.

Now I was here in Toronto, and the actual report was about to be considered.

Dr. James Downey presented the report and accepted some questions before Chairman Barber opened the floor for discussion. A number of presidents came to the microphones, some for clarification, others in strong opposition to the recommendation; some with unfortunate misinformation, while others, particularly from religious colleges, spoke in our favour.

A few recurring concerns appeared to be most pressing. For example:

- Is "academic freedom" clearly understood and stated?
- Should it be possible to hold faculty to "extra-academic" commitments?
- Was it true that TWU gained university status by 'doing an end-run' on the BC University Council by pushing a Private Members' Bill through the Legislature?
- Is it true that TWC would not hire a Sikh or a Jew?
- Could this young institution attract and hold qualified faculty, if they had to agree to such a draconian 'Faith Statement'?

It was quite obvious that our Faith Statement was most problematic, in spite of the clearly stated Academic Freedom Statement that settled the issue for some. Gradually the focus became 'required extra-academic commitments', many of which had been dropped from most universities in years gone by. Chairman Lloyd Barber chose to call on the president from a respected affiliated college. He simply asked, "Mr. President, I know that you have a number of well-known faculty members who are priests. Do your faculty members have to sign some kind of religious agreement in order to be professors?

His response was, "No, our faculty don't have to sign any religious agreement. However, if priests who are also professors should choose to marry and leave the priesthood, they can no longer be members of the faculty."

This proved interesting, as conversations quickly began. Surely this was an example of what would be called an 'extra academic' requirement. If so, it must then be that any university could have unique standards or policies that might not hold for other institutions. Are there not some institutional sovereign rights?

There was very little further discussion before someone moved to table the issue. A 'second' followed, just as the chairman was asking for some latitude. Dr. Barber was saying, "With your permission, it seems to me that it would only be fair to give this young president an opportunity to respond, after all that he has heard today." He looked to those wanting to make the motion, got no response, then looked to the back of the room where I was sitting and said, "Oh, come on up here, Dr. Snider. We want to hear from you."

This was unexpected! I'd heard several negative, and even some harsh comments directed to our college and to our intentions. We were, as the chairman said, young and unknown. Perhaps the best thing I could have hoped for would be that these leaders might have the same opportunity the evaluation committee had in visiting our community and our campus. I needed to share some of our vision. I wanted to be their friend.

I thanked the Chairman, and added a soft apology that we'd been unable to provide a larger and clearer picture of our Trinity Western community. I said I hoped we'd be able to do so in days to come; but for now I'd try to correct a few misconceptions:

- I'm sorry about the mistaken notion that Trinity Western might 'do an end-run' on anybody. In fact, a spokesman for the B. C. Universities Council visited us on two occasions, and it was he who informed us that the Council didn't have the legal right to deal with private institutions. Thus, we were left with only one other choice: a private member's bill, which was thoroughly and publicly reviewed.
- The question about the quality of our faculty who would choose to come to a faith-affirming University deserves a positive response. Our faculty has doubled in numbers in recent years. They haven't come because of large salaries or fancy facilities, but because of our mission to intentionally develop quality Christian leaders; our community intent to build up one another; and our commitment to academic excellence. We're pleased to welcome the growing number of experienced professors and researchers who choose Trinity Western. You should also know that many, if not most of them, are graduates from your universities.
- Would we hire a Sikh or a Jew? No, not likely; any more than we would want to hire a 'cultural Christian'—someone who simply comes from that background. We might welcome such people as visiting scholars, because we don't intend to be doctrinaire, *i.e.* imposing some philosophy or doctrine on others without regard to other considerations. In short, we look forward to welcoming qualified faculty who want to become, on our terms, members of our unique community.
- Finally, among the many colleges and universities that have come to this conference from across Canada and the United States is a coalition of Christian colleges. We have close relationships with many of these fully-accredited institutions that have great academic traditions. Besides that, they have varying faith statements and student-centred community standards to

challenge and stimulate all their members to personal development. I think it would be unfortunate if in Canada, Christian colleges like those weren't available to the large number of families who now think it necessary to send their children to the United States for higher education.

There were questions pertaining to the possibility that Trinity Western might actually be the only such institution in Canada. Several seemed to agree that this could certainly be so, especially since Catholic colleges don't attract many Protestant students.

I thanked the Chairman for the opportunity to speak. He was gracious, and then followed up on the motion to table the recommendation to approve the membership of Trinity Western College.

The vote turned out to be a bit awkward. A voice vote was not determinative; a hand-raising vote was too close to be certain; finally ballots were distributed. It was obviously a close decision; but finally, the recommendation was tabled. I was dismissed from the session.

Picking up the pieces

I was hardly outside the door before I started thinking of my colleagues back at TWC. They would certainly be wondering what had happened. I immediately called Ken Davis. We'd worked closely together, and he would report to our community at the Friday Student Chapel. It seemed like I had a moving picture in my mind of all that had happened, including the words of the various spokespeople. I transferred that picture to Dr. Davis, who in turn would pass it on to the campus.

My first thought was that I shouldn't leave the area. Instead, I'd wait to meet any who might want to talk to me. Several friends would probably sense my disappointment, and they might have some suggestions. We all understood that a 'tabled item' might never be brought back to the next meeting.

I felt a little like a pastor standing by the door at the close of a service. Many passed by quickly, but some stopped to talk or just to wish me well. Finally Dr. Downey came by and we shook hands. His immediate comment, "You spoke very well" was followed by, "I think my colleagues made a mistake today—well, maybe not a mistake. They just tabled it; you can still try again."

Without even thinking I responded, "Well, Jim, we have to realize that Trinity wasn't on trial today; AUCC was. Someone from the media is waiting for me right now, to receive the results of this meeting. People from all across the nation have been praying for us at this time, and when the word gets out that AUCC has discriminated against this Christian college, which met all of the criteria for full membership, AUCC will look bad."

"You can't let that be published! It wouldn't be good for Trinity!" Jim said.

"It wouldn't be good for AUCC," I responded quickly.

Dr. Downey and I reminisced briefly, and he asked where I could be reached. I wrote out the phone number for where I was staying, and we agreed that I wouldn't release any statement until Monday morning, when I returned to Langley.

Others spoke with me, the most memorable being the Chairman, Dr. Barber. He threw his big arm around my shoulder and let me know that he thought we ought to be a member. He told me he'd attended a Lutheran college, which sounded much like Trinity Western; and he urged me to strive to gain membership for the good of AUCC.

"Don't give up!"

It was time to go. The reporter who was to publish the results of this important day for Trinity Western took me away from the large hotel and the many conference guests. We stopped at a little restaurant not far from the hotel, and as we entered, I noticed three public telephones (they were still in vogue in those days). It occurred to me that I should call my mother-in-law, where I was staying, to let her know what I was doing. I called, but before I could greet her she talked excitedly about a phone call that had just come in for me. She said that someone from AUCC had called and had left a number that I should call back.

I was soon talking with Dr. Allan Gilmore, Executive Chairman of AUCC, whom I'd never met. His first question was, "Dr. Snider, Where are you?"

I assumed that he'd been looking for me, and answered, "I did leave the hotel, and I'm not quite sure where I am; but it's just a few blocks away."

His laughing response was also an invitation: "Well, how would you like to come and have lunch with some of us who don't know where we are, either?"

It took very little time to return to the hotel and up the many floors to the office space reserved for the Conference. The warm welcome I received felt like returning to long-time friends. I hadn't met these people, but they'd spent considerable time evaluating the report on TWC, and then approving and forwarding it to the AUCC members. I saw them as friends.

The lunch was prepared and the intended conversation began immediately. (I learned later that some of the executive members had planes to catch in the afternoon; hence the rush). An early introductory question wondered if I might be able to "help AUCC get out of the dilemma in which we find ourselves." The

French legal expert was heard to say, "This is no good. Either we accept Trinity Western, or we will have to evaluate all our religious colleges!"

I was asked directly what I thought might help to resolve the issue. My first thought was that I'd have to be assured that our application would be lifted from the table at the next meeting, which was scheduled for March. Then I thought we might add pertinent information to enhance our application. Someone asked about any research we were doing, since we hadn't spent much time clarifying that area. Fortunately, I was able to report on a number of research projects on our campus, and about research partnerships on other campuses in a variety of fields. This proved to be a winning suggestion for additional information.

Finally we concluded that we'd prepare a joint statement for the media, which would state clearly that Trinity's application would be brought to the table at the very next meeting; that Trinity Western would report more fully on the research being done; and that both Trinity Western College and AUCC would actively invite and welcome presidents and deans, as well as other administrators and faculty, to visit our campus and learn the merits of this institution as reported by the examining committee. The report to the media was prepared, on the basis of that afternoon's discussion, primarily by the Executive Chairman, Allan Gilmore, and by me as the President of Trinity Western College. It was released the following week to the national media.

However, Dr. Gilmore also wisely observed that in the interim, we should obtain assurances that none the three presidents of B.C.'s major universities would object to our admission. We still had a long way to go.

29

Perseverance pays off

While it was disappointing that we hadn't been granted membership, in spite of the report that Trinity Western had met all of AUCC's requirements, I'd come away with the Executive Director's word that our application would be considered again at the next general meeting. The intervening six months wouldn't be idle!

The campus community took things in stride. They'd do just about anything to help, and seemed confident that God knew what He was doing. They'd work hard to prove their abilities, and to maintain their intention to live our Mission. That is, after all, the "Trinity Western Way"!

We were pleased to have a visit to our campus by Dr. Allan Gilmore, the Executive Chairman of AUCC—whom by now I considered a supportive friend. It was interesting to learn that Dr. Gilmore was a former Baptist pastor—in the same church Ken Davis had pastored in years gone by! He was pleased with what he saw and learned about TWC, and gave some helpful suggestions. He was a man of integrity, and it was he who had encouraged us to consult B.C.'s other university presidents.

Dr. Davis and I laid out a plan to make our institution better known. Most Canadian universities were in the central and eastern provinces. Neither of us knew many of the other presidents personally, so we began to arrange to meet as many as possible in our western provinces. British Columbia, with three universities, was the place to start.

The President of UBC, Dr. K. George Pedersen, was a former Academic Dean at the University of Victoria, President of the University of Western Ontario, and more recently had been President of Simon Fraser University. He was well aware of our history and reputation. Indeed, TWC, as a junior college, had always closely cooperated with UBC. Dr. John Parnell, the long-serving registrar at UBC, had established the agreement that enabled Trinity Junior College students to transfer their credits to UBC.

We also made an appointment with Simon Fraser University's President,

Dr. William G. Saywell, an historian in Asian Studies. We hadn't known him personally, but he gave us an hour to make our case. As a fellow professional historian, Dr. Davis sought to show the historical validity of the kind of university-college we were and intended to be, and its unique and ongoing value to the academic community and to Canadian society as a whole. We didn't gain his total support, but he agreed to neutrality; he wouldn't oppose our application.

Everything then hinged on the President of the University of Victoria, Dr. Howard Petch—a scientist who had strongly and vocally opposed our application. I'd tried to get him to visit our campus and our faculty personally. He didn't set up an appointment, noting that he was too busy. Finally, Doctor Davis felt led to call him personally, because he knew him well. Dr. Petch had been Ken's Academic VP at the University of Waterloo, and among other things had assisted him in resolving some Science/Arts financial problems while there. Ken told me later:

"Dr. Petch responded immediately as an old friend would, but he was totally surprised to learn of my involvement at TWC. After some further discussion, I asked him, as a personal favour, to pay us a visit before the next AUCC meeting. After a long pause, he agreed to take an hour while on his way with his wife to a weekend break in the Okanagan."

He came, looked over the campus quickly and then went to the Science Department, his major interest. Our department of excellent, well-trained and well-prepared faculty were waiting as a group in the Science Building. Ken introduced him and went back to his office to pray and wait… and wait… while Dr. Petch grilled them carefully, professionally, on all aspects of their training. More time passed—well over an hour.

Finally, Ken said, he came back to Ken's office, sat down, and began to talk quietly. He related to Ken that he had been raised in a devout Baptist home in rural Ontario, and his early university training was at McMaster College—which at that time was a small Christian college, much like TWC. He said TWC was a fine college, and that he'd erred in speaking against its application for admission to AUCC. He assured Ken Davis that he'd reverse that.

And he did, being the first to speak when the matter was raised at the next Association meeting in 1984.

The days went by quickly. There was no sign on campus, that I could see or hear, of a martyr complex, or of "being hard done by" as a community. We had several interested visitors and we heard that in some universities, questions were raised about us at their Senate meetings. Dr. Davis and his staff provided an excellent review of our research projects, on campus and in collaboration with other universities; as well as writing, artistic design, production and publishing that might be expected in undergraduate studies.

All of this was soon to come to a conclusion. Dr. Gilmore graciously arranged for my accommodations in Montreal for the March, 1984 meeting. Things were quite different from my former visit: I'd been registered as a guest, and I was present for the whole meeting. Dr. Gilmore introduced me to several presidents, and I found it interesting that some small groups were apparently discussing our membership. I had no responsibilities that I knew of, and decided that "they also serve who only stand and wait."

And wait I did—but not for long. Dr. Arnold Naimark, President of the University of Manitoba, had been named the next Chairman of AUCC. He had a special way of making everyone feel relaxed.

The Trinity Western issue soon came up, and once again Dr. Downey was asked to summarize the membership report and its recommendation. Nothing had really changed. The report had determined that Trinity Western College met all criteria for full membership. In subsequent discussions, it had been pointed out that only a couple of years previously, two renowned consultants had established the criteria at considerable cost—and AUCC had approved them.

It was also found that Trinity Western, ever since its founding, had a Faith Statement to which all faculty and staff were to adhere. Questions had been raised about the acceptability of an institution requiring "extra-academic criteria" for its faculty.

Dr. Naimark thanked the members of the Examining Committee and opened the floor for discussion. There were ready speakers. I had no idea what to expect.

I felt great relief in seeing Dr. Petch rise to speak. He wanted to speak first, since he had been first to speak on the previous occasion. He wanted it known that unfortunately, BC's university presidents had been misinformed. Trinity had not "made an end-run on the Universities Council." TWC had, in fact, welcomed a Council spokesman to the campus, and had been correctly informed that the Universities Council had no jurisdiction over private or non-government institutions. Trinity Western had no alternative but to ask an MLA to carry forward a "private member's bill", which opened the process leading to Trinity Western's achievement.

Dr. Petch said he'd initially wondered about the competence of the faculty of the recently chartered four-year Christian college. But now he affirmed the faculty he'd met as not only well qualified, but people excited about their community, who welcome the opportunity to challenge the very bright students being drawn to this institution.

I wasn't in a position to say anything; but I felt certain Dr. Petch would have agreed that these were the kind of faculty who not only teach subjects in their disciplines, but teach people; and influence them to become the kind of people God had uniquely created them to be.

The President of McMaster University was next to speak. His was a carefully prepared talk that spoke of our great historical values, and the role that religious institutions have played in shaping our culture—and which should be preserved.

A few others spoke of having visited or learned in some way about Trinity Western and its good reputation. Only one president asked for more information. He wasn't sure our Academic Freedom Statement was adequate; so he asked if it could be read in whole, one more time. I was pleased to hear the request, and listened intently with all of the members—whose silence, I guessed, must have signaled approval of the statement… or just that no one wanted to discuss the matter further.

As I recall, a member stood and said, "If the Examining Committee said they had some concern, or maybe some uneasiness about the required Faith Statement, and the Executive Committee said the same thing, why then would these committees forward this recommendation?"

There was some talk that we at the back couldn't hear; but someone—perhaps the Chairman—reiterated that Trinity Western met or exceeded all AUCC's criteria. Someone called for the question. Dr. Naimark established the voting procedure; the vote was taken, and Trinity Western College became a full member of the AUCC.

There were other business items on the agenda; but I was content to breathe deeply, and though I appeared to be listening, my thoughts were on God's goodness!

The meeting finally closed. The Chairman immediately walked toward the table where I'd been sitting. Others stepped up to congratulate and welcome me, but this was the first time I'd met Dr. Naimark. He reached out in his jovial manner and shook my hand as he said, "Welcome to the club, Dr. Snider. I understand that you are a graduate from the University of Manitoba."

"Yes indeed!" I responded happily. "Three times."

"I didn't know that, but you're certainly welcome back. We have many more degrees you could get."

Then he said somewhat reflectively, "You know, it's very interesting; most of us, as presidents, have visited and learned a lot about many other universities through the years; but in just this short time, after what you have just been through, *everyone* knows about Trinity Western!"

I knew it was a compliment. I also knew that it described the way that God often does things. We certainly couldn't take the credit! What we would do, though, was to express our gratitude to God. After all, the whole Trinity Western project was, and is, in the words of the Apostle Paul, **to the Praise of His Glory**.

Lloyd Makaroff, the first full-time campus pastor, stands behind the pulpit speaking to the students in the Cal Hanson Chapel.

30

TWC becomes TWU

By the year 1985, we were becoming frustrated about being a "college". The confusion of TWC being a four-year, degree-granting university-college, along with the province's many two-year applied and junior colleges, needed to be resolved. We had already informally dropped the "college" title for general usage in our conversation and literature, even while we were anticipating our legal status change, which had not included the title "university".

Dr. Davis took the initiative to write to Dr. McGeer, the provincial Minster for Advanced Education, to seek some name redress, so as to distinguish between two-year colleges and four-year degree-granting university-colleges. It seemed easy enough, but we received no response.

So it was that our administration began the process of achieving a solution by political action, by a Private Member's Bill which would change TWC to TWU. The bill, sponsored by Rita Johnston, MLA—who would later, in 1991, become the Premier of B.C.— seemed to go well until just a few days before the Private Bills Committee, which was to introduce it at the final session, found that a strong and unexpected negative reaction had arisen. Clearly, this threatened the bill's success to such an extent that the committee thought that perhaps it might be better for TWC not to proceed.

As the committee met on the last evening, it recognized that the root of the problem seemed to be a fear that it was too soon, and some feared that a bill turning us into a full-fledged university might lead to cheap graduate degrees, which would be hurtful to B.C.'s academic reputation as a whole.

During their final session that evening, the committee phoned Dr. Ken Davis at his office at Trinity Western for advice, After a quick desperation prayer for help, Ken's immediate response was to suggest strongly that they make three amendments, and then proceed with the proposal. And these were:

> 1. that TW agrees not to proceed to the offering of any graduate degrees for a period of five years;

2. that every proposed graduate degree program thereafter must first be examined and approved by three professors in the proposed field, one from each provincial university; and then the recommendations, if positive, be forward to the Minister of Education for final approval to proceed;

3. that conditions 1) and 2) do not apply to graduate programs in religious/theological studies.

These recommendations met with their approval, were added to the bill as amendments, and allowed the bill to proceed successfully. Indeed, they became the operative principles carefully followed in our graduate academic programming ever since. So it was that in 1985, by government action, TWC became TWU.

Paul Wong founder and director of the Masters in Counselling program. Dr. Snider on the right.

Don Page visiting with students.

TWU Archives

PART V

Bringing the vision into focus

*The vision must be clear; but so must be our plans for attaining it; and so must be the hope and optimism of the constituency that provides support. One of the most important things we strove to teach our students, by example, was the difference between a critical **spirit**, which is usually quite negative, and a critical **mind**, which must be keenly analytical—but always with a positive orientation towards the realization of the goal, whether building a university, or discovering the truth.*

—Neil Snider

31

TWU as a faith-filled academic community

*From an address by the late Dr. Harro Van Brummelen,
founding Director of the TWU School of Education*

When I came to Trinity Western in 1986, it was a step of faith, both for the University and for myself. In my interview with senior administrators, they wondered how someone from a Reformed Church background would fit in.

Accepting that contract was a step of faith for me, too: at many faculty meetings, Dr. Ken Davis reported on TWU's fundraising results—followed by a prayer session, since it was far from clear whether we would exist the following year!

But I never regretted my step of faith. It's been a blessing and a joy to work for a common purpose with exceptional colleagues and wonderful students. When I reflect on my TWU involvement over the years, I can point to several highlights. One was going to the Supreme Court of Canada to ensure that Canada's faith-based institutions could continue to play a responsible role in the public square (See "Part VIII" on page 243). But just as significant, in my view, was the undertaking to establish core values that anchor our learning community.

Harro Van Brummelen

In 1998, President Snider and Academic Vice-President Don Page agreed that our Mission Statement needed elucidation. Executive Vice-President Guy Saffold and I were charged with leading a process to choose and define the core values that would guide Trinity Western into the future. That process became one of the finest I've experienced at TWU. Why? Because the whole community was engaged: faculty, staff (from Student Life and Academics to facility maintenance), students, administrators, and Board members. We conducted surveys, in which people expressed what they thought our core values should be. We held workshops where various groups gave input.

After we'd agreed on the basic core values, we considered the strategic implications of each. Writing teams then drafted papers to explain how each core value would affect our life as a Christ-centred academic community. The draft papers were distributed for final input, and eventually the Board of Governors approved each paper.

The process took three years; but those years were a time of deepening our perception of what TWU is all about. It was a time of building a strong internal sense of institution-wide collaboration and commitment.

Fairly early in the process, a consensus developed around five core values:

- Obeying the authority of Scripture;
- Pursuing faith-based and faith-affirming learning;
- Having a transformational impact on culture;
- Servant-leadership as a way of life; and
- Growing as disciples in community.

But when we were just about to finalize these, the late Professor Barbara Pell had an observation that, as usual, could not be ignored. She asked: "What is a university that doesn't have excellence as a core value?"

I answered that our core values were ones that made us distinctive—but *every* university says that it pursues excellence.

Barbara was unfazed: "Well, then we'd better include excellence—and define it in a way that's unique to Trinity Western."

She won the argument, and *striving for excellence* became our sixth core value.

I believe this set of core values still anchors us, so I'd like to point out a few highlights for each.

> **First, obeying the authority of Scripture.** The Bible gives us a view of the world and our place in it, by which we are to "[take] every thought captive to the obedience of Christ."[1] The Scriptural themes of God's creation, the fall of humanity and Christ's redemption shape the basic perspective governing what we do at Trinity Western. As a community of faith, we foster confidence in the authority of the Bible—not only among students, but also within the church and the larger community.

---
1   II Corinthians 10:5 (NASB)

Further, we base internal decisions and practices on Scriptural principles such as respect, integrity, and fairness.

Second, pursuing faith-based and faith-affirming learning. Faith-based learning and scholarship take place on the premise that we are called to unfold God's created and ordered reality—and to do so within the framework of biblical principles such as integrity, justice, compassion, peace, stewardship, and respect for the dignity of all human beings. Faith-affirming learning initiates students into the evangelical tradition, but also encourages them to critique and renew that heritage as they embark on their own faith-based quest.

Third, having a transformational impact on the culture: the Bible makes clear that God calls His followers to be personally renewed by the Spirit, and then to influence the culture by "[seeking] the peace of the city...."[1] As Christians, we seek righteousness, justice, and mercy; and, especially, freedom for the oppressed and support for the vulnerable. We encourage students to be a positive influence on the culture—even if their influence, like ours, will be a limited one until Christ's return.

Fourth, servant-leadership as a way of life. Drs. Snider and Page deal with the importance and implications of this core value in Chapters 41 and 42.

Fifth, growing as disciples *in community*. This core value embodies all others, yet was the most difficult to draft. The authors of the first draft saw discipleship in an important but narrow sense: reaching out with the Great Commission in order to lead others to Christ. But follow-up discussions led us to see that in an academic setting, discipleship also includes a resolve to apply learning and scholarship in ways that make a positive difference: speaking out knowledgeably on key issues in our disciplines, and doing works of service. Our discussions helped to bring together our Student Life staff and our faculty, to see how both were involved in nurturing discipleship, even if with sometimes different emphases.

Finally, striving for excellence. How can we describe this in a distinctively *Christian* way? Well, the key became excellence in the *Christian* mind; but not purely *intellectual* excellence. As the paper states, "We believe that thoroughly Christian minds can exist fully only

---

[1] Jeremiah 29:7 (KJV)

in thoroughly Christian people. Therefore, we strive for excellence *as a community*, upholding high standards of whole-person development; a community where we pursue academic excellence on the basis of integrity, care, and mutual respect."

To what extent have these core values influenced our graduates? I could give many examples of graduates in any of our programs who have made an impact for God within the framework of these core values. We have graduates serving in Ottawa, serving in overseas countries throughout the world, serving the destitute in inner cities, and serving in small and large corporations right here in British Columbia.

But in my mind, one particular example stands out.

Ten years ago, two business graduates came to me. "Dr. van Brummelen, we've prayerfully considered where in the world a Christian voice is most needed, and how we can be a meaningful influence there. That country is Rwanda, where the 1994 genocide killed more than a million people. We don't know anything about education, but we believe that God calls us to start a school there to train future leaders for Rwanda. How do we go about it?"

I must admit that with our School of Education just starting up, and myself being quite involved in training Christian teachers in the former Communist countries, the best I could do was to encourage them, and provide them with names of people who could be helpful in setting up a school in Africa.

By the grace of God, these two young men, Richard Taylor and Jeff Komant, have accomplished more than they ever dreamed! And a large part of the reason is that they were rooted in and committed to TWU's core values.

The core values we developed more than a decade ago at Trinity Western still anchor our learning and our living in community, both within and outside the University. We published the papers in a booklet that's still used to orient new faculty. I hope and pray we'll continue to use these values to guide our thoughts and actions. They're rooted in Scripture; and, when implemented, they help to prepare our students for a life of service: to God, to their neighbours, to their communities, and to society-at-large.

And that's what Christian higher education should be all about.

> *The late Dr. Harro van Brummelen had a history in Christian education long before coming to TWU; he'd been the head of FISA, the Federation of Independent School Associations in B.C., and a leading figure in establishing and administering schools run by Christian Reformed churches. He is greatly missed at TWU.*

32

CTP: our 'Critical Time Period'

By Dr. Guy Saffold

Right from the beginning, we recognized that unless we built greater financial strength, it would be impossible to manage the growth. In the mid-'80s, we declared four months a "Critical Time Period" (CTP), during which maximum effort must be exerted to strengthen TWU's financial position, both short- and longer-term. Dr. Howard Anderson, who had earlier assisted in development of the TWU Mission Statement, now returned to give leadership to the CTP. Two high-level marketing teams were established, one to work on building enrolment and the other to raise $590,000 to meet urgent needs.

The following year was dedicated to a strategic capital funding campaign to raise the funds needed to provide a new library building and a science centre. The Board and administration went to work—and to prayer. The CTP proved successful, clearing the way for the much-needed capital fund drives.

By September of 1990—two years ahead of schedule—the "impossible" dream of "1,300 by 30" unfolded before our eyes, as 1,358 students enrolled for studies. By TWU's actual thirtieth anniversary, the number had swelled to 1,553—far surpassing the original plan. Not every element in the plan had been fulfilled; perhaps most significant, we hadn't been able to mange all that growth "debt-free" as had been hoped; but a large flow of contributions had kept the financial picture manageable, and TWU was financially sound. Truly, it had been "no human plan" but rather one birthed in a God-given vision and achieved with His provision.

Two decades (plus two years) of student enrollment statistics

Year	Enrollment	Year	Enrollment	Year	Enrollment	Year	Enrollment
1974	358	1980	553	1986	955	1992	1,495
1975	374	1981	668	1987	1,109	1993	1,558
1976	400	1982	742	1988	1,175	1994	1,721
1977	437	1983	805	1989	1,228	1995	2,005
1978	452	1984	777	1990	1,276		
1979	504	1985	838	1991	1,358		

These efforts were also rewarded over time. In 1999, the stirring music of a bag-piper led a procession across campus to break ground for the Norma Marion Alloway Library, which was constructed and dedicated in 2000 to great celebration.

Onward to 'TWU 2001'

In late 1991, the TWU Strategic Planning Committee prepared an initial draft plan, and in fall of 1992 it was circulated to the entire campus community for review and feedback. Extensive reviews over the following months triggered investigations of capacities, implications, and possible alternate strategies. In the fall of 1993, the plan was again circulated to the full faculty and staff for review and revision.

One result of rapid growth was that plans needed continual updating. Since each planning process led to substantial fulfillment, our planning horizon had to be extended again and again. As we approached the 1992 goal of "1300 by 30", we were already thinking ahead to the turn of the millennium. Drafting began for the vision and plan we called 'TWU 2001'. If it was perhaps overly cute to link this to having 2,001 students by the year 2001, the plan was nonetheless ambitious, the result of a highly inclusive campus-wide effort to think forward to the next phase in TWU's expansion.

'TWU 2001' called for an intense focus on quality—a goal that would, within a few years, be anchored in a well-defined core value of "pursuing excellence in university education." The plan called for quality in spiritual development, as well as academic development, recognizing that these two goals, linked together, constituted the most important distinctive of a TWU education. The University was to be "mission-driven", and outstanding in leadership development, with an emphasis on service to the Christian community and the wider community and culture.

An emerging emphasis was on strategic partnerships with the growing number of organizations that wanted to link with TWU in various ways. Opportunities were increasingly coming to us, and it was necessary to choose wisely among the many possibilities. We could engage in only a few of the most strategic possibilities. The Associated Canadian Theological Schools (ACTS; see Chapter 36), which had become the third-largest theological school in Canada, was in the process of expanding to include six partner seminaries. They included the University's own Evangelical Free Church of Canada, the Baptist General Conference, the Fellowship of Evangelical Baptists, the Christian and Missionary Alliance, the Mennonite Brethren, and the Pentecostal Assemblies of Canada. Wycliffe Bible

Translators had linked with TWU to develop the "Canada Institute of Linguistics" (CanIL; see Chapter 56), with a vision to train Bible translators and literacy workers. "A Rocha", a Christian organization concerned with environmental stewardship, was partnering in projects with the University's Biology program. In Education, we were partnering with the Society of Christian Schools in British Columbia.

Continuing dream, on-going realization

To be honest, we tended to put too many visions into the mix at the same time—more than could be accomplished. However, if not every objective was achieved, many others were fulfilled in depth, and often more richly than even anticipated. We were at times too optimistic about how quickly things could be done; but in other cases, goals were realized more quickly than imagined, as people bent their efforts and passion to moving plans ahead, and God opened unexpected doors.

We were planners because we wanted to be doers. But in doing, we were constantly reminded that something much larger than any of us was underway as part of God's purposes. In the end, we were continually amazed and deeply thankful for what God had continued to do in raising TWU to new levels of achievement and impact. God was truly at work; so rather than claiming credit for what had been done, it often seemed that we were only bystanders, watching the Lord do one amazing work after another. TWU truly was developing "to the praise of His glory."

Through all of these cycles of planning and implementation, the original dream that gave birth to Trinity Western continued to thrive, taking new forms as the institution matured and expanded; but always with the same goal at heart: developing godly Christian leaders who would serve in the marketplaces of life with a transforming impact on the world around them.

But now we must return to the earlier years, to "fill in the blanks"—to see the actual fulfillment of the detailed planning that carried us onward.

33

Dr. Don Page comes to TWU

Trinity Western University was known to Dr. Don Page, because he had been a convocation speaker, and had spoken at some fund raising events for the University. We had invited him to consider becoming Academic Vice President in 1979; but at that time, the timing wasn't right because of his responsibility to look after his recently widowed mother in a nursing home in Ottawa. Fortuitously, Dr. Ken Davis took up the challenge. He was clearly the right man for handling the challenges faced by a junior Christian college trying to launch four-year degree programs and also to gain recognition by the AUCC as a university in the faith tradition.

Also fortuitously, the 1980s would turn out to be Don Page's most rewarding and instructive years at External Affairs. It was a time in which he would hone his negotiating and consensus building skills, which would become assets for his later work at TWU. In addition, he was reluctant to leave his leadership of the Public Service Christian Fellowship (PSCF), a series of regular prayer meetings for Members of Parliament and senior civil servants.

Over the course of the next few years, several things influenced Don's change of heart. His work on the history of the External Affairs Department was at a dead-end, and when a decision was made to downsize the Historical Division by transferring its research work to the operating divisions, he

Don Page

seriously began contemplating a return to the university world, having previously taught at the University of Saskatchewan's Regina Campus. That possible move, however, was interrupted by the Deputy Minister unilaterally transferring him to the Policy Development Bureau to work on the government's proposed foreign policy review.

"That gave my tenure at External Affairs a whole new meaning," he recalls, "but I also knew that officers did not survive for any lengthy period in that Bureau because of the pressure to produce policies and speeches of high quality on short notice. At the same time, my work with the Public Service Christian Fellowship was beginning to lag, and I longed for someone else to give its 38 Bible Study and Prayer Groups fresh direction and impetus. It seemed that the time was right for me to pass the baton.

"Through my position with the PSCF and work with the Great Commission Prayer Crusade, I was in close association with many Christian MPs who, along with me, began wondering what we should be doing to replace ourselves as Christians in government service. We pondered over where Christian MPs would come from in the future.

"I was also concerned with a troubling trend that was emerging at External Affairs. Every year about 4,000 aspiring diplomats would write the entrance examinations. We would interview about 400 of the best and then hire six to twelve of them. In short, we had the very best university graduates, most of whom had more than one degree, and fluency in foreign languages.

"In a peripheral way, I was involved in their subsequent training to become foreign service officers and I very quickly became disillusioned by these intellectually brilliant recruits making personal decisions that got them into trouble, based on the situational ethics that they had learned in their university education."

Don reasoned that there had to be a better quality of graduates whose ethics were directed by a Christian moral compass. He and his Christian colleagues in Ottawa kept saying, "Someone needs to do something about these problems." He recognized the problem, but didn't see himself as part of the solution, beyond raising the issue with Christian leaders with whom he came into contact.

"I certainly was not contemplating leaving Ottawa, as I was now at the pinnacle of my career, having just drafted the Mulroney government's foreign policy statement and was busy explaining it to audiences all across Canada as well as to senior officials in other government departments through my adjunct appointment to the Canadian Centre for Management Development."

In the Autumn of 1988, Dr. Ken Davis indicated his desire to step down from being Academic Vice President, for health reasons. Don was still in the midst of charting possible foreign policy scenarios, depending upon the outcome of the November federal election and the simultaneous presidential election in the United States, when I called and asked if he would now consider coming to TWU as Academic Vice President.

"I was too busy to consider the possibility at that time," Don recalls, "so the next month Dr. Snider came to Ottawa to put the offer to me directly. His most penetrating question to me, and one that resonated with what I had been thinking was, 'What are you doing to replace yourself?' While I admired what was happening at TWU, I had many questions about the future direction of the University and especially its commitment to develop the kind of quality Christian leaders that we needed in Ottawa and elsewhere in Canada.

"I did agree, however, to visit the University to look at the possibilities, as long as it was understood that I would be doing so on my own account, so that there would be no obligation on my part to the University. Moreover, any move to Langley would have to be a family decision, and at this point the family was not united on making such a move. We needed to check it out and to discern God's will for such a dramatic move and change of direction.

"The date was set for January, but that didn't work out, as the Prime Minister was contemplating a cabinet shuffle and I was ordered to remain in Ottawa. Finally, by the end of February, the timing was right and the whole family went to Langley. The boys were keen on skiing at Whistler while Annabelle and I went through interviews and looking at housing possibilities.

"It became very clear that I would have my work cut out for me if I were to undertake the task of leadership development at the university. The faculty were cordial, but skeptical that anything good could come out of Ottawa; and some wondered aloud if I might be 'just another lackey of the President.' The administration and two Board members did their best to assure me that all would be well once I arrived.

"Leaving Ottawa wouldn't be easy. The boys were fully engaged in their schooling in Ontario, and had girlfriends there. Annabelle loved her ministry with Christian Women's Club and we had many close friends through our church. After much prayer, I decided to follow Gideon's example and to put out a fleece. I would consult 21 major Christian leaders across the country to see what they would advise.

"Ten very firmly said 'You must go because we see the need for Christian leadership development, and you have the requisite academic credentials and experience to make it happen.' The other 10 said 'Absolutely not!' They questioned why I would leave my position of influence in Ottawa, where my work could impact thousands around the world, as well as the Prime Minister, for work in a little known University in far-away Langley B.C.

"The Hon. Jake Epp was the only one who sat on the fence. He knew of my work in External Affairs and the PSCF, but he was also attached to TWU through his daughter attending the University, and himself having received its honorary doctorate. So much for the fleece. I was still on the fence, as was my family.

"I felt that I could go either way while Annabelle and one of the boys were opposed to such a move. Over time and after much soul-searching and prayer, we came together on this and decided that if the University still wanted me, we would make the move."

In the meantime, the University had to go through its internal processes to determine whether it would formally extend an offer of employment. By April, that had taken place and Don and Annabelle came back for a more serious look at Langley and the University. It was clear that the President and Board of Governors wanted someone who would work to fulfill the Mission Statement of the University to "develop godly Christian leaders".

"In the minds of most faculty," Don recalls, "the Mission Statement was a great theme for the President's chapel talks and for fund-raising, but it was little more than a fanciful idea as far as the academic work of the University was concerned.

"Upon my arrival, I was determined to make the development of godly Christian leaders the cornerstone of what I wanted to accomplish. How that would be accomplished wasn't immediately clear to me, but I knew that it would not be easy when, at my first meeting of the Academic Council, and every meeting thereafter, I decided to give a devotional on leadership. That was, after all, what I had been doing for years through the PSCF.

"I no sooner finished my inaugural devotion when a senior faculty member and department chair announced that 'we are "godly Christian leader-ed" to death on this campus', to which an equally senior leader pronounced a very audible 'amen'.

"I indicated that I understood what they were saying, but I was about to change that by making the Mission Statement a living reality in all of our educational pursuits. To which, there were some audible guffaws and smirking laughter. So much for a friendly welcome to their new Academic Vice President!

"One thing was clear to me, I had not come to TWU to manage the status quo; I was there to make a fundamental change in the academic culture, to what

I hoped would be a better future for the University and, most important, for its graduates."

This was to be a course that would set TWU on a different track, yet retaining the respect of our university peers. We would still focus on academic excellence and the integration of our faith with our disciplines, as other Christian universities did, but our added value for a TWU degree would be in leadership development that would enable our graduates to be recognized as a step above graduates from other universities, as they were equipped to take on leadership positions in their places of employment. There had to be a demonstrable benefit in coming to TWU that could not be found in other universities.

Notwithstanding God's extensive preparation of him in government, and his leadership of Christian fellowship within government, it would be this focus on producing godly Christian leaders that would be the hallmark of Don Page's service to TWU. We were confident that God was behind this addition to our leadership team.

In Memory—Six ornamental flowering cherry trees were planted outside Douglas Centre in memory of the six members of the TWU community who gave their lives on March 5, 1991 when their two Cessna 172s, returning from a class trip to California, crashed in a snowstorm near Bellingham, Washington.

PART VI

Learning through tragedy

34

Our aviation disaster

In the spring of 1991, as the campus was readying itself for final examinations and anticipating the celebration of our 11th graduation service as a University, our community was plunged into the greatest tragedy we had ever known. Beyond any doubt it was among the deepest tests of faith in our sovereign God we ever faced. Even today, so many years later, my memories of those days are clear and the sadness, although much healed with passing time, is unforgotten.

By the 1990s we were experiencing great success in building TWU into a mature university. It was tremendously exciting and encouraging. Remarkably, despite the rapid growth, our campus community remained close knit, joined together not only in classes but in sports, Bible studies, many social events and the day-to-day academic life of a busy university. Our program in Aviation that enabled students to earn a commercial pilot's license was among the closest group on campus. Aviation students were often seen going to classes wearing their uniforms as they shared the hard work of this intensive combination of university studies and flight training. The demanding training inspired unusually close camaraderie.

The tragedy began late in the afternoon of March 5, 1991 as five of our single engine Cessna 172s, which had been on a training flight to California, took off from Everett, Washington heading north on the final leg of their trip. Soon they would reach their home base. The last portion of their flight was a small hop across the mountains south of Bellingham, Washington. It was there, when they were less than 30 minutes from home, that everything began to go wrong.

On departure from Everett, the weather report had called for an 8,000-foot ceiling with fifteen miles of visibility—excellent flying weather. Suddenly, as they neared the mountains, without warning and all at once, they found themselves in the worst weather they had ever seen. An unpredicted snow storm had whipped up, hiding the mountains and reducing visibility to zero. Later it was said that the "snow hit so hard and fast it left the planes without a chance."

Senior flight instructor Bob Chapman, leading the journey from one of the planes, quickly contacted the other four with an urgent message to turn back. Chapman's plane and one other landed safely at Bayview Airport in Washington. A third plane received radar assistance from the Vancouver Area Control Centre and achieved a safe landing in Abbotsford, B.C. There was great and growing concern, however, because there had been no acknowledgement of the radio message to turn back from two of the planes, each carrying a pilot and two passengers, which were now overdue and unaccounted for.

Ivan Pettigrew, Director of the TWU Aviation Program, was quickly notified. A search and rescue operation was launched by authorities in Washington State and anxious hours passed. Efforts were made to contact any airports where the missing planes might have landed. By the early hours of the next morning, however, there was still no word, and hope was fading. Ivan notified Academic Vice President Dr. Don Page that the two missing planes were now feared lost.

Don rushed to campus and engaged a set of emergency protocols to manage what was clearly going to be a major crisis. The switchboard was opened in the early morning hours to manage a growing flow of communications. Effective liaison was established with the search and rescue operation. Dr. Guy Saffold came in to manage communications with the media, who were already arriving on campus in significant numbers. The simultaneous loss of two aircraft was a major story.

By far the most difficult task fell to those who had to notify the families of the missing aviators. Aviation student Terry Townsend, 34 years old, who had left the Lethbridge Police Department to respond to God's call into mission aviation, was married to Shelly, and was the father of two young children. Ivan Pettigrew and another Aviation Department administrator went to the Townsends' home to give Shelly the news personally. Even before they arrived, however, Shelly had turned on the radio and learned that two planes were missing. She called the University. Dr. Page had to tell her that her husband was on one of the downed planes and probably dead.

As day dawned on March 6 the search and rescue teams, some in helicopters and some travelling on horseback because of the dense mountain terrain, reached the crash sites. The tragic news that had been feared was confirmed. There were no survivors; all on both planes had perished as their planes shattered against the mountainsides.

The first plane had crashed into the side of Chuckanut Mountain at about 7:30 p.m. the previous evening. Student pilot Jeff Helzer, 24, a first-year student, was killed along with Teena Daly, 22, a fourth-year student, and Terry Townsend. About ten minutes after the first crash the second plane went down in thick forest just south of Bellingham. It carried Graeme Seath, son of TWU Board chairman Malcolm Seath and his wife Margery, and a 24-year old TWU aviation graduate, who had become one of our flight instructors. With Graeme was Danny Penner,

18 years old, from White Rock, B.C.; and 21-year-old Al Karim Merali, a first-year student from Outremont, Quebec.

By 11 a.m. that Wednesday morning, the time of our daily chapel service, the gymnasium was packed with students, staff and parents, as well as representatives from the federal, provincial and municipal governments, and mourners from across Canada. Dr. Page gave a brief account of what was known, acknowledging that we couldn't explain why this ghastly accident had happened; but affirming that, as Christians, we trust in the sovereignty of God, who knows all things. Scripture was read, and prayers were offered by Student Life Vice President Tom Bulick and others.

As these early events were unfolding, I had been in Edmonton attending a meeting of the Association of Universities and Colleges of Canada (AUCC). I, of course, returned to campus immediately; but before leaving was able to inform my fellow university presidents of the disaster. They were quick to communicate their condolences.

The next few days were emotionally draining as our campus family responded to these painful losses. There was hardly a person among us who had not known one or even several if not all of those who had died. In the midst of many phone calls and visits, I set to work with a heavy heart planning for a campus-wide memorial service on Friday.

An especially deep and moving time was a gathering with all the parents in one of the side rooms of the gymnasium, where we could talk and pray together before going in for the memorial service. At the service the president of the student council spoke, as did Board chairman Malcolm Seath, who thanked God for the wonderful son they had been given, and for his godly influence on students. The AUCC was represented by Dr. William Saywell, President of Simon Fraser University. Later, Dr. Saywell, who was visibly moved by the service, sent a most thoughtful letter of condolence.

Speaking to parents, faculty, staff and students, I meditated on our anticipation of being reunited in the life to come, and stressed the unusual family relationships that develop so quickly within a campus community, especially when its members share belief in Jesus Christ. More than a purely human organization, members of such a campus community are part of a dynamic organism: "People of the Way," as the first-century church was called. The service included well-known hymns that spoke of our faith and confidence in God. The memorial service was summed up with the words, "God is sovereign. We leave our beloved in our Father's hands, for they are now with Him Who has called them home."

The event was carried nationwide on the noon news. After the story aired on

Global television, the broadcast crew quickly switched to a commercial break—because they had all dissolved into tears. Numerous other media reports paid tribute to how the faith of the whole campus community strengthened them in their time of grief.

After any tragedy and its immediate shock and grief, the much longer process of healing must begin. For Malcolm and Margery Seath, parents of flight instructor Graeme Seath, healing and sustaining faith came through a grief support group called HOPE. "It was a wonderful support in those first months to have people who were going through the same thing," Malcolm Seath recalls. Through all the years since, he has been part of that organization, speaking about his journey, and helping others along theirs. "My story is one of how God worked—not so much to give me the answers, as to take away the questions; but how He has restored my faith; and better still, how He has refined my faith," he says.

The TWU Student Council took the initiative to plant six flowering cherry trees between the Larson Lounge and Douglas Hall, to honour the six who had given their lives. Beneath those trees is a monument and plaque. It reads, *"Oh I have slipped the surly bonds of earth... put out my hand and touched the face of God,"* from John Magee's well-known poem about aviators. And as long as their bereaved classmates were still attending the University, the anniversary of this tragedy was marked every year by a special chapel service.

Twenty-five years after those terrible days, the cherry trees have grown thick and spread their branches wide, arching gracefully over what are now some of the most central walkways on campus, each year faithfully setting forth their magnificent blooms for all to see. In 2016, for the 25 anniversary of the tragedy, Colleen Little wrote a memorial piece for the University's magazine. "For 25 years," she wrote, "those trees have stood—always to weather the winter, blossom for the spring, and remind us of the lives past and the memories that endure."

For me, the tragedy of those days has always stood as a reminder of the need for genuine biblical faith in all circumstances. There were so many occasions when we rejoiced and celebrated as we saw God support the growth of Trinity Western with His generous and often unexpected provision. On this occasion, in a moment of deep grief, our community was challenged to trust our God, even though we could not understand the reasons for what had happened.

We had to learn to mourn as well as rejoice *to the praise of His glory.* He is faithful, and His love endures forever.

ACTS Graduation, May 2003

PART VII

Growth through graduate programs

The undergraduate program of a university teaches students how to think, and how to explore and evaluate ideas; but it is the graduate program, where the sum of human knowledge is constantly being enhanced by research and study, that makes the institution a real university. In graduate programs, students become their professors' colleagues in such research.

—*Neil Snider*

35

Graduate pastoral and theological programs

In 1980, as I was just starting my third three-year term as President of Trinity Western University (as it formally became in 1985), we began receiving requests from pastors for continuing education courses to help them enrich their ministry.

We had just graduated our first four-year class; enrolment was growing rapidly; and we knew that moving into a four-year program meant we needed to seek accreditation for our degrees, if they were to truly benefit our graduates. But accreditation and degrees meant leaving behind our junior college history, and elevating our curricula to the level of a true university of the liberal arts and sciences—very different from a Bible college, which had been the educational foundation for many Canadian pastors. We didn't want to add to the impression in the Canadian higher education "establishment" that Trinity was "just another Bible college"; and it was widely feared that answering the request of pastors for ministry-enriching courses might do just that.

But neither could we ignore such requests, as a Christian institution devoted to preparing Christian leaders for service to the community.

The answer was to develop a plan that would elevate ministry training to university level, the same as we planned to do eventually for Christian teachers, nurses, doctors, lawyers and business professionals.

It was into this milieu that God had sent exactly the right man for both objectives: a scholar intimately familiar with the curricular demands of higher education, and also himself a pastor: Dr. Ken Davis.

In those turbulent years in the early '80s, Ken Davis not only served as our Vice-President and Academic Dean—a heavy workload by itself—but he also played a key role in preparing Trinity Western for membership in the Association of Universities and Colleges of Canada (AUCC). And at the same time, he took on the challenge of laying the groundwork for Trinity Western's Institute of Graduate Studies, and later of ACTS—the Associated Canadian Theological Schools and Seminaries.

Our founding and funding denomination, the Evangelical Free Church of America, and its smaller branch, the EFC of Canada, had their seminary in Deerfield, Illinois: Trinity Evangelical Divinity School (TEDS). If we were going to offer EFC pastors and others university-level courses as ministry enrichment, it would make sense to do so in cooperation with TEDS. But how?

Through long months of increasingly complex negotiations, Ken applied his expertise to careful planning, answering repeated requests from TEDS for details of course planning, budget estimates, faculty outlines and more. Often, months went by between requests from Deerfield for more data. Patiently, he reviewed and revised—and waited. In 1983 and 1984, he crafted a plan to create a Canadian TEDS—"TEDS(Can)", it was tentatively called—making use of both Canadian and American faculty and course outlines. But over and over again, when it seemed that agreement was almost within our grasp, new challenges were raised.

Eventually, Ken Davis turned all his planning into a design for an Institute of Graduate Studies at Trinity Western University. The plans so carefully prepared to provide graduate-level theological and ministry studies for Canadian pastors wouldn't go to waste. And as TWU matured as a University, there was less and less reason to look elsewhere for validation.

By 1985, Trinity Western had successfully made the transition to a four-year program, had been granted the authority to issue its own baccalaureate degrees, and had been accepted as a full member of AUCC. Now Ken Davis could turn his skills and experience to helping the University add graduate programs and degrees to its offerings.

By January of 1986, we recognized that if TWU were to fulfill its mission and strengthen its graduates for witness in Canada, it would require a much larger support base. We called a conference of leaders from several mission-compatible evangelical Canadian denominations to consider a further step into evangelical higher education in Canada. The meeting was attended by our founding denomination, the Evangelical Free Church of Canada, and also the Fellowship of Evangelical Baptists, the Associated Gospel Churches, the Baptist General Conference, the B.C. Baptist Fellowship and the President of Northwest Baptist Theological College and Seminary (NBTC/S).

The primary purpose was to encourage other Believers' churches to recognize TWU as *their* university. With broader support among compatible evangelical churches, much more would be possible than any single denomination could achieve: and thus a much greater impact on Canadian culture would be within our reach.

As the first such meeting came to a close, President Harris of Northwest Baptist Theological College and Seminary noted that all six groups present were struggling with the need for training to upgrade pastoral ministries. Would TWU be willing and able to help also in advancing cooperation and understanding in this area of Canadian-oriented, relevant ministry training? After a brief discussion on this and related issues, it was agreed by all to ask Dr. Davis to prepare yet another paper on this subject, for the next leaders' meeting, encompassing this added concern.

The second denominational leaders' meeting reported back unanimous support for TWU and its mission. It then went on to focus on needs in the area of seminary-level pastoral training. Two groups (the EFCC and BGCC) had seminaries available, but they were located in America; and both found them of limited help in increasing the effectiveness of their ministries in a Western Canadian context. It was too expensive to go to the U.S. seminaries; and too few graduates ever returned to Canada. The AGCC had no ministry school in Canada. The BC/Alberta district of the Fellowship of Evangelical Baptists of Canada had a wonderful Bible college; but its seminary, although of fine quality, was small and struggling financially. From this base, the meeting focused its attention on a paper submitted by Dr. Davis, entitled *Pastoral Preparation for the '90s*.

That paper set out Dr. Davis' vision for a consortium of Believers' Church seminaries, able to mount a full set of seminary programs. The idea was "do-able"; only 35-40 percent of the total cost would have to be borne by each seminary; it could provide graduate-level pastoral training; each member of the Consortium would be responsible for its own autonomous seminary, and its share of combined faculty; each participating denomination would have a significant portion of its instructional curriculum taught by "TEDS(Can)". The Consortium would not itself be a seminary, but would provide the teaching unit for all the seminaries; each seminary would be affiliated with TWU for supervision of the academic quality of all Consortium courses and programs; and all degrees would be granted jointly by both the University and each particular seminary.

Dr. Davis ended the paper with this challenge:

> "… in the face of militant, up-surging Secularism and Paganism in a country largely unevangelized, such as Canada is, and where Believers' Church evangelicals are largely in small groups of… scattered assemblies, it is almost sinful—and certainly lacking in obedience and vision—not to be able to set aside a few differences for the sake of a

limited co-operation that could enable the provision of an accredited, 21st century-relevant, biblically faithful training program for leadership and pastoring; one able to enhance greatly the effectiveness of our primary mission *i.e.*, the effective witnessing to and evangelization of Canada, by pastors who are unapologetically committed to the New Testament objective of planting Kingdom-witnessing Believers' Churches. We could do it together—if the vision is from Him, and we are open to it."

Thus the seeds of the ACTS consortium of seminaries at TWU was planted—to open in 1988 and to become, in only a few years, the third-largest seminary in Canada!

The Agreement—Signing the affiliation agreement between TWU and ACTS. Back row (L to R) Bruce Traub, Ken Davis, and David Fairbrother. Front row, Neil Snider, Gerry Kraft, and Doug Harris, 1987.

36

ACTS: a bond of love, a passion for ministry

By Dr. Guy Saffold

In the fall of 1988, two dozen students and a small group of professors gathered for the first time in an aging portable building sitting on temporary blocks next to the Trinity Western University gymnasium.

The plumbing in the old building had mysterious quirks, frequently announcing its presence with a shockingly loud banging. The building's two classrooms, stuffy and poorly ventilated, were too hot in the summer; but that problem balanced out because in the winter they were far too cold. As a result, the average annual temperature was perfect!

It was impossible to grow lonely in the building, because small noises from inside the walls were ample evidence of the small residents who loved to chew on any bits of paper that were left out. One of the early professors, working diligently to complete his PhD studies, was heard to worry that the mice might gain a taste for the paper his dissertation was written on. A colleague assured him that his topic was too complex to be digestible, even for a mouse.

It was the first semester of operation for a brand new educational ministry called ACTS: The Associated Canadian Theological Schools at Trinity Western University. If the building was not all it could be, the atmosphere was permeated with excitement. A tremendously creative partnership among TWU, Northwest Baptist Theological College, and Canadian Baptist Seminary, this little start-up venture in theological education had quickly drawn national attention.

The vision was brief but clear. That small first group, working with a deep bond of Christian love, believed that if they worked together, shared resources together, and put the Kingdom of God first, together they could develop a seminary that would make a powerful contribution to building the church of Jesus Christ, in Canada and throughout the world.

Fosmark Centre—Honours two brothers, Carl and Lee Fosmark and their families. Carl was a charter member of the Enchant (AB) Church, the first Evangelical Free Church in Canada. He became pastor, and still later with his wife, Bertha, gave leadership to the Free Church in Canada, becoming its first Superintendent. Lee and his wife, Hattie, having a passion for souls, an optimistic spirit, and an ability to evangelize, gave their lives to the local church and to church planting.

That initial sense of vision and passion led to successes that attracted students from across the country. The original two dozen students became four dozen the next year. Very soon it was no longer useful to count by dozens, because by the third year of operation enrollment had surpassed 100 students.

With growing enrollment, the facilities had to be expanded. In the fall of 1990, the magnificent new Northwest Baptist Theological College building was completed, adding much-needed classroom and office space. In September 1993, when the 20,000 square foot Fosmark Centre opened, the ACTS group left the old portable buildings for the home it still occupies today.

The old portable building, however, carried on serving by becoming the first home for the newly-developed Canadian Institute for Linguistics, an extension of Wycliffe Bible Translators, which had partnered with ACTS to offer a breakthrough Master of Arts degree in Linguistics and Exegesis. The CanIL team rolled up their sleeves, thoroughly remodeled and upgraded the old portable, set it on new foundations, and launched into their ministry of training Bible translators and literacy workers for the global church. In not too many years, CanIL enrolled its own contingent of 150 students, who were taking linguistics courses from CanIL and courses in biblical languages and exegesis from ACTS. The success of that program eventually led to construction of another major facility, The Harvest Centre, located next door to the Fosmark Centre. The partnership between the ACTS Seminaries and CanIL has deepened and flourished over the years. Their full story is told in Chapter 56.

The ACTS Seminaries began by offering a basic set of theological degrees: a Master of Divinity, a Master of Religious Education and a Master of Ministry. Before long, we launched a fine program in counseling from a ministry perspective. The roster of programs grew, along with the enrollment. A Master of Theological Studies degree program cultivated skills in biblical and theological research. A Master of Arts in Cross-Cultural Ministries coordinated with the Master of Applied Linguistics and Exegesis in training Bible translators and others to take God's Word to the ends of the earth. A Master of Theology program provided advanced training, equivalent to the first year of doctoral studies.

Neither was that the end. Enrolment grew further, and eventually ACTS was able to launch its own Doctor of Ministry degree, and a Master of Christian Studies program with special emphasis on leadership for ministry.

Later, the Canadian Pentecostal Seminary was formed—the first seminary ever in the Pentecostal Assemblies of Canada (PAOC). Although it remains an independent seminary, it has now begun to draw on the resources of ACTS to serve its students.

A survey taken for the tenth anniversary of ACTS revealed that of the first 64 ACTS graduates, seventeen had gone into church planting, and nearly all the others were serving effectively in some form of pastoral, church or missionary service.

It was also discovered that ACTS graduates had begun to distribute themselves around the globe, serving in England, France, Germany, Finland, western and eastern Europe, many countries in Africa, India, Sri Lanka, Vietnam, Hong Kong, Taiwan, Japan, and Korea.

In the spring of 1997, a visiting team from the Association of Theological Schools (ATS) spent three days carefully reviewing every facet of the ACTS operation. Their report was positive, and the ACTS consortium gained full accreditation with ATS. In 2002, that initial five-year accreditation was renewed for another ten years without a single notation of deficiency.

Over the years, ACTS has continued to develop and change. Today this unique and effective partnership includes Canadian Baptist Seminary, Mennonite Brethren Biblical Seminary, Northwest Baptist Seminary, and Trinity Western Seminary. ACTS programs have deepened and been renewed. The original faculty have aged, and younger professors have joined. ACTS graduates have continued to post a remarkable record for service. The original vision has never faded. Today that vision is most clearly and simply expressed in the ACTS mission statement:

> *To develop godly servant-leaders who have a love and burden for people, based on a strong commitment to Jesus Christ, the Word of God, and the ministry of His church, who will energetically strengthen, revitalize and aggressively multiply communities of effectively ministering believers in Canada and around the world.*

Large achievements grow from small beginnings if they are infused with vision, and pressed forward with energy and faith. ACTS began in an entirely unremarkable old building, but the vision was clear. It has since become one of the finest ministry training centres in Canada, combining an emphasis on practical skills, leadership, and Kingdom growth. The growth and development of ACTS occurred more rapidly and with more strength and scope than we could ever have anticipated. It was yet another evidence of what can happen by working "to the praise of His glory."

And that old portable building? The continuing needs and programs of TWU won't let it go. You can still find it on the original site, essentially totally replaced but still in operation, providing a home for the Exam Centre & athletic offices.

37

Preparing Student Life for the 21st century

Dr. Tom Bulick was a significant figure in the implementation of TWU's philosophy of "Total Student Development"; and he brought several creative people into the Student Life program. In the spring of 1986, when he was nearing the end of his PhD program at Dallas Theological Seminary, he contacted a pastor and friend in Southern California, Mike Fisher, to inquire about ministry opportunities in his area. Years earlier, Mike and Tom had ministered together at Grace Bible Church in Dallas when they were both in the ThM program.

"When I re-contacted him," Tom recalls, "I didn't know of his involvement with Trinity Western University.

"He told me the University was searching for a Vice President for Student Affairs. Arvid Olson had resigned that position to help establish a college in the Philippines, and Trinity was seeking a suitable successor. So I phoned Dr. Snider, introduced myself, and explained why I was calling. That serendipitous call set in motion a chain of events that resulted in a rather unlikely outcome."

Tom first visited TWU over the American Memorial Day weekend in May, accepted the position when it was offered to him in June, and moved to Langley at the beginning of August. His wife, Ruth, and one-year-old son, Zach, joined him in October.

"I say the outcome was 'unlikely'," he explains, "because my education and

Tom Bulick

experience were in biblical studies and church ministry, rather than student personnel and personal work. It was Trinity's disciple-making mission that made for a good fit—and subsequently, for a dozen years of fruitful ministry."

Those key values, Tom elaborated, included:

> "**First, we *valued mission***. We valued the express goal of the University, captured in the Mission Statement: 'to develop godly Christian leaders.' What's more, we valued the contribution Student Life made to accomplishing that mission. In our view, Student Life was not ancillary, but integral to mission accomplishment.
>
> "**Second, we *valued disciple-making***. We recognized the crucial connection between discipleship and formation; consequently, we defined mission accomplishment in terms of student development outcomes. God's purpose for believers is succinctly summed up in Romans 8:29, "*For those God foreknew he also predestined* **to be conformed to the image of his Son**, *that he might be the firstborn among many brothers and sisters*" (NIV). Our transformation into the likeness of Christ is His purpose for us.
>
> "The process we go through to become like Christ can be viewed in terms of training, development, or holiness. When viewed in terms of training, we call it discipleship; in terms of development, formation; and in terms of holiness, sanctification.
>
> "We viewed 'to develop godly Christian leaders' as disciple-making—but rather than define our objectives in terms of spiritual disciplines, we defined them in terms of student development outcomes like competence, interdependence, mature relationships, identity, purpose, and integrity that includes spirituality.
>
> "**Third, we *valued community***. We recognized the power of relationships to transform lives, and concluded that development takes place best in community.
>
> "I remember a leadership team meeting in Chilliwack: in answer to the question, 'Who are you and why are you here?' we all began by talking about the person or event in life—or perhaps a book or course—that was the answer. After everyone had shared, it dawned on all of us that everyone had mentioned another person—in some cases, a person unaware of their influence.

"**Fourth, we *valued leadership***. We recognized that of all the strategies for disciple-making and student development, involvement in student leadership was the most effective."

Two hires proved strategic to the trajectory of Student Life at that time—one near the beginning, the other near the end. In our search for a new Campus Pastor, we interviewed Malcolm Cameron—and were immediately convinced his persona and gifting were a perfect fit for the position.

But Malcolm was unmarried, and because the Campus Pastor was expected to pastor faculty and staff as well as students, and also to serve as liaison to local churches, some thought Malcolm lacked the gravitas for the job. We heartily disagreed.

Indeed, we'd been searching for someone *just like* Malcolm: someone who would laser-focus his attention on the student body; so we hired him as Director of Campus Ministries. In the years that followed, Malcolm moved chapel services to the gymnasium—a risky decision, but it soon proved to be a wise one. Second, he transformed campus chapel into *Student* Chapel. As a result, student attendance and student leadership in chapel more than doubled. In my opinion, the impact of Malcolm's leadership and the importance of his legacy simply cannot be overstated.

A key movement during this time was an all-out effort to increase the number of students in leadership positions, in part by increasing the number of positions. It began at an early leadership retreat on Thetis Island. Students had completed their group presentations. As Allan Kotanen, Dave Stinson, John Wassen, Malcolm and Tom were discussing the success of the retreat, and specifically talking about the value of student leadership to mission accomplishment, Tom remembers it was as if they all said with one voice: *since involvement in leadership is the most effective strategy we employ, why don't we increase the number of student leadership opportunities? Why don't we double the number of student leaders on campus?*

It didn't take long to brainstorm a five-part strategy to make it so. The Student Life team agreed:

1. to expand the number of student leaders in existing positions;
2. to create as many new positions as we could justify based on need, *e.g.*, commuter assistants, academic advising assistants; recreation services assistants, discipleship group leaders;

3. to create position descriptions for each new position, and assign Student Life staff members to supervise and mentor the student leaders in each one;

4. to expand student leader training to include leaders in new positions; and

5. to debrief the experience with them at the end of the year.

There were approximately 100 student leaders at that Thetis Island retreat; we more than doubled that number during the 1990s.

Another key movement during the '90s involved convincing third- and fourth-year students to remain part of the campus community by offering them appropriate housing. Freshmen and sophomores lived in dorms. Seniors lived in apartments. However, there weren't enough apartments to meet the demand for senior housing, and there was no junior housing at all. So the Student Life team proposed expanding "senior housing" and creating an entirely new "junior housing", enabling juniors to live in dorm-style units, but prepare their own meals. Third-year students, who really wanted to live on campus but otherwise might have moved off, now had the option of preparing at least some of their own meals. It was an immediate success.

The new Mission Statement made it imperative for TWU to develop a holistic understanding of curriculum, including both formal studies and the many campus experiences outside of class called "Student Life". We developed one of the strongest Student Life programs at any Christian institution in North America, and constantly laboured to integrate Student Life with academic studies for fulfillment of our mission.

This led, around 2000, to establishment of a unique set of four "collegia" for commuter and graduate students, to provide these groups of students with an anchor to campus activities, events, and social life, similar to that which residential students enjoyed more naturally. The Collegium was pioneered on our campus by Sheldon Loeppky, Student Life Coordinator, who would later help to organize student living at TWU's Laurentian Leadership Centre in Ottawa. 'Collegium' is from a Latin root meaning 'a gathering place'. In Marlie Snider's honour, and remembering how my wife's gracious hospitality had always helped to bring the campus community together, the students christened the first freestanding collegium 'The Marlie'. The name has stuck.

Another strategic hire was Dr. Ken Kush. Years earlier, Ken had been the Director of Community Life at Trinity Western. After leaving, he completed his doctoral program at the University of British Columbia, and then served as Director of the Student Counseling and Resources Centre at UBC.

Ken Kush had training and experience in student personnel, and he had skills and experience conducting research. He had excellent professional connections in the broader academic community. Before leaving, Tom Bulick hired Ken as Director of the Career Centre. This would set the course of Student Life for nearly a decade. Little did Tom know, at the time, that he was hiring his successor! Ken gave leadership to the Centre and brought a much-needed expertise to Student Life. Like Malcolm Cameron, Ken Kush was the right person, with the right skills, whom God had prepared and provided at an opportune time. His remarkable story of God's grace in preparation, is our next chapter.

38

Realizing 'Total Student Development'

Student Life helps TWU earn A+ in academics—seven years in a row!

Ken Kush was first recruited by Arvid Olson in 1978, when Arvid was Dean of Students, to become TWC's Resident Director of Student Life (a position that soon expanded to Director of Community Life); and together they worked to implement the concept of Total Student Development.

Ken had graduated from Ontario Bible College in 1976, planning to teach—but teach what? His first thought was History, so he went to the University of Waterloo to seek the counsel of History Professor Dr. Ken Davis. Dr. Davis was then helping Canadian Bible college graduates transfer their credits to university.

"I discovered I could either do another two years at the University of Waterloo, and get my BA," recalls Ken Kush. "Or I could invest the same two years at Wheaton College to earn an MA with a major in Organizational Development—*real leadership stuff*—*and* get a second major in Counseling Psychology. That was a no-brainer. I went to Wheaton."

When he graduated from Wheaton in 1978, Ken had three opportunities: to teach at a college in Buffalo; to teach at a Pentecostal Bible college in southern Ontario; or Arvid Olson's offer to help develop the Student Life program at TWC. Although it paid the least (only $600 a month), he chose Trinity Western, "where I could teach, practice counseling psychology, and practice Organizational Development; there was so much more range of opportunity! So I packed my Pinto station wagon with everything I owned and drove across Canada to a place where I'd never been before.

"My focus was on being intentional about ministering to students… creating a taxonomy of developmental tasks… doing an assessment of each student in each dorm, in relationship to the developmental tasks in the community there—asking 'what can we do to help these kids grow?' This blended right into discipleship—developing the whole person.

"Arvid put my office strategically across the hall at Seal-Kap House from TW's Acting Academic Dean, Dr. Deane Downey. Because of his relationship with Arvid and with Allan Kotanen, he was sympathetic when I told him students were saying, 'We're spending so much time studying this (psychological aspects of human relationships); can't we get credit for it?' We were able to get them third-year credits for Religious Studies 370 and Psych 361—'Applied Helping Skills'. Imagine: Student Life getting academic credit!"

Ken stayed at TW until 1984, when he enrolled at UBC to complete his PhD in Counseling Psychology, and later joined their Student Services staff. He says, "I went to UBC like Moses went to Egypt: not in a reed basket, of course; but to acquire the learning of the mainstream."

In all, he was there ten years. "I built connections, and learned so much… and when I went to conferences with other counseling directors, because I represented UBC, doors opened! I went to the Canadian Student Services Centre, and the Director of Student Services at the University of Manitoba took me under his wing… although still young, I was being acknowledged as an equal."

While Ken was at UBC, the Director of Student Counseling retired, and Professor Marv Westwood was appointed Interim Director while a committee searched for a replacement. Prof. Westwood hired two graduate students—Ken was one—to propose a model for Student Development at UBC. Their plan incorporated ideas Ken had experienced at TWC. At UBC's Counseling Centre, he also worked with a psychiatrist from UBC's Health Centre, and the chairman of the search committee suggested Ken should apply to become Director of the Counseling Centre; he did—and won the position, in spite of his age (32), with a mandate to implement the model he'd helped write.

When Ken returned to Trinity Western (now TWU) in 1997, Student Life staff had exploded; they had 300 student leaders in residence.

"But," he remembers, "all the units of Student Life were then operating in 'silos'—each function operating independently, instead of coordinating—we needed to integrate across all the various functions that related to student life.

"One question that confronted me was 'How can we do all this, and still do our jobs?' My answer was, 'If you're not "doing all this", you're not doing the *real* job. The real job is working with academics to develop the whole person in every student.'

"We did an assessment, and came up with a plan that, instead of focusing on the services or programs, concentrated on the *outcomes*: what's our contribution to the Mission Statement? What's the *educational* function of Student Life?"

Looking around the Student Life boardroom today, you can read the answers on the annual theme banners that still festoon the walls:

- Serve One Another
- Called to a Higher Purpose
- A People of Integrity
- Authentic Learners, Passionate for Truth
- Engage Your World—***Lead**!*
- A Mind to Lead, a Heart to Lead
- Growing Disciples with a Living Hope
- Act in Faith, Run with a Purpose
- Renewing our Minds, Becoming like Christ
- Living Well; Pursuing Wholeness
- Thriving in Wholeness, Seeking Peace

Ken became UBC's delegate to the Canadian University Survey Consortium (CUSC). In 1992, while talking with the Director of Housing from the University of Manitoba, Garth Wyman, at a conference, they discussed popular magazine "ratings" of universities. "There's coming a time when we'll have to measure student experience, so they can compare," Ken said. "We'll need data; surveys of students' experiences; retention; first-year experience; senior year experience…"

Garth asked, "Why not establish our own ratings?" But they knew universities wouldn't be eager to participate, because they don't like to be compared competitively.

Later that year, about a dozen Canadians from that conference met again at Calgary, and developed a survey to evaluate student experience information that the universities could share internally, as a research tool to improve their performance. Out of that meeting grew the Canadian University Survey Consortium (CUSC), which is limited to universities that are members of the Association of Universities and Colleges of Canada (AUCC).

At that time, AUCC wasn't happy with consumer magazines that provide "university" editions, ranking universities—first, second, third, *etc.*—in various categories, such as academics, science, research, and student life.

When Ken returned to TWU, he continued to be a part of those consultations; and remained a member of CUSC. He suggested to Trinity's leadership that TWU should participate in those surveys, which were being done in a three-year cycle:

one year looked at students' freshman-year experience; another at their senior-year experience; and yet another at students' overall impression of their full four-year experience.

The CUSC criteria were taken from UCLA's Dr. Chip Anderson's 'Five Cs':

- Course selection: which courses, when?
- Connection: becoming part of the academic and social life on campus;
- Confusion: "What's expected? What's 'normal'? What's happening to me?"
- Confidence: overcoming self-doubt; regaining optimism; and
- Career selection: Which career path will fit and fulfill me? What factors need to be considered? (5- & 7-year plans)

When the *Globe and Mail* (one of Canada's national newspapers) decided to do an annual 'rating the universities' issue, they employed CUSC's data… and Trinity Western University rated A+ in academics—and attained that level seven years in a row!

Ken Kush and the TWU Student Life team made many other contributions as the University grew. When the student population became more than 50 percent commuters, it was recognized that things had to be adapted to help commuters feel part of campus life. The 'collegium' (a concept Dr. Guy Saffold brought back from Seattle University) serves that purpose. TWU has also had a growing number of international students—and a new collegium, called 'The Globe', a place for international, Canadian and American students to meet and mix informally, serves that need.

"Student Life is set up on a 'community' model," says Ken Kush: "It comprises meals together, conversation and games, and exchanges of ideas. And we were always aware that longitudinal studies of outcomes tell us that one of the most important things students are looking for is ***spirituality***. So we ask, 'What's the University's contribution to students' spiritual development? What is the added value of a university education at TWU?'

"Our larger purpose, from our earliest days, has been to help all students become disciples—and disciple-makers."

39

Athletics and leadership

On another front that quickly caught people's attention, Trinity Western's Athletics Division moved from B.C.'s college league to Canada's national university league, where we had to compete with universities 10 to 20 times our size, and much better endowed with expensive athletic facilities. In explaining this move to a skeptical faculty, many of whom thought we would almost certainly be losers, Don Page pointed out that, just as in academic endeavours, "You don't have to be big to be good." But we also knew it would take a lot of hard work for our athletes, just as it did for our faculty. However, Don promised that he and his academic guiding coalition would do everything possible to support the athletes.

In the first six years in this level of competition in the Canadian Inter-university Sports (CIS) league, all but one of our varsity teams ranked at one time or another in the top ten in the country, and made the Western Canadian playoffs. Our women's soccer team and men's volleyball team won national championships; and our men's soccer team won a silver medal. Each team had set the nationals as their eventual goal—and some achieved it long before they expected to! As in other aspects of the University's growth, a vision was realized through a well-executed strategic plan. Equally important, every coach and every team was committed to the leadership development of their players, as part of our university's value-added mission.

But without a benchmark in either time or level (or both), how would we know whether the desired change had been accomplished?

Spartan Athletics History

TWU wanted to enter the CIS for two principal reasons: we wanted our teams

- to enhance the image of TWU across Canada, using sports as a platform; and
- to compete on the same level on which TWU wanted to compete academically: TWU was now a university, so we wanted to align with and compete against other universities, not just colleges.

Murray Hall, Director of Spartan Athletics, was the prime architect of the move to CIAU (Canadian Interuniversity Athletics Union, now CIS—Canadian Intercollegiate Sports); others were Steve Scholz, Associate Director of Athletics; Ron Kuehl, Don Page, and Harvey Ouelette from the TWU Executive; Cam Lee and Jeff Suderman from Admissions; Kim Gordon; and TWU Board members Wayne Nygren and Allan Skidmore, who were all very supportive of the move.

Spartan coaches at that time were Kerby Court (women's basketball); Stan Peters (men's basketball); Carol Hofrer (women's volleyball); and Ron Pike (men's volleyball).

Many new opportunities resulted from TWU's move to CIAU/CIS:

- Spartan Athletics changed from recruiting mostly from students already attending TWU, to recruiting off-campus and across the country.
- TWU coaches now had a voice at the national level.
- Spartan teams became successful relatively early: winning CIS medals as such a small school really turned heads across the country, in other universities and in the media.
- TWU administrators and Admissions counselors sensed greater awareness of TWU as a result of our teams traveling and competing across the country. *Maclean's* magazine wrote that "TWU punches above its weight", drawing still more favourable national attention to the University; TWU Admissions benefitted from the fact that we could now recruit CIS-level student-athletes, many of whom wouldn't have considered TWU when we played only in the B.C. College Athletic Association.
- TWU also benefitted in terms of student retention, as student-athletes now had five years of eligibility.

Having competitive teams in the CIS allowed us to partner with the Township of Langley in building the Langley

Ron Kuehl

Events Centre, thus bringing CIS Championships to town, with economic and tourism benefits for both the Township and the City of Langley, as well as more local and national exposure for TWU.

Our teams now have more chances to travel, and thus to have an impact throughout the world. Connections nationally have led to international opportunities, including in missions; and playing at a higher level has gained TWU more respect. The change also created sponsorship opportunities with national corporate partners that wanted to be associated with the highest level of competition in the country. "Brand exposure" for Spartan Athletics and TWU increased greatly: our teams travel across the country weekly; and when our teams defeated bigger university teams, they gained more exposure for TWU in the media, both locally and nationally, and with both sports organizations and the Canadian public.

Murray Hall

As our teams improved, more organizations wanted to partner with us; and as we grew the Spartan Athletics Golf Tournament, the more competitive we became, and thus the better impression we made on highly influential sponsors from top corporations across the country—to the point that they wanted to recruit our athletes to work for them, and their executives and employees considered TWU for their children. Ultimately, as these contacts led to our partnership with WirelessWave, with their many corporate connections, ours became one of the most unique and successful golf tournaments in Canada—and successful corporations always want to be associated with other successful organizations. So our continued success in the CIS helped us to grow the golf tournament. And through the growth of the golf tournament, we also helped to establish relationships between some of our corporate golf sponsors and the University, opening the door to partnerships to which we previously didn't have access.

Creation of the 'Complete Champion Approach'

Another opportunity that came about largely through our move to the CIS was development of the "Compete Champion Approach" (CCA). We realized that we needed to differentiate ourselves from other universities if we were to compete against them in recruiting, athletics, and other critical areas. This forced us to evaluate what was already unique about Spartan Athletics, and that gave us a tool to plan how we'd achieve our goals. This became a great recruiting tool for our coaches, and helped give us a foundation on which to build our new CIS program. It helped us focus on key areas of development so that we could be very strategic in how we supported and developed our athletes, and in how we used our resources and time; it also gave us a very clear direction and focus, which made us stronger at a time when we might have been overwhelmed by the move to a higher level of competition.

Our athletes and coaches at that time should be recognized for their willingness to venture out and "stick it out"—being willing to train harder, take more knocks and play against better opponents until we were good enough to compete and win (for example, women's volleyball had two years of losses before they won their first CIAU match… now *that's* perseverance!) These people were pioneers, who weren't sure what they'd face; but they stood up to face it head-on, regardless—and did whatever it took to prove that we deserved to be in the CIS.

Trinity Western University Spartans: strong, united, determined & faithful

Spartan Athletics at TWU seeks to be one of the University's centres of excellence. Fully supporting the University's Mission Statement, Spartan Athletics has set its goal to develop godly Christian leaders equipped to succeed in dynamic environments, persistently pressing to the very edge of their abilities, shaping and transforming sport and culture, while growing in their personal relationships with Jesus Christ. Four vision statements articulate our goals, characterized by four impact words and supported by a strong financial model:

1. **Transformation** • *Spartan Athletics will transform lives.*
   There will be a pervasive climate of whole-person development as we intentionally work with our student athletes to become great competitors, committed scholars, mature Christian leaders and full participants in their communities upon graduation.

2. **Servant-Leadership** • *Spartan Athletics will have outstanding leadership & leadership development.*

We will be a highly effective team of servant-leaders that reflect our mission and values, committed to learning, modelling and teaching effective teamwork and servant-leadership.

3. **Collaboration** • *Spartan Athletics will be a valued partner.*

    We will work collaboratively and proactively as a strategic partner with all campus departments to support the goals and initiatives of others.

4. **Recognition** • *Spartan Athletics will be widely recognized.*

    Spartan teams and staff will be widely recognized locally and nationally for our outstanding model of higher education athletics and for positive contributions to local and broader communities.

5. **Resources** • *Finance and Facilities.*

    Spartan Athletics will be supported and sustained by appropriate facilities and a solid financial model.

The Complete Champion Approach is to help student-athletes use their God-given talents and intellect to live a life of significance, experience true personal success and powerfully influence their families, teams, communities and cultures.

40

Launching the Nursing Program

Nowhere is the application of Christian compassion as visibly evident, or as needed, as in the profession of nursing. When the Registered Nurses' Association of B.C. asked TWU to create a nursing program, how could we not be excited to have God respond to their need through us?

In the mid-1980s, the Government of British Columbia recognized a serious shortage of nurses in the province, at the very time when a significant shift in nursing education was developing. Hitherto, the focus of most programs had been on the care and management of illness. But at this time, there was growing interest in care and management of the healthy, requiring a high level of interpersonal patient care that could be achieved through a liberal arts and science educational base.

The Registered Nurses Association of British Columbia (RNABC), responsible for regulating the practice of nursing in the province, had decided that by the year 2000, the minimum requirement for registration as a nurse should be a baccalaureate degree in nursing. At that time, the only baccalaureate program leading to nurse registration in the province was at the University of British Columbia.

In March, 1987 the Executive Director of the RNABC sent a letter asking if Trinity Western University would consider developing a four-year baccalaureate program in nursing. This would be a huge undertaking for the University, as there was no resident expertise in the area; and unlike many programs that arose out of faculty interest and expertise, it would require fitting nursing education into our Christian liberal arts and science framework, but with accountability to external regulatory bodies.

How do you begin a nursing program? And how would we, as a private Christian university, connect with local provincially-funded health providers? These and other questions were on our minds. For guidance, Dr. Ken Davis asked Dr. David Sterling to begin an extensive investigation of nursing programs in B.C., Alberta and Ontario. Based on their experiences with curriculum development, David Sterling and Ken Davis decided that a Bachelor of Science in Nursing, with an emphasis on public health and personal patient interaction, would fit well with the University's mission for developing graduates who could serve locally and internationally. The University's interest in nursing education related especially to the non-technical side of the profession, in which the emphasis would be on patient-nurse interaction in such fields as home care; gerontology; school, family and community nursing; as well as hospital and clinical care.

TWU had been blocked from starting its long-envisioned nursing program for lack of the funds to build the additional science and specialized nursing labs essential to the program. We needed at least three-quarters of a million dollars, more if possible.

Dr. Guy Saffold and I had earlier travelled to the provincial legislature in Victoria to visit MLAs with an appeal for assistance. There was a shortage of nurses in the province, and our case was that TWU could prepare them at no operating cost to the province, if only we could get some initial capital funding to start the program. We visited MLA Bill Reid and laid out the case for a contribution of one million dollars to start the nursing program. We weren't very optimistic about success, but we'd been told it might be worth our while.

To our surprise, Mr. Reid quickly agreed, and said that it would not take very long at all to get TWU a cheque for a million dollars. He could do this, he said, because he had some power of direction over the B.C. Lottery Fund, which had surplus cash that he felt could quite appropriately be used to start a nursing program.

With this information, our hopes—which had been rapidly rising—sunk as quickly as they had gone up. There was no way TWU could take money raised by gambling! We asked Mr. Reid if the government could perhaps supply the funds in some other way. No, that would not be possible, he said, puzzled over the University's response. We thanked him as graciously as we could, and left his office. Once we were further down the hall, Guy Saffold turned to me and said, "Neil, did we really just turn down an offer of one million dollars?" We laughed together: there had never been any question of saying 'yes'. But just as Mr. Reid had probably never had an offer of a million dollars refused, this was also my first time turning down a million dollars!

The next step was to get acceptance of what we were planning from the three local hospitals where we'd need to operate clinical practice opportunities (Langley, Surrey, and Abbotsford hospitals). They were reluctant to use their scarce resources to support TWU clinical instructors at their hospitals without additional government funding. David Sterling worked very hard to establish positive relationships with the local hospital administrators, emphasizing that a highly professional nursing faculty at TWU could be an asset to the hospitals, by adding another source of professional expertise to their own professional development programs.

In March, 1989 B.C.'s Minister of Advanced Education and Job Training announced that funding would be provided for developing 300 additional baccalaureate seats. We also developed clinical placement arrangements with a number of community health clinics.

David Sterling's exhaustive preparatory work left us with probably the greatest challenge that we would face in launching a nursing program: where would we find qualified Christian faculty with advanced degrees in nursing, who were also university teachers and knew how to begin and sustain a Christian nursing program? PhD programs in nursing had just started in Canada in 1991. Moreover, even if we found qualified faculty, would they want to come to a start-up program in a small Christian university, when there were so many opportunities for them in larger and more established programs in prestigious universities? For advice, we turned to the University of Prince Edward Island and Red Deer College, institutions of somewhat similar size to TWU that had recently launched nursing programs.

The founder of the nursing program at Red Deer was a Christian, who gave us additional spiritual insights into what we needed to do to embed our beliefs into the program so as to attract Christian faculty. Their faculty's collective insights became very valuable, as we discovered that we had significantly underestimated what it would cost to launch a program that required so much expensive medical equipment, and with a very low student-to-faculty ratio.

Our Assistant Dean of Science, Dr. Jack Van Dyke, and Dr. Don Page had to refashion our plans in order to make the dream a financially viable reality. Even more challenging, for Jack, was having to defend the substantially increased costs at the annual budget planning meeting of the Academic Council, where there were many competing needs for every spare dollar the University could raise.

It was obvious that only through Divine intervention could we find and attract qualified and thoroughly Christian nursing faculty. Our prayers were answered in the person of Dr. Julia Emblen. Julia was then directing the nursing program at Trinity Christian College in Illinois, and had experience in previously starting another nursing program. She was first contacted by David Sterling to find out how we could locate qualified faculty; but we also discovered that she wanted to return to her roots in the Northwest, following the recent passing of her husband. We couldn't have been more blessed than to have Julia as our first Director of

Nursing. She arrived in 1992 to begin putting our vision for the program into practice.

Building a qualified faculty was a monumental task for Julia and Jack Van Dyke, as Dean of the Faculty of Natural and Applied Sciences, where the nursing program was to be situated. Jack's wife was a nurse, so he was well aware of the challenges we faced. Once again, God brought us the most amazing faculty to begin the program. Dr. Beverly Robinson was experienced in providing nursing care to Aboriginal and northern communities. Dr. Landa Terblanche had recently moved to Canada from South Africa, where she had directed the nursing program in a military hospital. Professor Catherine Harwood came to us from the nursing faculty at the University of Western Ontario. Local nurses with Masters' degrees—Karen Johnson and Gwen Rempel—joined the faculty to bring their expertise in gerontology and pediatrics, respectively; and Marjorie Drury taught nursing fundamentals to first-year students.

Thanks be to God, before our first graduating class enrolled, we had assembled one of the most qualified teams of nursing faculty anywhere in the country. Not only were they academically qualified, their expertise and experiences dovetailed remarkably. This was very important for obtaining recognition for the program, and credentialing for our future graduates from the RNABC and the Canadian Association of Schools of Nursing.

Because of their specialized knowledge and different scheduling requirements connecting the University to local hospitals, nursing faculty tend to be entities unto themselves. Since our nursing faculty came from such diverse professional backgrounds, there were priorities—*e.g.*, philosophies of nursing care, and teaching methodologies—that had to be reconciled. Jack Van Dyke played a very important role in developing a homogeneous nursing faculty, and integrating them into the broader culture of TWU. Our nursing faculty have, on several occasions, won TWU's annual Ken Davis Outstanding Teaching Award.

Of course, we needed more than qualified faculty; we needed the physical laboratory resources and spaces to mount such a program. The story of how we received from the government the capital costs for constructing a wing on the Arts and Science Building to house the new nursing program is remarkable: after turning down a million-dollar grant from provincial gambling funds, and after the tragedy of losing five Aviation students and their instructor, TWU unexpectedly received $750,000 for the Nursing Program's needs.

Adding nursing students to our existing science courses meant a need for more science laboratories, especially in biology. Several donors stepped forward to renovate our existing labs: in particular, the Neufeld family covered the rest of the renovations to bring all of our science labs up to par, as we renamed and dedicated the Anna and J.G. Neufeld Science Centre on campus.

In September of 1993, TWU accepted our first class of nursing students. That was another miracle, as we had no assurance, when we launched into this enterprise, that enough students would choose TWU over other, more established baccalaureate nursing programs. The Admissions Department had been tracking enquiries about a possible nursing program, and were able to turn the applicants into *bona fide* students who filled our classes to capacity.

The direction of the nursing program is best reflected in excerpts from a 1993 submission to the RNABC on Curricular Planning and Design for the Nursing Program:

> The purpose of the TWU nursing program is to prepare graduates who are competent and safe to practice in multiple settings, providing nursing leadership in home, hospital, community and other environments where nursing care is offered.
>
> Graduates are prepared to provide for spiritual needs, integrating Judeo-Christian values through their practice. The graduates' caring behaviours are directed toward health promotion, maintenance, and health restoration actions, including biological, psycho-social, and cultural dimensions....
>
> The educational experience should cultivate knowledge and personal development in order to glorify God and to serve mankind.... The liberal arts foundation provides the basis for developing the whole person, with religious studies pivotal in establishing values related to artistic and scientific dimensions....
>
> Christian nurses are motivated by values reflecting Christian love, in the sense of the wounded healer exemplified by Christ. The nurse cares for persons providing altruistic love, personal presence, honesty, integrity, empathy, trust, faith, hope and courage.
>
> Professional Christian nursing practice is characterized by a high degree of commitment to serve the needs of all persons at every stage of the age spectrum and at all points along the wellness-illness continuum.

The quality of the Nursing Program can be seen in our graduates, whose pass rates for the Canadian RN licensing exams are among the highest in the nation.

Employers consistently comment on the high quality of our nursing grads. According to comments from employers, patients and clinical staff, what distinguishes TWU nurses is their deep compassion and dedication.

One of the faculty, with responsibility for clinical education, and later the chair of the program, Dr. Barb Pesut, observed, "Hospital staff will often stop me and ask where we get our high calibre of students; because they are just overwhelmed by the compassion, hard work and interpersonal skills of all of our student nurses."

Over and over again, our nursing graduates have demonstrated the value of learning their nursing skills and professionalism in the context of a Christian liberal arts environment that emphasizes service to God's glory. Trinity Western University has been faithful to its mission to develop and provide godly Christian leadership in nursing for more than two decades.

The quality of the nursing program is also seen through the report of the Education Approval Committee of the RNABC in 1998. The committee interviewed 13 employers of our nursing grads and concluded, "Comments about attitude and interpersonal relationships were overwhelmingly positive. Their ethical behavior, critical thinking and problem-solving were described as highly effective." Interviews with patients cared for by TWU nursing grads indicated: "Responses were all positive, and described graduates as calm, caring, enthusiastic, careful, available, supportive and professional." Hospital preceptors who observed our student nurses "rated student characteristics as 'good' to 'excellent' in terms of preparation, knowledge, skills, judgment and attitude."

> *"I am presently interning in the research, policy, and planning department of the Canadian Medical Association. I know that the work I am doing is making a difference in the lives of Canadians, as well as fulfilling my dreams. It's only been a few weeks, and I can only imagine what will happen in the future!"*
>
> —JESSICA SENN,
> NURSING GRADUATE,
> FALL, 2005

The path to success wasn't always an easy one. Nursing students were required to complete community health-care learning, to meet the required outcomes of a baccalaureate level nursing degree. During the early years of the TWU Nursing Program, however, there were difficulties in securing clinical teaching placements in traditional public health units. This obstacle required our faculty to work extra hard to establish alternative clinical education opportunities in non-traditional settings such as Aboriginal health, rural health, parishes, nursing units within Federal Corrections, a safe house for women fleeing violence, youth clinics, and other similar settings. Initially, it felt like a huge stretch to create community nursing practicums in settings where nurses didn't usually have a role. Students, however, gave powerful reports about the quality of learning in such innovative settings; and this provided the rationale for a whole new way of looking at the value of such non-traditional placements.

Through sharing these student experiences with regulatory bodies and other nurse-educators, the Innovative Clinical Placements Research Team (ICPRT) was born. Through three phases of studies, including a national research study that surveyed every university and college baccalaureate nursing program in Canada, the ICPR team demonstrated that student learning in such non-traditional settings not only met educational requirements, but also equipped students with skills and knowledge beyond what traditional community health settings could offer. From the outset, TWU's nursing faculty were active members of the ICPRT, and over the years 2001-2010, the team published six papers, an ambitious national survey, and almost 20 presentations at provincial, national and international conferences. TWU Nursing was definitely on the cutting edge in researching, using these non-traditional clinical settings and presenting their validity in student learning. Based on their research and experiences, most nursing education programs in Canada have now incorporated such settings into their curricula.

Before long, the Nursing Program became one of the flagships for fulfilling TWU's mission. From the outset, it had been hoped that our talented and dedicated nursing faculty would extend TWU's reach and mission far beyond our campus and the local hospitals. Mission-minded Julia Emblen was the champion for this development early in the program's evolution. Through her experiences in the United States, she developed a particular interest in parish nursing, sometimes known as congregational nursing or church nursing.

Parish nursing points people to Jesus as our Great Physician. It's a compassionate healing ministry for those who seek to be whole in body, mind, and spirit, done primarily through health counseling and spiritual or pastoral care for people facing health challenges, while acting as a liaison between the faith community and the medical community. Julia herself developed the courses for training parish nurses, and offered them to other nurses through weekend workshops and conferences sponsored by TWU. Several nursing students, supervised by Julia, also provided summer nursing care to congregations. Through Julia's efforts, TWU became the pioneer in Canada for such training.

In 1997, TWU hosted a conference of the Nurses' Christian Fellowship Canada (a ministry of Inter-Varsity Christian Fellowship) to introduce the first graduating class of nurses at TWU to this wider ministry. The breadth of our Nursing Program's outreach can be seen in the many conferences where TWU has hosted or been represented.

In 1999, we hosted a conference on spirituality and health care, and another on "What is the Baby-Friendly Initiative?" In 2001, our nursing faculty made a presentation to the Meaning Conference on "Spiritual Health Interventions to Restore Meaning" that was later published in the *Canadian Nurse Journal*. That same year, a conference was sponsored on "Promoting Excellence in Nursing." In 2003, TWU hosted the first-ever conference in Western Canada on "Camp Nursing: Putting the Puzzle Together." And for many years thereafter, TWU's Darlene Pankratz was a regular presenter at camping conferences.

As new faculty were added to the Nursing Department, their expertise expanded—as when, in 2000, Dr. Sheryl Kirkham (the Governor General's Gold Medal winner at UBC) joined us and introduced ongoing Faith and Nursing Symposia that attracted both national and international attendees. Her research focuses on the areas of culture, religion, equity and health, with particular attention to how difference is negotiated in clinical settings, including in the context of end-of-life care to people with chronic life-limiting conditions. Her ground-breaking research has led to her receiving the College of Registered Nurses of B.C. Award of Excellence in Nursing Research in 2010, and more recently her induction into the prestigious Royal Society of Canada—a first for a TWU faculty member.

As Catherine Harwood remembers, "At provincial and national nursing conferences, professors from other nursing programs would regularly come to TWU faculty to say how glad they were that TWU was on the program, because they learned so much from them." Once again, it proved that "you don't have to be big to be good at what you do in honouring God."

Overall, the entire nursing faculty and student body have benefited from their research and awards in their study of religion, culture and spirituality in health care. It's also significant that our nursing faculty have won the annual Ken Davis Excellence in Teaching Award more often than any other department in the University.

A unique part of TWU's nursing program is the emphasis on missional nursing to underprivileged populations. This was first begun in 1995, when through a local Registered Nurse, Suzanne Taylor, some students at the end of their junior year went on a nursing missions trip to Belize. That program has continued since; and has included trips to Romania, Guyana, Zambia and a remote Aboriginal community in Canada. These experiences, combined with the global and missional mindset of faculty and students alike, have contributed to the way so many of our nursing graduates are serving around the world. In 1998, Julia Emblen was recognized by the RNABC for her efforts in placing nursing students in cross-cultural and traditionally under-served populations. TWU's Nursing Program was the first in Canada to do this, and it has now become part of most nursing education programs.

The strongest affirmation for what the Nursing Program has accomplished comes from the graduates themselves. Sarah Walker graduated in 2000, and has worked as a nurse in Maple Ridge; and thanks to the encouragement of Julia, has ministered to HIV patients as an acute medical/palliative care nurse, helping patients and their families face the possibility of death without destroying their hope for a miracle.

"God is constantly reminding me," says Sarah, "that I must not take away hope; and that He is in control of my patients."

Since graduating in 1997 from the program, Rick Sawatzky has made a career of nursing and says, "Education at the TWU School of Nursing has provided me with the foundation for studying both the practice and science of nursing, and integrating that with values and beliefs that find their roots in faith-based traditions." And that's why all past and present faculty have invested so thoroughly to make this program a success—***To the Praise of His Glory***. Since graduating from TWU, Rick has gone on to earn his doctorate, and now teaches in the nursing program at TWU. He holds a Tier 2 Canada Research Chair in Patient-Reported Outcomes, and in 2015 received two significant grants: a three-year, $310,000 grant from the Canadian Institute of Health Research (CIHR)—the first-ever CIHR operational grant awarded to TWU; and then another CIHR grant of $735,139 over four years for a project focused on seniors with complex care needs.

Like so many other programs at TWU, our Nursing Program has put our Christian education onto the world stage—which has not gone unnoticed, as students from all over the world want to study at TWU.

(In writing these reflections, I'm grateful for input from Drs. Don Page, Julia Emblen, Sonya Grypma, Catherine Hoe Eriksen (Harwood), Sheryl Kirkham, Rick Sawatzky, Landa Terblanche, and Jack Van Dyke.)

41

TWU's MA in Leadership

Having tackled the mission for servant-leadership development at the undergraduate level, we now turned our attention to graduate studies. The idea of a graduate degree in leadership had been tentatively approved by the Board of Governors as early as 1988, in its thinking about possible graduate studies for the future; but no action had yet been taken—we had made an agreement with the provincial Ministry to defer implementing graduate studies for five years. What galvanized the University into action were discussions at the AUCC of dividing member institutions into three categories. By this proposal, if we didn't have graduate degrees, TWU would have been relegated to a third tier of colleges.

Ken Davis, Don Page and I were determined that must not happen. While we couldn't match the work of the large research universities, we wanted to be recognized as a university in the second tier; and that meant having graduate studies programs, in addition to those from the seminary. The first proposal was for an MA in Counseling Psychology, as we already had the faculty to make this possible. This was to be followed by programs in Leadership, and then Biblical Studies. But each of these programs would have to be self-sufficient in revenue generation, so as not to be a drain on the University's undergraduate budget; so the Director of Graduate Studies, Don Page, would have to raise all start-up costs.

> *"I've gained the confidence to tackle large projects and manage crises in a way that produces good results for my company and earns me the trust of my colleagues. Incredibly, since the start of the program I've been honoured to receive two promotions and three salary increases."*
>
> —Kyle Barker,
> MAL Business Stream,
> 2008

The model for the MA in Administrative Leadership was based on the very successful work of the Executive Leadership Development Institute (ELDI), and the task of developing the proposal was given to Dr. Guy Saffold. Students with at least three years' working experience beyond their undergraduate studies would be invited to embark part-time on a 25-month program to develop their leadership skills. From the outset, the guidelines were very clearly established:

- The program would focus on development of Christian leaders, not leaders who happened to be Christians;

- It would emphasize experiential learning, rather than only the study of leadership theories;

- Its leadership model was to be found in Jesus' example of servant-leadership;

- Faculty must have not only the qualifications for teaching at the master's level, but actual experience in leading organizations; and

- The program's academic rigour should allow MA graduates to pursue doctoral studies in leadership.

Dr. Don Page, the Director of Graduate Studies, designed the program so that students would take several courses of two weeks each over three summers, then another five courses on-line, followed by a major project involving application of their learning in their places of employment. The first four on-line courses would specialize in Business, Education, Christian Ministry, and Health Care (the Student Ministries and Non-Profit streams were added later).

This was the first on-line program ever offered by TWU, and it wasn't without its problems. We went through five platforms in the first few years, trying to find one that would be easy for students and faculty to navigate. Thus, every semester was also a huge learning experience for faculty, none of whom had ever taught on-line before. Those first students deserve a lot of credit for persevering while we tried our best to work out the glitches that sooner or later seemed to appear in every platform we tried, until the University finally developed its own platform.

"The MA in Leadership experience has added so much to my personal, professional, and spiritual development that it is hard to articulate just how life-changing it has been. I expect I will be continuing to consolidate the learning from this program for the rest of my ministry and beyond."
—Beverly Woodland, MAL Christian Ministry Stream, 2010

We'd originally thought of hiring someone to establish and lead this new graduate program; but as we went through the development stages, Don Page became so excited about its potential that he decided to resign as Academic Vice-President, to direct the MA in Leadership Program. It also meant that he had to give up leadership of the ELDI, as both programs would be active in July. It took two years to divest all his responsibilities, but in the summer of 1999 he was ready to lead the program—by teaching its first course.

The program began as a Master of Arts in Administrative Leadership, to satisfy educational authorities who wanted that designation for credentialing. When they relaxed this out-dated designation, we switched the name to the more accurate Master of Arts in Leadership, since our focus was on leading, rather than administration.

The program began with a full cohort, and within a couple of years we were adding a second cohort to meet increased demand. In the first five years, we found that 70 percent of those in the Business Stream received a promotion in their place of employment before they'd even graduated! Clearly, employers were recognizing the value of MA in Leadership training.

Leadership development recognized

We also knew that we needed an externally-recognized peer evaluation that would show the wider academic community what we'd achieved in the leadership development component of our Mission Statement. At the beginning, we didn't know exactly what form that approval might take. Members of the AUCC knew what TWU was trying to become—and so did the Economic Council of Canada, which, in the meantime, applauded any and all efforts at leadership development in Canadian universities, which they considered vital for meeting the country's economic needs.

By December of 1994, the AUCC and the Economic Council of Canada decided to showcase the best of university education in Canada to a group of visiting university chancellors and presidents from other countries. Eleven of the 90-plus universities in Canada were selected for visits: in Western Canada, UBC was chosen for its research, and TWU for leadership development.

In the half-day that the delegation spent with us, Dr. Paul Chamberlain demonstrated how we taught leadership through Philosophy by an emphasis on ethical decision-making; Dr. Dave Rushton explained that in Music we involve students in the organization of musical performances; Dr. Michel Mestre showed how we taught all 26 leadership characteristics identified by the Economic Council of Canada through our Business courses; and in Education, Dr. Harro van Brummelen, Dr. Joy McCullough, and Dr. Ken Pudlas demonstrated (by an elaborate chart) how every Education course at TWU contributed to some aspect of leadership development, to enable our Education graduates to become leaders in their schools.

Dr. Deane Downey explained how we used our capstone Interdisciplinary course to solidify our leadership principles in the minds of graduating students, by practicing teamwork through cross-disciplinary student projects.

The true measure of the value of the program was not just in what it had done for the individual graduates; but also in what, as servant-leaders, they could now do for others. Many graduates applied what they had experienced and learned to developing servant-leadership programs for their own organizations. This was especially true in the non-profit organizations, as they set up leadership development programs where none had existed before. Of particular note were programs established for the Salvation Army, Youth With A Mission (YWAM), Mission Aviation Fellowship, Wycliffe Bible Translators, and many churches.

In 2004, Pan African Christian University in Nairobi asked if they could adopt the program, and Stan Remple and Don Page taught them how to teach the program in Africa. Don wrote their introductory textbook on servant-leadership, entitled *Effective Team Leadership: Learning to Lead through Relationships*. Since then, hundreds have graduated from this program in Africa; and for these graduates, the MAL faculty in Canada designed 26 three-day models for taking the MAL teaching into their places of employment. In 2004, Don Page passed the directorship to Stan Remple, who proceeded to take the program to China, while Don continued to teach in both programs.

The MAL program is all about raising up and equipping leaders who, through their serving leadership, will make the world a better place to live for all of us. And that's exactly what the graduates of the MAL program are doing in their own spheres of influence.

42

TWU rated 'foremost in leadership development'

It takes a leader to train leaders. Such educators are like top sergeants in an army: they've learned, and they know how; so they can lead, and show how. Dr. Don Page had come to us from a career in the upper echelons of the federal civil service, where he also organized Bible studies and prayer groups for Members of Parliament and federal government employees, and advocated the importance of Christian principles in government policies. When he became our Academic Dean, the Mission Statement goal of training Christian leaders "for the various marketplaces of life" took flight!

But the importance of leadership development still needed to be recognized by our academic peers; and for some, so did the very existence of Christian, faith-based universities in Canada.

Trinity Western University was different—but it was still largely unknown outside of university presidential circles, even though we had been accepted into membership in the AUCC in 1984. It seemed we had to prove, over and over, our academic credibility as a university. We were determined to raise the University's profile by getting our Academic Dean onto the agenda as a presenter, respondent, or panelist whenever possible at meetings of the AUCC and the Council for Christian Colleges and Universities (CCCU); and whenever possible, to tie this to our vision for leadership development. By doing so, Don Page was able to gain academic approval for our faculty, and also credibility for the idea that leadership development is a legitimate academic pursuit. This was ground-breaking in Canada, as no Canadian university at that time offered a degree in leadership development.

In many ways, the AUCC functioned as a presidents' club, in which we were already well known as a unique private Christian university. But this recognition didn't translate into many benefits for us in the academic sector: our graduates weren't always accepted, either because other academic leaders still hadn't heard of

TWU, or because they had an ill-informed opinion of us. Here, the goal was to demonstrate that TWU is a viable academic institution, whose graduates should be admitted—indeed, welcomed—into graduate schools. This was done through discipline-specific articulation meetings and the semi-annual meetings of the Academic Vice-Presidents, at which we sought name and credential recognition by being an active participant on every program.

Many good things were happening on our campus—things from which we thought our AUCC colleagues could learn. We had to demonstrate that we had something to contribute to university education—something in which they would be interested. One example: there was a lot of discussion among universities about how to educate students with disabilities, without being discriminatory. UBC had set up a special department for developing new pedagogical means; but it didn't answer the fundamental question of what standards must be reached, for persons with different kinds of abilities to graduate with a specific major. At TWU we'd had a particularly difficult case in the music department: to determine how music theory must be demonstrated by a music major with coordination disabilities. The case had led to physical threats against one of our faculty, and even a case before the British Columbia Human Rights Tribunal!

We did a lot of research into how other universities handled similar challenges, resulting in a 40-page legal submission to the Human Rights Commission. Our experience, and our exoneration by the Commission, was precedent-setting—and of great interest to our AUCC colleagues, because we'd preserved the academic integrity of the degree. By this, and other interventions, AUCC could see we were qualified players in the academic field; this led to our graduates being more freely accepted into prestigious graduate schools.

While we were studying what other Christian universities were doing in student leadership development, the president of the CCCU, Myron Augsberger, asked Don Page to do a study on why CCCU members had an increasing turnover rate among university presidents and academic officers. Many reasons were given, but most prominent by far was that incumbents didn't feel adequately prepared for the leadership responsibilities of the position, after they had assumed it. Don was asked to initiate and direct CCCU's new Executive Leadership Development Institute (ELDI) for training new university presidents and academic officers in leadership.

The ELDI was so successful that the declining longevity trend in Christian university leadership was actually reversed. Once again, this added credibility to TWU; equally important, it helped develop many curriculum resources for our own servant-leadership development. Curriculum and methods used at every leadership development institute in North America were examined (such as the Center for Higher Education Research and Development, The Center for Creative Leadership, the Greenleaf Center for Servant-Leadership, the National Center for Post-Secondary Governance and Finance, and every American university program for leadership development).

> **We needed an externally recognized peer evaluation that would show the wider academic community what we'd achieved in leadership development. At the beginning of this journey, we didn't know exactly what form that approval might take.**

As previously mentioned, in December of 1994, the AUCC and the Economic Council of Canada decided to showcase the best of university education in Canada to a group of visiting university chancellors and presidents from other countries. During their visit to TWU, Don Page outlined how we teach leadership across disciplines; which moved the head of the visiting delegation to announce that TWU was "the foremost university in the country for leadership development"—thus everyone on campus knew our benchmark had been reached! This led quickly to other universities—the first were the Universities of Manitoba and Alberta—sending delegations to TWU to learn how we did it, before they began their own leadership development programs.

This wasn't a one-time celebration, however. At every faculty or departmental meeting or retreat, we sought to get leadership development onto the agenda, so we could be aware of what our people where thinking and feeling, and what progress was being made. Academic VP Don Page and I knew we couldn't be everywhere or at all faculty and staff meetings, so we relied on Don's faculty "guiding team" to carry the discussion and give us feedback. This wasn't a "witch-hunt" to learn who the holdouts were; but rather, a means of fine-tuning our thinking and communications: "*Why* are some not seeing the benefits of this change, and what can we do to make those benefits clearer?" The burden of proof was always on Don and his guiding team.

Specific Examples
One of the power-brokers among the faculty was a hold-out. In the end, it wasn't the large number of meetings Don had with her, but two quite unrelated events that brought her on-board.

First, her son took a class from Don, and he applied the leadership development being taught there to his part-time job. When he told this to his mother, she began to see a practical, not-so-academic perspective of the change.

Second, Don had spoken frequently about what biblical servant-leadership looks like; but at a Staff/Faculty Day, when he contrasted the selfish, "command-and-control" type of leadership that Jesus frowned upon with the kind of servant-leadership He advocated, she suddenly grasped what the course proposed. Hitherto, she'd always argued that "You can't teach leadership principles through Shakespeare's plays"—because that wasn't why he'd written them. Now there was something more than the fine points of English literature to be learned from studying Hamlet and Macbeth: there were also powerful leadership examples and lessons that could be applied in today's society—and isn't that what our mission is all about?

It took almost six years, but she was then on-board with TWU's leadership goals. We were all glad we'd persevered. She was an excellent teacher, with much to offer the University. We were glad that she hadn't taken her considerable talents elsewhere. She became an ally, and a dear friend in this endeavour of anchoring leadership development into our academic culture and practice.

We also had a few faculty who needed to shift their emphasis in the classroom from their teaching to student learning. At the same time, they needed to see that what university students need isn't just the knowledge and skills of the discipline, but preparation for serving God *through* their disciplinary training and practice. And that's where leadership development comes into play—not taking anything away from what was being taught, but adding value to it.

One day, as Don Page was walking across the campus, a history professor showed him the last question on an examination: "Evaluate the leadership role of Alexander the Great." Don asked whether his students had learned everything he wanted them to know about Alexander; to which he replied, "Yes—and more." For some time, we'd argued that students would have a fuller appreciation of historical characters if they could see them through a leadership perspective. And it would also help them evaluate modern political leaders for whom they might be voting. This history teacher now understood the value of what we were doing, and became an influential member of Don's guiding team.

Accomplishing the vision for leadership development also had a profound impact on another change in the academic sector: as Academic Dean, Don had inherited a structure of ten academic divisions. It was time-consuming for many managers, who did a lot of administrative work for little results. The ten divisions were consolidated into four faculties, each headed by an Assistant Dean—who now had more time and resources to handle administrative duties. Over time they were empowered to become leaders instead of managers; and by so doing, they could give better direction to the leadership development mandate. That also gave Don more time to invest in the development of the leadership skills of the Assistant Deans.

Teaching servant-leadership by example

The Academic VP's role was to invest in serving the well-being of the Deans, who would do the same for their department chairs, who would in turn invest in individual faculty members, who would invest in their students. This was the culture of servant-leadership, modeled by the way Jesus washed the feet of His disciples.

This model only works, however, if everyone is committed to advancing the mission of the University; and discussions at all levels of the organization had to centre around how best to do this. That's why the TWU Mission Statement had to be the essential part of every faculty recruitment.

One of the biggest obstacles to seeing the vision develop was getting all departments to focus on leadership development in their curriculum revisions. Many just didn't know where to start. We could appreciate their dilemma: they hadn't been trained as academic leaders, and only a few had read articles or books about leadership. They were discipline-specific experts, not students of leadership theory or practice.

What they knew about leadership had come from watching their predecessors, who weren't always paragons of servant-leadership. We realized we had to help them to get going in the right direction. Don Page did this with the input of his guiding team, designing three questions for each department or academic discipline—the answers to which would be the beginning of their curriculum statement on leadership development.

The questions were specific to each academic discipline we taught, but in general followed a similar pattern. For example, the Philosophy Department faculty were asked to write a short essay answering the following three questions:

1. **How does the teaching of philosophy advance the mission of TWU to develop godly Christian leaders?**

2. **What aspects of your teaching could most impact the practice of good servant-leadership?**

3. **How and when can you introduce these aspects into the your curriculum with actual examples as teaching lessons, either or both good or bad?**

The department's response focused on good ethics and character, and their curriculum objectives were revised accordingly. There was no longer any excuse for inaction, and everyone got into the discussion at departmental meetings and faculty retreats.

Attitude training was just as important as skills training. Our academic leaders had to be coached on how to deal with negative attitudes towards change. Practicing empathy and seeking to understand others became critical skills. These leaders then became coaches for others who had difficulty getting their minds and hearts around the desired changes in how they taught their courses. Don's guiding team had built enough trust and credibility by this time to sustain the effort until positive results from the change could be observed. As Don Page has so lucidly put it:

> "Successes in reaching our leadership development goals were also publicly recognized and celebrated. When the achievements of some of the older, more experienced faculty were recognized, it became a powerful encouragement for younger faculty to demonstrate what *they* could do. Every advance in leadership development was linked to the University's success as an institution; to its fund-raising potential; and above all to the betterment of our graduates. We also highlighted faculty who had taken on leadership roles in professional associations. Money was made available to leaders who wanted to host a professional development meeting on our campus, as a means of raising the University's profile in that profession. When faculty received promotions or tenure, their contribution to leadership development was noted and publicized.
>
> **"Servant-leadership isn't about developing followers, but developing other servant-leaders.** For example: our choirs were well-recognized for outstanding performances under the baton of choral director Wes Janzen, who had always conducted the choirs when they performed with professional musicians from the Vancouver Symphony Orchestra and CBC Chamber Orchestra. One day, I challenged him, as a servant-leader, to develop student conductors who could conduct these world-class musicians. It would be a huge stretch, and certainly one that made everyone nervous. I remember sitting in the audience some time later, watching four of our students conduct the choir and orchestra. They were great—and the concert-master publicly told them so! That was servant-leadership development at its best; these music majors would go on to graduate studies in music and to become leaders in church worship ensembles and choirs, and other professional performance positions."

43

TWU as a 'national learning laboratory' in Leadership Development

By Dr. Don Page

Through influencing the national academic culture, TWU was becoming a "learning laboratory" on leadership development. We had the benefit of Executive Leadership Development Institute (ELDI) experience, which enabled us to bring into our meetings the best practices of other Christian universities. We also used devotions on biblical leadership examples and themes in committee meetings, and frequently sprinkled leadership quotations to keep ideas and discussion flowing along the lines of the intended change.

We also knew that we needed some proof of the value to our students of what we were teaching about leadership, as well as the leadership opportunities they had through a variety of student-directed campus activities. Although every course was now being designed to advance the theme of biblical leadership development—and we had 22 courses designed to produce leaders in professional disciplines like Business, Nursing, Education, and Human Kinetics—we still didn't have a cross-disciplinary course in leadership for our student leaders. So I introduced and taught that course on the interdisciplinary foundations for servant-leadership.

Deans and department chairs were encouraged to put leadership development and practices on their reading lists and meeting agendas. Recognition was given to faculty who introduced leadership into their professional development planning. Graduates who exemplified serving leadership in their jobs were featured in University publications. Honorary degrees were awarded to those who exemplified Christian leadership principles. Thus we began to take servant-leadership beyond the existing literature on the subject. How could servant-leadership be introduced into the foreign cultures into which some of our students were going? How could churches learn to function as a team?

As a learning organization, we contributed to this broader application of serving leadership.

Several steps were taken to anchor servant-leadership development into the culture of the University. We had developed six core values around which TWU was to function, and one of them was "Servant-Leadership as a Way of Life". This core value statement was to be used as a benchmark for evaluating everything we do. It was given to every new employee, and was made available to all students.

Leadership development was also included in the criteria for faculty recruitment, and in evaluations for tenure, promotion, and all leadership positions. A year-long new faculty workshop, which faculty were given course relief to attend, was developed for bringing new faculty into the operating culture of the University. Included in its curriculum was how to make servant-leadership development a reality in classrooms, through modelling as well as teaching. An annual monetary prize and a certificate were instituted, to be given to faculty during graduation ceremonies for innovative teaching ideas leading to leadership development.

For students, two much-publicized annual awards were given to those who, in the opinion of their peers and professors, best exhibited the qualities of biblical servant-leadership. At a special chapel, followed by a luncheon ceremony, they received a statue of Jesus washing the feet of Peter; a substantial monetary reward; and a gift to a charity of their choice. At any given time, 25 percent of our students are involved in some leadership experience on campus. The training for these positions now involves training in servant-leadership, by staff who have graduated from our master's program in serving leadership.

44

TWU's Laurentian Leadership Centre

Many hands in the leadership at TWU responded eagerly to the vision for a campus in Ottawa. TWU students could serve as interns to Members of Parliament—even Cabinet Ministers—and also in social service and media organizations, where they might learn to impact the culture and policy of our nation! One of the central figures was Don Page, former policy- and speech-writer for Canada's Ministers of External Affairs.

Don Page had come to TWU with a dream that had been birthed from his experiences in hosting university interns and co-op students in his office at External Affairs. Eager and talented university students came to intern with the federal government, only to find that the work that they were assigned was all too often primarily of a clerical nature, and didn't make use of nor enhance their learning or skills.

When students were assigned to Don in the Policy Development Bureau of External Affairs, he put them to work doing research for policy statements and speeches, or drafting portions of speeches under close supervision. He soon saw that there was plenty of room for students to gain valuable experience from internships, and opportunities for future employment in the public service. He also recognized the possibility and benefits of introducing Christian students into government service.

Shortly after coming to TWU, Don discussed with our Administrative Committee a proposal for establishing centres in Ottawa and Victoria where our students could gain exposure to government service; I took it to the Board of Governors, who in 1990 approved the idea in principle. However, we couldn't make it a reality at that time, because the Ontario Government's regulations prevented any out-of-province university from offering degree programs in Ontario without their approval. When Don shared our idea with officials of the Ontario Government, they offered us the possibility of establishing such a centre—in

Timmins, Ontario! It was clear that they didn't want any competition for students in the same cities as their provincial universities; and locating in Timmins certainly wouldn't advance our objectives.

When the Harris Government took office in 1995, it announced that new regulations would allow out-of-province universities to offer programs in Ontario. It took quite some time for the government to decide on the approval process under the *Post-Secondary Choice and Excellence Act;* but TWU was first on the applicant list. This was both good and bad. There were long-drawn out bureaucratic discussions before the Ontario Government established its regulations; but in the process, TWU had the opportunity to review the proposed regulations and make suggestions—which were accepted.

It would be two years before final approval was given to TWU for the Laurentian Leadership Centre in Ottawa. Along the way, we had to answer seemingly pointless questions such as how would we guarantee that there were enough chairs in the classroom, etc. Library access was also of concern to the appraisers. We had neither the space nor the resources to develop a full on-site library for the courses we taught; however, through the inter-library loan system our students had access and borrowing privileges at the excellent libraries of nearby Ottawa and Carleton universities. We also had to put up a bond for every student attending, and prove that academic records were securely stored off-campus. These were cumbersome issues to deal with, but our responses proved that we were a legitimate university, capable of operating in Ontario.

In the meantime, Ron Kuehl, the head of our Development Department, had been looking for a suitable location and building in Ottawa. Don Page had suggested Sandy Hill or The Glebe, both areas close to Parliament Hill. Available properties however, didn't match our needs for accommodations and classroom space. Then in 2000, Ron "happened" to sit next to a real estate agent on a flight to Ottawa to see his family, and learned of the availability of the Laurentian Club building on Metcalfe Street, right in downtown Ottawa. In financial difficulties, due to declining membership, the Club had ceased to operate as a club for the business élite in Ottawa, and was anxious to sell its property. The initial asking price of $2.9 million had been reduced to $2.3 million, with some of its treasured assets sold off to pay taxes and upkeep in the meantime. The only catch: the closing bid had to made within two weeks!

On returning to TWU, Ron persuaded me to ask our Board chairman Alan Hedberg to join me in a hasty trip to Ottawa to see the property. This was also the time of the B.C. College of Teachers' challenge to TWU before the Supreme

Court of Canada (see Chapter 48, "The Legal Challenge" on page 245), so Ottawa and its importance was in our purview.

The location was ideal, being within walking distance of Parliament Hill; but the building, although structurally strong, would require repairs and upgrading. A long-standing leak in the roof had caused significant water damage to two rooms on the third floor. Nevertheless, the decision was made to offer $1.3 million.

Although it was a closed-bid process, we knew the Club had already received bids from two embassies and another educational institution. The highest bid was from Libya, who wanted it for their embassy. However, there was no way the Club would sell their beloved, historic building to the dictator, Moammar Gadhafi!

Actually the Laurentian Club wasn't anxious to sell it to any embassy, as it would then become the national property of the country that purchased it; and that meant that even though the City of Ottawa had declared it an historic building, it could be remodeled as they pleased, without regard to preserving, for example, the ornate hand-carved woodwork that surrounded many of the windows and doors, the seven marble fireplaces, the stained-glass windows, and the original tapestry that covered the main walls of the public reception areas.

The building had been built by John R. Booth as his residence in 1909, when he was Canada's greatest lumber baron. No expense was spared in making it a signature building on the Ottawa landscape. What the Club liked about the TWU bid was that the interior would be preserved, along with the name "Laurentian"; and the intended purpose was also appealing to them.

Several members of the Club's executive said that when they met in the third-floor boardroom to open the TWU bid, a door leading to storage cabinets in the eaves of the house suddenly swung open, after years of being jammed shut! The club members took it as an omen that Mr. Booth would be pleased if TWU's bid were accepted. And so, in May 2001, TWU suddenly found itself in possession of the historic Laurentian Club building. In the documents prepared by the Historic Sites and Monuments Board of Canada (October 24, 2005) outlining the importance of the Booth House as a national historic treasure, the following description was given of the building:

> The John R. Booth Residence is one of the finest architectural examples of a Queen Anne Revival style building in Ontario. Once home to John R. Booth (1827-1925), a prominent Canadian lumber baron and businessman in the early 20th century, this Victorian home stands out for its excellent design and state of preservation. The Queen Anne Revival style was created for comfortable, often luxurious living. Virtually every

available building material was used to enliven the surfaces: terra cotta, shingles, clapboard, half-timbering with stucco infill; rough fieldstone; pale smooth stone and rich, red brick. It was the most eclectic type of all revival styles with details including: Tudor, Venetian, oval and bay windows, half-timbering, shaped pediments, ribbed chimney stacks, columns and applied decorative structure. The Queen Anne Revival style was most popular for domestic architecture, but was also used for apartment buildings, resort hotels, public institutions and commercial structures.... The John R. Booth Residence is as impressive today as it was almost one hundred years ago. It has two principle façades, shaped gables and a square corner tower, which is an unusual feature of the Queen Anne Revival style. Inside, the house displays rich woodwork, delicately carved over-mantles, paneling and a beautiful sculptured staircase. There are eight fireplaces, some finished with Italian marble, and many of the walls are draped with tapestries.... Architect John W. H. Watts enhanced the design by adding a square corner tower surmounted by finely sculptured finials to create a house of baronial grandeur.

While the acquisition was in keeping with the Board's earlier approval of a centre for TWU in Ottawa, the building alone didn't make a program. In the meantime, Don Page had stepped down as Academic Vice-President in order to direct the new Master of Arts in Administrative Leadership degree, and also to serve as acting Dean of Graduate Studies. The centre in Ottawa needed a champion, if was to get off the ground; someone with contacts and the credibility in Ottawa to secure internships in important government and political offices in Ottawa. Don agreed to take on the challenge half-time, and passed on his responsibilities for Graduate Studies to Ken Davis, who was still with ACTS.

Before the remodeling could begin, an environmental assessment had to be done; a buried oil tank, abandoned since 1946, was leaking. The Club took responsibility for that cleanup. Fortunately, the oil had not leaked under the adjacent apartment building, and the only disruption was to the parking lot. It took a full year for the building to be put in shape for the arrival of its first students in September, 2002. The former servants' quarters and club storage rooms on the third floor were gutted to make way for five dormitory rooms and accompanying washrooms. The commercial kitchen had to be reconfigured. The basement was converted into another dorm, laundry room, and storage. The main public areas were kept largely intact, with fresh coats of paint, and tearing up the worn plush carpet on the main floor. The carpet turned out to be a blessing in disguise, as it had protected the original wood flooring, which was refinished; it was made of three-inch flooring, according to Mr. Booth's standards.

Over the course of 2001/2002, a local contractor oversaw work on the building, with finishing details managed by designer Sandi Hall. Student Life Coordinator Sheldon Loeppky purchased most of the things the students needed in the kitchen and for recreation, as well as for the live-in on-site apartment for the full-time Student Life Leader; Don and Annabelle Page coordinated these efforts. Many unwanted items had to be disposed of or refurbished for students' use. Long hours of hard work turned into a labour of love.

Our investigation into who John R. Booth was turned up a great Christian servant-leader—an ideal role-model for students who would be living in his house! His business acumen, as Canada's foremost lumber baron and railway magnate, was well known in the Ottawa valley; a street and building in the city are named after him. How he conducted his business is important for students of leadership to learn. Above all, he cared for his employees, at a time when there were no social and health insurance schemes. For example, when fire destroyed much of his lumberyards on Bretton Flats in Ottawa, he kept his workers on the payroll until the restoration gave them back their jobs. If employees were hurt on the job, as they frequently were in the lumber and railway businesses of the early 20th century, he undertook to look after their families—and he was the largest employer, by far, in Ottawa.

Never one to broadcast his philanthropy, John Booth built a wing on the hospital, and was the largest donor to charitable causes in the city. He never owned more than two suits—one for Sunday and one for work—the Sunday suit replacing the work suit in due time. He was a faithful member of St. Andrews Presbyterian Church, and his personal Bible was well-worn, with many notations in the margins. His motto, *"God Helps Us"* is still engraved on the door of a cabinet at the entrance to the grand staircase.

When he died in 1925, Prime Minister Mackenzie King said: "Mr. Booth was indeed one of the Fathers of Canada; it is not too much to say that it is to men of such sterling worth and indominitable will as he possessed, more than aught else, that we owe the development of our Dominion." Hundreds of his employees walked behind his casket on a cold December day, and thousands more lined the streets as they moved from his house to the burial site in Beechwood Cemetery. He truly is a great role-model for our students, being known—for his industry, generosity, and fairness—as a devout Christian gentleman.

The original team managing our program was made up of Dr. Don Page as

Executive Director, Dr. Paul Wilson as program director, and Sheldon Loeppky as Student Life Co-ordinator. Paul Wilson came to us with excellent credentials on Parliament Hill, having been Director of Research for the Reform Party, and someone who could carry on the work of securing top-notch internships, as well as teaching the course on Canadian Government, for which he was well-suited, with plenty of personal insights and experience. By design, Sheldon Loeppky stayed at the LLC to get the program up and running for the first semester; then his job was turned over to Carmen Meir, a TWU graduate well acquainted with Student Life.

The purpose of the LLC is best captured in the program's mission statement:

> The Laurentian Leadership Program advances the mission of Trinity Western University by enabling a community of upper level students to acquire an enhanced understanding of God's call on their lives as leaders, through first-hand leadership experiences in Ottawa as they practice the principles of Christian servant-leadership. It does this by:

1. Providing a full semester of degree-based learning through academically approved courses and internships;

2. Offering students learning internships in business, government, political, media, and non-profit organizations;

3. Fostering dialogue between students and national leaders and various agencies in Ottawa;

4. Enabling students to see how their Christian values and beliefs are articulated and used in the public square through engaging the culture and technology;

5. Providing a community-based environment where students reflectively consider their Ottawa experience in terms of who God is calling them to become, as Christian servant-leaders; and,

6. Preparing students for future service or employment opportunities in national and international arenas.

The first students arrived in September, 2002, just as the final touches were being put on the renovations. In the mornings, they would take three courses on Canadian Government, Canadian Culture, and Ethics in Decision-Making. Each afternoon, they would be at an internship associated with their major. While the majority of these internships were on Parliament Hill, there were also internships in high-tech companies in Kanata; media outlets; non-profit organizations; and government departments which are scattered throughout the National Capital Region.

Every office receiving an intern had to sign an agreement that the intern would only work on policy issues and research. There was no pay involved, so the offices didn't feel they had to get direct benefits from the interns' work. And not every office qualified to have an intern, especially on Parliament Hill. Five MPs had been asked to identify offices, regardless of party affiliation, where members or executive assistants were working on cutting-edge proposals. From these lists, only one-third of the MPs were identified as having offices suitable for an LLC intern. Students had to keep a daily record of the work they were doing, and what they learned. These journals were reviewed regularly by the Director of the Laurentian Leadership Centre, who also went on-site to check on how each internship was progressing.

Instead of having interns confined to their offices, MPs were encouraged to take them to committee meetings, party meetings, and to social events, such as the Governor General's reception in Rideau Hall for the opening of Parliament. The interns were prepared in advance for these events through special protocol training.

The LLC students were also introduced to local customs through visits to the Supreme Court of Canada, Rideau Hall, the Rideau Canal, Kingston, the Thousand Islands boat cruise, the War Museum, the National Art Gallery, the Museum of Civilization, Montreal, attending John R. Booth's church in Ottawa, and an Ottawa Senators hockey game. And in Spring, they went skating on the canal and sampled the maple syrup harvest. There were always touring and cultural activities students could attend at the National Arts Centre. Because of the LLC's central location in Ottawa, special guests were invited to speak to the students, both in and out of their classes; some stayed over in the guest suite to further enhance the students' learning opportunities.

The official opening of the LLC was October 9, 2002. It was a gala affair, held at the prestigious Chateau Laurier Hotel, with the Hon. Preston Manning, MP as guest speaker. Also in attendance were senior administrators from the University, and MPs and Senators who'd had our students as interns. A highlight was the presentation by the Booth family of the original (and now restored) painting of John R. Booth that would once again hang in the foyer of the Centre. Tours of the facility were given by the students throughout the weekend, along with a breakfast for local pastors, to acquaint them with TWU and ACTS, and our presence in Ottawa.

From the very beginning, it was determined that students coming to the LLC should not be charged more than if they were on TWU's Langley campus, taking the normal course-load of 15 semester hours. While our charitable status prevented us from earning a profit from our operations, the difference between tuition income and operating costs was made up by renting ground floor rooms to groups wanting a prestigious location for meetings, and from rental of parking spaces—for which there were many eager takers. Many students chose to remain in Ottawa following their Spring semester at the LLC, because they had job opportunities following their internships; so student life continued throughout the year. In short, it was a financially viable operating centre, once the initial purchase price had been raised.

The LLC gave TWU a "branding identity" in Ottawa. From being virtually unknown in Ottawa, TWU and its LLC became known to every Prime Minister, Governor-General and most Cabinet Ministers and MPs, because of the students' presence in or near their offices. Good staff and faculty, and careful recruiting from our most suitable students, ensured that they appreciated the unique opportunity they'd been given, and how important it was to perform well so the tradition could be continued. It wasn't long before LLC students became the preferred source from which MPs sought executive assistants and staffers. Placing our students became easier as time went on, as MPs couldn't get enough of our students to work for them. Every student has acknowledged after leaving the LLC that their experience and training there gave them invaluable assets for finding jobs on graduation. The work of the LLC in fulfilling the mission of TWU is best told through the testimony of the students themselves:

> "My experience at the LLC this semester has been amazing. I have been blessed with great co-workers and superiors within my internship, as well as caring and informed professors. Coming to Ottawa to participate in this program has given me a real understanding of what moving to a new place looks like. I have found that in coming here, I have managed the transition well. This, as a result, has given me confidence in planning the next steps in my life, whether that consists of seeking a job or entering into graduate studies."
>
> —Rachel Kohar, *History*; intern with the Association of Universities and Colleges of Canada (AUCC). Fall, 2011

"When you live at the LLC, you're living your education; the community, the classes, the downtown and the work is all about applying yourself to the lessons you have been taught. To no small extent, it forces you to engage the world while thinking about your and others' souls. To me, the LLC has been the perfect bridge to cross from the theoretical world of TWU to the practical world of politics, by equipping you to face this world, grounded in heavenly certainty."
—Tyler DeJong, *Political Studies*; Office of Bev Shipley, MP. Fall, 2009

"That which distinguishes a semester at the LLC from a 'normal' semester at TWU's Langley campus is your interaction on a variety of different levels with your peers, your professors and those whom you meet through your internship. A morning class about Modern Western Society would have me working through things intellectually, until I would get to work and be confronted with that society on a very practical level. As a Christianity and Culture major, I found the LLC to be a perfect fit."
—Nicole Den Haan, *Christianity and Culture*; Office of Brad Trost, MP. Fall, 2009

"Just as merely owning a toolbox will not build you a house, merely attending the LLC will not change your life. The LLC gives you every tool and resource possible, but you are the one who must show the initiative to use the tools available to you. The Laurentian Leadership Centre is the best program that Trinity Western University has to offer, because of its 'live, learn and work' environment. It has given me the best opportunities available, and has prepared me to confidently transition into full-time work as a political staffer. It has stretched me and grown me to adapt to the balancing act of a very busy, but fun life here in Ottawa. We have a tradition of excellence from the calibre of alumni who have come before us, and it is this precedence that opened doors to me, and will continue to open doors to future LLCers. I feel that I would not have had these doors opened, had I not attended the LLC, but tried to do it on my own. Trinity Western University is not just like any other university; we are called to a higher purpose 'for such a time as this', and the Laurentian Leadership Centre is an integral part of that calling."
—Jenna Andrews, *Communications*; Office of the Hon. Jason Kenney, Minister of Citizenship, Immigration and Multiculturalism. Spring, 2009

45

TWU's scholarly research in the Dead Sea Scrolls

For university professors, maintaining professional standing through active scholarly involvement in research, publishing and professional associations is very important. We had envisioned each graduate program eventually having a related institute, through which scholarly research by our faculty and their papers and books could be noted and published.

Very few Canadians know that TWU is now one of the world's premier centres for Dead Sea Scrolls research. And not long ago, the "little University that could" also acquired a matchless library of resources for study of the Septuagint; world-class Bible scholars now staff both Institutes, and world-class Bible scholars now come to Langley to study at them.

These developments began in 1994, when Dr. Craig Evans, then the Chair of our Religious Studies Department, came to Dr. Don Page, after attending the annual meeting of the Society of Biblical Literature, with an idea that he correctly understood could put religious studies at TWU on the international map. During a sabbatical leave, Craig had been working on a proposal for establishing a Master of Arts in Biblical Studies degree (our third graduate program). That MA degree could be greatly enhanced, he argued, through the simultaneous creation of a Dead Sea Scrolls Institute that would conduct cutting-edge research on the world-famous Scrolls—and, to our delight, particularly on the biblical portion of those Scrolls.

In his enthusiastic way, Craig laid out an ambitious plan whereby the joint launch of the MA in Biblical Studies and the Dead Sea Scrolls Institute would enhance our biblical research through a connection to the Scrolls, which were already attracting international scholarly and media interest. It could, he reasoned, make TWU a leading university in the field; and that would attract graduate students who wanted to study the Dead Sea Scrolls under the guidance of world-class Qumran scholars.

This was not to be taken lightly, as Craig was perhaps the University's most prolific scholar, as well as a superb teacher and a valuable and fully-engaged faculty member. While at the Society's meeting, he'd met Dr. Peter Flint from Southwestern College and Dr. Martin Abegg from Grace Seminary, whom Craig introduced

Martin Abegg, Craig Evans, and Peter Flint

to Dr. Don Page as world-renowned scholars working on the Dead Sea Scrolls. And here was the clincher: they might be interested in coming to TWU, if we could offer them graduate teaching as well as undergraduate classes; would we give them a call?

There was one catch to this however: how could we get the Academic Council, representing all academic disciplines on campus, to agree to support two appointments to the same department in one year? It was only through combining the MA proposal and the Dead Sea Scrolls Institute that we could provide enough tuition dollars to make these appointments, for any new graduate program had to be financially self-sufficient and not draw on undergraduate revenues. At the outset, Craig had already arranged that half of Peter's salary could be covered through teaching joint courses at ACTS. As to the start-up costs, Craig assured us that we could raise these through faculty-sponsored conferences.

Marty Abegg had been introduced to the Scrolls while taking a seminar at The Hebrew University in Jerusalem with Emmanuel Tov, who was assembling and editing scroll fragments containing the books of Joshua and Jeremiah. At that time, the Scrolls were well-known; but after 40 years, the bulk of them were still unpublished.

Upon returning to North America to continue his graduate studies at Hebrew Union College, Professor Abegg learned that HUC professor Ben Zion Wacholder had acquired a secret printed concordance of every word appearing in the Scrolls. As part of his doctoral research, and as a "gift" to Wacholder, Abegg reconstructed several unpublished copies of a text from the concordance. Dr. Abegg typed each word into his computer until he had reconstructed whole texts; and then, together with Wacholder, they published the texts to worldwide acclaim.

From the *New York Times* to *Newsweek*, Marty Abegg was dubbed the "scroll-buster" and the "man who freed the Scrolls."

Dr. Peter Flint had come to Notre Dame University from South Africa, because Notre Dame had the largest number of scholars studying the scrolls. He was granted admission to the underground vault at the Rockefeller Museum in Jerusalem where, as co-editor of the Psalms Scrolls, he began the painstaking work of deciding which pieces belonged to which manuscripts, and comparing the text to the standard biblical text. From Notre Dame, Dr. Flint, a consummate visionary, had gone to Southwestern College, where he'd established a very successful series of "Scrolls and Bible" seminars that related the Scriptures, early Judaism and Christianity, to the Dead Sea Scrolls.

1995—when Marty Abegg and Peter Flint arrived at TWU—was a memorable year, for it launched one of our greatest research initiatives, undertaken by the co-directors of the new Dead Sea Scrolls Institute under Craig Evans' leadership. While both Marty and Peter published several books based on their research, probably their most significant one was *The Dead Sea Scrolls Bible* published in 1999. The Dead Sea Scrolls offered confirmation of some Old Testament texts and added missing psalms that were more than 1,000 years older than any previously discovered biblical manuscripts. Along with their commentaries on these 220 texts, most of which had never before been translated into English, their first-time publication has allowed us to read the Bible very much as it was in the time of Jesus. Or, in the words of the great Biblical scholar, N.T. Wright, in his review of *The Dead Sea Scrolls Bible* for Century One Bookstore: "Here is a book we will soon wonder how we did without. Bible scholars will find it essential; students will find it stimulating and exciting; anyone interested in the beginnings of Judaism and Christianity will find it fascinating."

The scrolls are just part of the literary heritage of ancient Judaism; but they offer very valuable insights into the broader cultural matrix of this Old Testament period. As Dr. Abegg has written in an article in *Biblical Archaeology Review*:

> Scrolls scholarship remains an ideal launching point for an academic career... The scrolls... are ideally suited to serve any university's biblical, Jewish, theological, and religious studies programs. Qumran scholarship requires Greek, Hebrew, Aramaic, the study of the foundational texts of Judaism and Christianity, knowledge of the early church and rabbinic

> Judaism, as well as familiarity with Israelite religion… it's hard to imagine another research focus that would equip the early-career Biblical Studies scholar with such a broad preparation.

And from Peter Flint:

> The value of the scrolls… extends beyond academia. My work in this field rests on the unshakable conviction that the Dead Sea Scrolls are foundational to understanding the origins of Judaism and Christianity; and are, therefore, part of the underlying fabric of contemporary Western Culture. The Qumran finds provide exhilarating views of the past—an essential quality for academic posts in any sub-discipline of Biblical Studies—as well as plug us into larger questions of relevance to theological and religious studies. Questions about wealth, poverty, ethics, identity formation, community dynamics, and gender, to name a few, are only recently being asked of the Dead Sea Scrolls… It will be up to our current colleagues and the next generation of scholars to continue to read, research, and write about what the eminent scholar, William Foxwell Albright, famously called "the greatest archaeological find of the twentieth century."

In 2004, Peter Flint was named as a Tier 1 Canada Research Chair in Dead Sea Scrolls Studies. Hitherto, Religious Studies hadn't attracted much attention from the élite selection committee. Thus, Peter's appointment was very significant recognition in Canada for the discipline, as well as for TWU.

Because of his scholarly work on the Psalms and Cave One Isaiah Scrolls, Peter's chair grant was renewed in 2011. His ongoing research is contributing to the scholarly understanding of the evolution of both Judaism and Christianity, thereby ensuring that the Dead Sea Scrolls Institute at TWU will continue to be one of the world's leading centres for Dead Sea Scrolls research.

In 2015, seven former students who had gone on to earn their PhDs, and friends of Marty Abegg, published a *Festschrift* entitled *The War Scroll: Violence, War and Peace in the Dead Sea Scrolls and Related Literature: Essays in Honour of Martin G. Abegg on the Occasion of his 65th Birthday*. One of the contributors to this volume is Craig Evans, who had moved on to Acadia Divinity School and more recently to Houston Baptist University. All three of these pioneers continue to be very active researchers in Dead Sea Scrolls and beyond.

The legacy of Marty, Peter and Craig, and other members of TWU's Religious Studies Department, can be seen in the phenomenal amount of research inspired through the work of the Dead Sea Scrolls Institute, and their sharing of that research through publications and conferences.

Just one month after he arrived at TWU, Peter Flint persuaded his new colleagues to sponsor what would become the first of several semi-annual seminars on the Dead Sea Scrolls, with over 300 people attending the first one. Attendees came from churches, the Jewish community and the general public. These high-profile seminars not only gave our own faculty an opportunity to showcase their scholarship; they brought noted scholars from around the world to our campus.

For the past 12 years, upwards of 20-25 TWU alumni have met regularly at the annual meetings of the Society of Biblical Literatures to share their ongoing research, thereby enhancing the value of their collective work. It's not surprising that at least ten papers are presented annually by TWU alumni and professors at these conferences. A similar representation can be found at the Canadian Society for Biblical Studies, where fully 20 percent of participants are TWU students, graduates or professors. And the work will not end. There are literally thousands of fragments at our fingertips, listed as "miscellaneous" or "unidentified" in almost any volume of *Discoveries in the Judaean Desert* (DJD) series that are ripe for (re)discovery. Marty Abegg has remarked on "the number of times professors from other universities stopped me to relate just how appreciative they are of our work at Trinity."

Thanks to Craig's initiative, our esteemed faculty began directed studies for doctoral students who wished to study under their direction as part of the doctoral program at the University of Manchester. Many of our MA graduates have gone on to other prestigious universities in the United States and Europe to obtain their PhDs. Dr. Flint's research is contributing to the scholarly understanding of the evolution of two of the world's major religions, and is ensuring that Canada's Dead Sea Scrolls Institute at TWU will continue to be one of the world's leading centres for Dead Sea Scrolls research. Here is the testimony of one of them, Kipp Davis:

> I arrived at TWU at the beginning of the academic year 1995, with the intent of continuing my studies for professional pastoral ministry; but with the important supplement of a robust programme for learning the biblical languages. It was with this motivation that I enrolled simultaneously in introductory courses to Hebrew and Greek, and where I met two of my long-time mentors, Marty Abegg—who would become my MA thesis supervisor, and Peter Flint—for whom I would later serve as a research assistant in my first post-doctoral appointment. My arrival at

TWU coincided with the first Dead Sea Scrolls symposium, and facilitated my introduction to the Scrolls, which have subsequently formed the kernel of my on-going research.

While my time in the MA programme was spent in the programme's infancy, the high level of training and extremely valuable personal attention I received, even in those early years, paved the way to my own academic achievements: from entry to my successful completion of a PhD at the University of Manchester, to a research appointment at the University of Agder in Kristiansand, Norway, to the publication of my first book and beyond. The lessons I learned as a TWU graduate student, and the long-term relationships I forged with Peter, Marty, and Craig Evans for 20 years now, continue to direct my ongoing endeavours; they have been indispensable for directing my own study of the intersection between Old Testament texts, Jewish and Christian religion, and the manuscript artefacts that form a heritage of my faith.

46

Septuagint studies land in Langley

The Septuagint, the earliest Greek translation of the Old Testament and one of the key religious texts of the third century BC, also has a high profile at Trinity Western University today.

Sept. 17, 2005, TWU launched the Septuagint Institute (SI), a centre for Septuagint research, translation, and publication. Two Toronto professors—among the world's foremost authorities on the Septuagint—donated their personal libraries to further research in ancient Greek texts at TWU and ACTS, making Langley the new hub for Septuagint scholarship.

"The launch of the Septuagint Institute is a truly historic event, not only for our campus, but also for Canadian and international biblical scholarship," said Robert Hiebert PhD, ACTS Professor and Director of the new Institute.

"This research centre is the only one of its kind in North America."

An international team of more than thirty scholars, including TWU and ACTS professors Hiebert, Dirk Büchner, Peter Flint, and Larry Perkins, have recently completed translating portions of the Septuagint into English—the first such translation in 160 years, the *New English Translation of the Septuagint*. The complete work was published in 2008 by Oxford University Press, and was featured at a conference of world Septuagint scholars in September of that year at the Septuagint Institute at TWU. The SI team contributes translations of the first four books of the Hebrew Bible: *Bereshiet* ("In the beginning"—Genesis, by Dr. Hiebert), *Shemot* ("Names"—Exodus, by Dr. Perkins), *Vayikra* ("And He called"—Leviticus, by Dr. Büchner) and *B'midbar* ("In the wilderness"—Numbers, by Dr. Flint).

When asked why this kind of research captivates him, Dr. Hiebert replied, "The Septuagint is a fascinating and important body of literature to study, because it is the product of what is likely the first major translation project involving religious literature in history. It's also the first translation of the Hebrew Bible into another language, and it provides us with insight into the Hellenistic Jewish community's understanding of its Scriptures in the three centuries before the time of Jesus.

Rod Hiebert (centre) with Peter Flint and Larry Perkins

"We know that the Septuagint was the 'Old Testament' of the early Church, because the majority of the quotations of the Jewish Scriptures in the Greek New Testament come from the Septuagint. And when the biblical author spoke in 2 Timothy 3:16 of 'inspired Scripture', the Septuagint would have had as good a claim as any Bible version at the time to be included in that characterization."

The Septuagint Institute works with and complements TWU's Dead Sea Scrolls Institute.

47

'Christian Leaders in Residence' program

By Dr. Don Page

Leadership development and campus life can be insular, so we wanted to expose our campus to prominent Christian leaders significantly impacting the very secular world into which most of our students will be graduating. To do this, we began a Christian Leader in Residence program, modeled on the Leader in Residence program at the University of Manitoba.

Each semester, we invite a prominent Christian leader to come to campus for three days. A dorm room in Macmillan Hall was remodeled into a guest suite, so the leaders can spend as much time as possible interacting with students. The program typically involves a chapel talk, during which the recipient receives an award; dinner with the student council executive; lunch with faculty associated with their area of expertise; one or more guest lectures in relevant classes; and an off-campus speaking engagement to raise the profile of TWU and give something to the local community, such as an address at a mayor's prayer breakfast. The chapel talk was to be the highlight, with the Christian Leader in Residence sharing his or her testimony, and showing how being a Christian is relevant in their business or profession. In between these scheduled events the leader is encouraged to spend as much time as possible with individual students or groups in the cafeteria.

Among the recipients have been: the Hon. Jake Epp, Minister of Energy Mines and Resources; Milton Fair, President of the Saskatchewan Wheat Pool; William Pollard, CEO of Service Masters; Judge Bob Conroy, of the Supreme Court of Saskatchewan; Gerry Organ, an all-time record holder in the Canadian Football League; David Ray, President of Apple Canada; Bob Kinney, President of Safeway Canada; Kevin Jenkins, CEO of Canadian Airlines; Diane Haskett, Mayor of London, Ontario; and John Kelsall, Vice-President of Operations at Canadian Pacific Railways. What each of these dynamic Christian leaders did was to show our students what it meant to be a Christian leader in the various marketplaces of life.

We also reach out beyond the campus through short-term missions projects, leadership placement and shadowing programs, and the Laurentian Leadership Centre in Ottawa for senior students who want to connect with the leadership of our nation. It's no accident that, on a per capita basis, more Trinity Western alums have been elected as Members of Parliament than from any other university in the country. We also have more of our leadership-trained students working in parliamentary offices than any other university.

Leadership development has become our distinctive as a Christian university built on excellence.

AT THE SUPREME COURT OF CANADA—Executive Vice President and Legal Challenge spokesperson, Guy Saffold, with Harro Van Brummelen, Dean and Professor of TWU's School of Education, pause on the steps of the Supreme Court of Canada, November 2000. TWU Archives

PART VIII

Meeting new challenges

There are two ways of finding the truth: by reason, or by revelation.

But we should always bring the fruit of our reasoning to the revelation for validation, not the other way around, for true revelation comes from a superior intellect. However, when any revelation is proposed, it, too, must be examined—even though ultimately, it must be accepted by faith.

But in a society dominated by militant Secularism, as ours is, there will always be Establishment bodies seeking to prohibit the acceptance of revealed truth, no matter how much it has been validated experientially. In such a case, the responsibility of the defenders of revelation is to state the defence firmly, but respectfully—and let the God of revelation contend for His truth. If we enter the lists with hubris, He may not respond. But if we meet our adversaries with appropriate humility before God, and with the assurance that He is the God of truth—and that therefore all truth is His truth—we can be confident that He will defend His own Word.

—editor

Many found it astonishing—since religious liberty and freedom of expression are both guaranteed in Canada's Charter of Rights and Freedoms, *which is an integral part of the Canadian Constitution—when a B.C. government agency, even after two of its own subcommittees had approved TWU's teacher training program, tried to reject it (not because of anything in the program itself, but only because of TWU's Community Covenant, by which scholars who so choose are able to live and study in a community where behavioural standards are conducive to learning). The team that defended Christian students' rights was inspiring: our lead lawyer was a TWU graduate; one of his assistants was a TWU faculty member; several TWU students took part; and our media spokesman was Guy Saffold, who in the next four chapters recounts our biggest legal adventure—all the way to the Supreme Court of Canada!*

—Neil Snider

Our legal team believed the arguments based on the *Canadian Charter of Rights and Freedoms* would be critical to the University's case. *Charter* law principles, however, apply only to persons and not to organizations. In order to raise these arguments it was necessary for our objection to be filed in company with an actual TWU student who could assert that his or her *Charter* rights had been breached. This was a difficult request to make of a student. Inevitably the student's name would become quite public, perhaps triggering harassment and maybe even damaging future prospects for employment as a teacher. With courage and faith, after prayer with her parents, Donna Lindquist—a wonderful young graduate of the TWU program—agreed to be that student. Ever since, the full name of the case has been *British Columbia College of Teacher versus Trinity Western University and Donna Gail Lindquist*. It was entirely consistent with the commitment of our graduates and the godly character of Donna Lindquist that when a need to stand for Christian values arose, she answered the call.

Dr. Guy Saffold

48

The Legal Challenge

By Dr. Guy Saffold

Trinity Western's acceptance into the AUCC, and its subsequent name change from Trinity Western College to Trinity Western University, ignited an era of rapid growth as we added both students and degree programs. Although we couldn't have foreseen the speed of our growth, we worked extremely hard to think strategically about programs that would have a "transforming impact on culture," as defined in our core values.

Our Mission Statement committed the University to preparing godly Christian leaders to fully engage in "the various marketplaces of life." Early on, we'd identified the field of Education as a high-priority area for program development; and, in 1985, we began to offer a degree program in Education. Students who completed this four-year degree could continue directly into the fifth-year Professional Development Program (PDP) that was in place at Simon Fraser University. This would provide them with the practical training that would enable them to be certified as elementary school teachers in British Columbia.

Under the outstanding leadership of Dr. Harro Van Brummelen, the Education Program grew rapidly, and our graduates compiled an exceptional record of achievement. Both we and the Education Department at Simon Fraser were very pleased with the results. Still, we knew that there was no guarantee that Simon Fraser would continue our joint arrangement indefinitely. Therefore, we began to take the necessary steps to enable Trinity Western to offer its own PDP program. However, just when this process seemed to be moving ahead smoothly, signs of the significant difficulties to come began to appear.

An application to the B.C. College of Teachers

The first difficulties were merely procedural. In 1987, Trinity Western made an application to the Ministry of Education for permission to operate its own PDP program, and it was greeted with the formal approval of the Ministry. The next step was to submit the program to the teacher certification body for the province, the British Columbia College of Teachers (BCCT). We submitted the application in 1988, anticipating reasonably quick approval; but were surprised when BCCT advised that it had yet to develop the evaluation criteria necessary to approve program proposals from private institutions. The process of developing those criteria, we were told, would likely take several years.

Although the delay was unanticipated and seemed unduly long, we agreed to withdraw our application for five years. Negotiations with Simon Fraser resulted in an agreement to offer a module of their PDP program on the Trinity Western campus, greatly increasing ease of access for our graduates. Despite this increased convenience, we continued to plan toward offering the program in our own name. When the BCCT announced in November of 1994 that the criteria were ready, Trinity Western had its application completed and submitted within 60 days.

Again, all seemed to go well at first. The BCCT process required four levels of review, beginning with the Program Approval Sub-Committee which gave our application a first look to see if it at least appeared to meet its standards. The result was positive, and the application moved to the second step: a visit by a BCCT Program Approval Team to the Trinity Western campus, along with another thorough review of the application. The intense effort and hard work of Dr. Van Brummelen and the Trinity Western Education faculty were rewarded with another positive recommendation, and so we moved on to the third step, a review by the Teacher Education Programs Committee.

We fully anticipated that this Committee would grant its approval. But, on May 17, 1996, it rejected our application, citing seven specific concerns that included insufficient library resources and, more importantly, a concern that Trinity Western's "belief systems" might have a negative impact on the capacity of TWU graduates to function within the public school system. That last concern proved to be the central issue. The committee was essentially assuming that TWU's Christian "belief systems" might be harmful to children in public school classrooms!

Dr. Van Brummelen responded to these concerns with a thorough and detailed document that addressed each item in depth. His response was brilliant, and in response, the BCCT Committee recommended approval of our Education program along with certain conditions, such as a period of evaluation and strengthening of education-related library resources over the first several years.

With that hurdle overcome, our application was forwarded to the fourth and final stage of approval, which involved a vote by the full Council of the BCCT. All seemed ready to go forward, and yet again, we anticipated approval to launch our own PDP program the following fall.

Unfortunately, it was not to be.

When Trinity Western's proposal reached the full Council of the BCCT, a firestorm broke out over our Community Standards statement which prohibits "biblically condemned" practices, including homosexual behaviour. On May 16, 1996, the BCCT Council rejected Trinity Western's proposed program. We immediately appealed for reconsideration, explaining that homosexual students are welcome to attend Trinity Western but, like all other students, their behaviour was be expected to be consistent with our belief that sexual intimacy should occur only between a married man and woman. The BCCT Council was not persuaded, and on June 29, 1996, it issued a final rejection of the program.

The Council's grounds for rejection were two-fold: first, it maintained that Trinity Western's prohibition of homosexual behaviour might lead to trained teachers who acted with prejudice against homosexual children in the public schools. It should be noted that, by this time, Trinity Western had been graduating teachers for more than 10 years, and there was not a shred of evidence to support this contention. Indeed, all available evidence pointed to the opposite conclusion—that Trinity Western-trained teachers were exceptionally compassionate and capable in dealing with all students. Nonetheless, the BCCT chose to believe that the public school system must be protected against the danger of "biased teachers, trained at TWU."

The second ground for rejection was the BCCT's contention that our community standards constituted "illegal discrimination" against homosexual persons. The Council said its mandate required it to decide issues "in the public interest," and in their view, the "public interest" was incompatible with granting approval (or an endorsement, as they saw it) to a program in which was embedded a "discriminatory principle."

Needless to say, the rejection was severely disappointing to our Education Department, coming as it did after literally years of diligent and careful work. However, disappointment must be accepted and worked through; far more dangerous to Trinity Western was the risk that the BCCT decision, if allowed to stand, would challenge the legitimacy not only of our Education programs, but potentially all our programs.

The rejection triggered an intense period of review, prayer, and planning within Trinity Western. President Snider and the Board of Governors concluded that the BCCT decision was critical to the future of Trinity Western and could not be allowed to stand unchallenged. Rather, Trinity Western *must* respond with the firmest objection. Accordingly, we filed an application for a judicial review of the decision by the British Columbia Supreme Court (in B.C.'s provincial court system, the provincial "supreme court" is the first court to which such applications are made).

With much prayer for guidance, and strong determination to defend Trinity Western's position, we quickly labelled this 1996 circumstance, "The Legal Challenge." It was a larger challenge than we suspected! For the next five years, we would be involved in what might well be the most critical battle in the history of our University.

Engaging the Legal Challenge

After we had made the decision to engage in a court challenge, the next most important decision was to select a lawyer to lead the process. For years, Trinity Western had relied with great satisfaction on the legal advice and services of Mr. John Cherrington. But after careful consultation with Mr. Cherrington, President Snider made a strategic decision to place the case in the hands of a young lawyer who was also a Trinity Western alumnus, Mr. Robert (Bob) Kuhn. (Years later, Bob would become the fourth president of Trinity Western University.)

Bob Kuhn and his legal team of Kevin Sawatsky (a lawyer and a Trinity Western faculty member in the School of Business) and Kevin Boonstra (a young lawyer, only recently called to the bar) began an intense effort to prepare our case for the B.C. Supreme Court.

At the same time, we realized that this type of legal case was certain to generate public interest, and it was imperative to prepare for the inevitable scrutiny of the media. Consultants were engaged to take a number of key leaders through an in-depth process of training in media relations.

I will not soon forget our media trainer. We had engaged an experienced journalist who fit perfectly the stereotype of a cynical, hard-bitten reporter, who was well-accustomed to asking probing and aggressive questions. Over several days, we were led through training sessions in media strategies and, most significantly, interviews before a TV camera. Drs. Snider, Page, Van Brummelen and I took turns being interviewed—or, should I say, being pummeled with questions by our reporter. He asked every hard and difficult question we could imagine. We tested and refined our answers over and over again.

As we came to the end of our media training, the consultants recommended that Trinity Western choose just one person to be the consistent spokesperson for the University. To both my surprise and dismay, I was the choice. The thought of

Bob Kuhn, Kevin Sawatsky, Kevin Boonstra

being grilled by reporters from print, radio, and television was not a welcome one. But my colleagues maintained that I was the best suited for this role and, in the end, after much discussion and with their sincere support and encouragement, I agreed.

Over the next five years, I would represent Trinity Western in literally hundreds of interviews that included almost all the major print, radio, and news outlets in Canada. Through all those years, I lived with a certain degree of dread that in some unguarded moment, I would utter a few poorly-considered words that would be seized upon as evidence against Trinity Western. Yet the intense period of preparation was invaluable, and so thorough that only once was I asked a question for which I was not prepared. In a larger sense, I had often stated, and taught my students, that sometimes God makes us wiser than we really are—a gracious and much-needed assist for me. It held true for my journey as the University's spokesperson. God was faithful and the much-feared verbal slips never occurred. He kept Trinity Western (and me) safe, right to the end.

49

Stating our case

By Dr. Guy Saffold

From May 5 to 9 of 1997, the Trinity Western case was heard by the B.C. Supreme Court, sitting in Chilliwack, B.C. On that first morning, I had an interview with BCTV, the provincial affiliate for CTV national news—as did Thomas Berger, the opposing counsel who was representing the B.C. College of Teachers (BCCT). Mr. Berger was confident, polished and a man of some presence, accompanied by his daughter, Erin, who was also a lawyer, working with him on the case. He had been a former leader of the provincial New Democratic Party (a political party with socialist leanings) and, after that, a justice of the B.C. Supreme Court. By comparison, I felt ill-prepared.

By 2:00 p.m., we were underway, with Mr. Justice W.H. Davies presiding. Our lead lawyer, Bob Kuhn, was very pleased with the assignment of Judge Davies, a long-time Chilliwack resident and a former partner in Bob's firm, Baker Newby. He was, Bob felt, one of the best we could have hoped for. Attending court with me were Academic Vice-President Dr. Don Page, Drs. Harro Van Brummelen and Joy McCullough from our Education Program, and several Trinity Western students.

Bob Kuhn, with the assistance of Kevin Sawatsky, began his opening statement to the Court by declaring that this case was about Canadians' freedom to think and believe according to their conscience, without fear that the government or its agencies might act against them.

The case was also about Donna Lindquist, a 20-year old Trinity Western student who had never in her life said or done anything wrong, but now was accused of wrong-doing by signing the Trinity Western Community Standards Statement, which affirms her religious beliefs.

Finally, he said, the case was also about Trinity Western University, an institution that hadn't done anything wrong, but rather, had over many years earned high academic respect as an accredited Canadian University.

The views of the BCCT, Bob argued, had no evidentiary basis. Not only has Trinity Western never been found guilty of discrimination, but there has never even been a complaint of discrimination. Yet, despite this lack of evidence, the BCCT was suggesting that Trinity Western University practiced discrimination so serious that it could not be trusted to operate a teacher training program. Even more surprising, the BCCT had reached these serious conclusions although its own subcommittees and teams after studying Trinity Western and its application, had recommended approval of the program. Indeed, it was only after its own committees recommended the program be approved that the BCCT suddenly concluded that Donna Lindquist was unfit, unqualified, and unprepared to teach in the public school classrooms of B.C.; and further, that Trinity Western University was unfit and unqualified to prepare her to be a teacher.

Bob then moved into a summary of facts in the case. He traced the process from its beginning, almost ten years earlier. He explained how a BCCT program subcommittee concluded there were sufficient grounds to authorize a Program Approval Team, which then assessed the program and recommended approval to the Teacher Education Programs Committee—which then recommended approval to the full Council. He pointed out that throughout this process, Trinity Western's character as a Christian university was known to the examiners, as was the nature of the Community Standards.

These issues were all carefully investigated, and none was found to be a barrier to approval. In fact, when the Teacher Education Program Committee recommended its approval on May 15, nine of the 20-member BCCT Council had agreed. Then, unexpectedly, one day later, on May 16, the Council rejected Trinity Western's application.

What had happened, Bob asked, in the 24 hours between the two meetings? Why had there been such a sudden and radical change in support for Trinity Western?

But when the University had inquired why the application was denied, the BCCT "was unable to further clarify or reconstruct the reasons for the decision." Bob suggested it was strange for a public body to have difficulty in explaining its reasons for so serious a decision.

Bob then traced Trinity Western's attempts to gain clarification, and the BCCT's persistent vagueness in response. He pointed out the BCCT's abortive and improperly balanced attempt to request legal advice from the gay community; its refusal to specify the nature of the legal issues reviewed, or even to clarify what laws were being considered.

Bob also pointed out that education graduates of nearby Christian colleges in the United States, which have standards similar to Trinity Western's, are accepted for certification by the BCCT. Why, he asked, would the BCCT accept graduates from these U.S. colleges without question, then behave in this startling way toward a fully-accredited Canadian university?

The legal argument Bob laid out was thoroughly prepared, and devastating in its critique of the BCCT's process. Furthermore, he said, the BCCT had construed its jurisdiction over-broadly; acted outside the legislature-authorized limits; made use of irrelevant information; failed even to attempt to gain relevant information; and engaged in numerous violations of procedural fairness.

If these egregious errors weren't enough to demonstrate the BCCT's unfairness, then the BCCT had surely exceeded the purposes for which it was established, by attempting to rule on the religious beliefs of Trinity Western University and Donna Lindquist. The Council had failed to consider B.C.'s Human Rights legislation, which explicitly protects religious freedom; and, instead of guarding *against* discrimination, BCCT had itself engaged in unjustifiable discrimination against Trinity Western and its students. This was also in direct violation of the *Canadian Charter of Rights and Freedoms*, Section Two, which protects freedom of conscience, freedom of expression, freedom of association, and equality before the law.

A number of organizations had made an application with the Court to be "interveners" in support of TWU's arguments, including the British Columbia Civil Liberties Association and the Catholic Civil Rights League.

Then Mr. Berger, representing the BCCT, began his assault on our position. He was about 60 years old, with gray hair, a dignified presence and a reputation for being an impressive and highly persuasive opponent in court. "Prepare yourself for a wild ride," Bob Kuhn told me as we entered the courtroom, "and pray that the judge will be able to think clearly."

According to Berger, Bob had made many elegant points about the rights and freedoms of Canadians, but had entirely misunderstood the essence of the case. The issue wasn't whether Trinity Western students would be "unfit" to teach in the public schools; but rather that they would be "unqualified" to teach in the public schools because their entire teacher training process had been conducted under the auspices of a Christian institution that holds a position toward homosexuals that is incompatible with "fundamental Canadian values."

He contended that requiring a portion of the teacher training program for Trinity Western students to be at a public institution was a simple, reasonable, and minimally intrusive safeguard to ensure they'd have experience in dealing with those who might be different from themselves.

As his speech wore on, his antipathy toward Trinity Western became visibly obvious.

"Just look at the 'Community Standards'," he fumed. "Look at the last paragraph," he said with great sarcasm. "This paragraph says to a prospective student: *REALITY CHECK! Did you think you were enrolling in AGU (Anything Goes University)? Did you think you were enrolling in IGU (Instant Gratification University)? Did you think you were enrolling in DAYPU (Do As You Please University)? Well, you're not! You are enrolling in Trinity Western University, and if you can't adopt these standards you should* **go away.**"

Court adjourned for the day before Mr. Berger could conclude, and it was agreed that he'd continue the following morning. With no ill will toward Mr. Berger, many Trinity Western supporters prayed that the purposes of those who opposed us would be frustrated. And we were soon to see those prayers answered

Mr. Berger further belaboured his arguments the next morning; and on a number of occasions, he seemed to lose clarity in his train of thought, leaving logical holes that left our jaws gaping. At times, he even appeared to contradict his own statements; and at other times, he made substantial errors in his statements of 'fact'.

To a certain extent, Thomas Berger had entered the courtroom as a Goliath: a man of large reputation and deep experience, who had powerful contacts and associations, and was a former Supreme Court Justice himself. By comparison Bob Kuhn, with Kevin Sawatsky and Kevin Boonstra, were our Davids, willing to challenge Goliath. They were young by comparison, and had neither Berger's reputation nor experience. But on this day, Goliath appeared to stumble badly. He was repeatedly interrupted and pressed by Justice Davies to explain gaps in his logic.

The day ended badly for Mr. Berger and his arguments. Bob warned us that it was too early to claim victory, as there was much more argument to come. But, for that day, we were all proud of our Davids. They had done an outstanding job.

On Friday, the fifth day of court, Mr. Berger concluded his arguments, and Bob rose to reply. He'd previously explained to us that a reply cannot restate, reiterate, or emphasize. Further, a long reply might invite a rebuttal reply from the opponent, and thus give them the last word, as no more speaking would be permitted. Instead, he'd told us that a good reply is short and concise, mentioning only the key points that need correction.

True to his words, Bob's reply met every criterion for a superb response. He stated that Mr. Berger had mischaracterized the arguments against TWU. Again and again he replied, "We do not believe this is what was said." It would therefore be important for the judge to review the actual submissions. Mr. Berger had also mischaracterized some of the most relevant legislation in a way that was prejudicial to us. Along with a number of other legal points, Bob reminded Justice Davies that the issue had created a cloud of uncertainty over Trinity Western University, and that the pall of this cloud caused damage that may well be irreparable. In order for the parties to gain finality, this issue must be resolved by the court.

With that, Bob concluded defense of Trinity Western's position.

Justice Davies announced that he would be occupied with other matters through the balance of May, but that he would likely be able to review this case in June. Our legal team was pleased with the court process, even though we didn't yet have a decision. But Bob invited all of us to share in a time of praise to God, thanksgiving for what had developed in court, and continuing our appeal for a just decision.

One of our group observed that our feeling of relief was akin to the sense one has after completion of the last final exam: a positive feeling of freedom that nevertheless has, buried within it, the recognition that the professor has yet to mark the paper and assign a final grade. I sent a message to the campus community that simply said, "Keep praying!"

50

The Court of Appeal

We'd come a long way. In September of 1997, Justice Davies of the B.C. Supreme Court had issued a ruling in favour of TWU:

> *"I am therefore remitting the matter back to the Council* [BCCT] *and directing that it approve TWU's Teacher Education Program for accreditation purposes, subject to the conditions recommended by the Teacher Education Programs Committee."*

It was a tremendous victory! We had felt like David tackling Goliath; and now, Goliath had been defeated! Justice Davies had not only rejected the arguments put forward by the BCCT, but had taken the additional step of ordering them to approve our program, subject to seven conditions to which we had previously agreed.

It could have ended there. But (not unexpectedly) the BCCT appealed the decision to the B.C. Court of Appeal. That Court agreed to hear the appeal, and was scheduled for June 15 to 17 of 1998, the following year.

There had been significant media coverage given to the case, so we expected a great deal of media interest during the Appeals Court hearings at the Robson Square Law Courts in Vancouver.

Media attention is always a mixed blessing. On the one hand, it gave us a larger audience when we made public statements in our defense. On the other, it kept drawing public attention to the fact that we had to defend ourselves and our University against the misperception of illegal discrimination.

When we arrived at court, I saw a large group of reporters and TV cameras, and immediately readied myself to answer their questions. But the media scrum showed no interest in us! Instead, they suddenly veered off in another direction where a provocatively dressed woman waved to them as she approached the doors to the court.

As it happened, our case had been scheduled at the same time as the case against

Gillian Guess, a comely Vancouver actress who was on trial for jury tampering. While serving on the jury of a murder trial, Ms. Guess was alleged to have had an affair with the defendant. The case was so sensational that media crews had flown in to Vancouver from New Zealand and Germany. Photographers were everywhere each day as Ms. Guess arrived each day in very tight and showy outfits.

So outrageous was her wardrobe, day by day (considering that she was on trial concerning an alleged sexual affair), that her lawyers developed an argument stating that she didn't have enough common sense to see what other people could clearly see—and therefore she should not be considered guilty! This "too-stupid-to-know-better defense" collapsed and failed. She was convicted and sentenced to 18 months at a women's detention facility colloquially known in court and media circles as "Camp Cupcake."

I mention this case because it was a huge benefit to us. It kept the media's attention elsewhere, and our case could proceed efficiently inside the courtroom, away from the cameras and reporters. This was much to our advantage, because the Court could then focus more on the issues, and not on public (or media) outcry.

There were three judges present: the Chair, Mr. Justice Goldie, with Mr. Justice Braidwood to his left and Madame Justice Rolls on his right. Thomas Berger was there, with his daughter Erin, just as at the first hearing. Our three-person legal team (Bob Kuhn, Kevin Sawatsky and Kevin Boonstra, as before) was present, along with representatives from the Catholic Civil Rights League and the B.C. Civil Liberties Association, which were both intervening in our favour. In addition, a large contingent from Trinity Western attended the hearing to offer their support, including Drs. Harro Van Brummelen, Joy McCullough and Bob Burkinshaw, plus a number of TWU students.

Mr. Berger began by saying, "M'Lords and M'Lady, it's an imperfect world. The College [of teachers] was asked to make a difficult judgment. It doesn't intend to prohibit TWU graduates from teaching. It merely says that you should take year five of your program at Simon Fraser University. This has worked well; let it continue. And that is, very simply, what this case is all about."

The balance of his arguments were the same as before: the BCCT believed teachers trained only at Trinity Western University wouldn't be adequately prepared to teach in public schools. Consequently, they should continue to spend at least one year in the rigorously secular Simon Fraser University program. Moreover, the BCCT believed it was not in the "public interest" for it to approve a program that, in their view, was based on discrimination against homosexuals.

Our legal team offered its effective arguments and then the B.C. Civil Liberties

Association argued, with clarity, on behalf of Trinity Western. Its submission to the Court stated:

> It is respectfully submitted that the issue in this case is not whether homosexuality is right or wrong; or whether one agrees with the Bible and the code of conduct of TWU. It is about whether an agency of the State, namely the Council of the College of Teachers, may assume jurisdiction over matters which are not expressly provided for under the enactment which confers jurisdiction on it. It is about whether that agency of the State can infringe fundamental freedoms without any evidence of any harm to anyone. It is ultimately about whether religious persons are free to become school teachers in British Columbia.
>
> One may not agree with the views contained in the Bible and TWU's code of conduct. Nevertheless, the teachers and students of TWU should be free to hold and express such views, and to associate with other like-minded persons, without fear of reprisal or state sanction."
> —*from the BCCLA Factum to the B.C. Court of Appeal*

Prior to his courtroom submission, Dr. Harro van Brummelen and I had a very interesting conversation with John Westwood, then-Executive Director of the B.C. Civil Liberties Association. He was most pleasant. I said that because of the BCCLA's strong secular orientation, this must be a difficult case for them to intervene in. "Not at all," he responded. "It's very clear to us that we should be here. We work from principles." The principled stand of the BCCLA, defending our rights even though they disagreed with our position, was most welcome.

In the end, the Court of Appeal ruled two to one in favour of Trinity Western. We now had two clear legal victories in our favour, and hoped that the BCCT might relent and agree to work with us to implement our final teacher training year.

But it was not to be.

In December of 1999, the rest of the world was concerned about an anticipated event called "Y2K"—the moment when the clock in every computer in the world would have to change from dates coded in the 1900s to dates for the new millennium. There was some uncertainty as to whether critical computers would continue to function.

At Trinity Western, however, our attention was fixed on the announcement just before Christmas that the Supreme Court of Canada would hear our case the following November.

We were on our way to Ottawa and the final leg of our "legal challenge."

51

'On the bird'

By Dr. Guy Saffold

"Five minutes to the bird!"

I was deep in the basement of the CBC building in Vancouver with Mr. Doug Smart, Registrar of the British Columbia College of Teachers (BCCT). Sitting shoulder to shoulder in front of the TV cameras, we were both wired with microphones and waiting for an interview by the hosts of the *CBC Morning Show* in Toronto to begin. Because it was to be a live interview, time had been booked on the Anik satellite, otherwise known as "the bird."

"Bird is locked," the technician called, and suddenly the satellite feed from Toronto appeared on our screens. A segment on healthy ways to cook vegetables was to be followed by our interview which would examine the Supreme Court of Canada case of *The British Columbia College of Teachers versus Trinity Western University and Donna Gail Lindquist*. Ms. Lindquist was essential to our case, since we were arguing that the BCCT's decision violated rights under the *Canadian Charter of Rights and Freedoms*; and since an argument under the *Charter* must be made on behalf of a specific citizen, Donna was bravely willing to be cited as the person at the centre of the case.

"What a jarring leap—from vegetables to religious freedom," I thought to myself. That sense of discontinuity only increased when the *Morning Show* hosts announced the segment on the TWU Supreme Court case, and promised that it would be followed by a *very special* segment on changing fashions in baby clothing. There I was—sandwiched in a 24-hour news cycle between vegetables and baby clothing.

Despite the surreal feelings of that day, our case was gaining national attention. We were headed to the Supreme Court of Canada, and knowledgeable observers were calling it the most significant religious freedom case to go before the Canadian legal system in decades. The outcome, it was predicted, would have a major impact on whether freedoms for religious organizations like Trinity Western would be protected, or significantly limited.

It had taken four years and more than a million dollars in legal and other expenses to get us to this place; but we were, at last, approaching the final decision that would determine the fate of our proposed teachers' education program.

Our segment began, and the hosts peppered both Mr. Smart and me with questions: "Why was the BCCT concerned about Trinity Western's position?" and "Why was Trinity Western so opposed to homosexual persons?" Mr. Smart and I were by now veterans of this kind of interview, having done it together several times. We each offered our usual answers.

He said the BCCT was concerned that Trinity Western-trained teachers wouldn't be adequately prepared for public school classrooms, and that our "discriminatory" Community Standards could not responsibly be approved by a body charged with guarding the public trust.

I responded that there was no evidence that the teachers we had trained—for more than 10 years—had ever been anything but excellent. Rather, I said, this case would decide whether Canada would continue to protect the religious freedoms of faith groups and individuals, or begin a dangerous erosion of those rights, which are guaranteed in Canada's *Charter of Rights and Freedoms*.

"The Supreme Court of British Columbia," I said, "ruled that the BCCT position was patently unreasonable. It's our hope that the Supreme Court of Canada will uphold that ruling."

Mr. Smart moved to respond, but the hosts jumped in and thanked us for being with them. The interview was over and the last statement had fallen to me—always an advantage in such situations.

"Releasing the bird," the technician announced. The hosts disappeared as the satellite link ended; but the journey to the Supreme Court of Canada would continue.

Throughout the year 2000, our legal team had worked hard to prepare our case. Under Bob Kuhn's leadership, our lawyers worked to focus and sharpen every point. We had to be prepared in every way.

For me and the Trinity Western media relations team, this meant a steady stream of interviews. The scope of interest in the case had increased as it rose to each new level of the court system. Now we were giving interviews not only to Canadian national outlets such as the CBC, *The Globe and Mail*, and Conrad Black's new paper, *The National Post*; but also to the *Wall Street Journal*, *The Washington Post*, and many others in the United States.

52

'The heart of the king is in the hand of the LORD'

By Dr. Guy Saffold

In September of 2000, I travelled to Japan to teach leadership at a conference for church planters at a spectacular retreat near Mt. Fuji. I tried to keep my attention on the men and women before me; but my thoughts kept flowing back to Langley, where Doris Olafsen and her external relations team were preparing a marathon cross-country media and prayer event that would be part of our final push before we went to the Supreme Court.

We wanted to put our case to the public, as we had been doing for several years, in an effort to raise both funds and prayer support. We needed to raise a significant amount of money to pay for the legal challenge; it had already consumed more than a million dollars, and there were more expenses still to come. Even more urgently, however, we needed prayer support, and our hope was that this tour would rally thousands of believers across the country to pray.

We had settled on the theme for the tour because we knew that, ultimately, our case was in God's hands:

> *"The king's heart is in the hand of the LORD, like the rivers of water;*
> *He turns it wherever He wishes.*"[1]

We wanted to remind our friends, donors, alumni, and the campus community to continue to plead our case before Him and to pray for the hearts and minds of the nine justices of the Supreme Court of Canada. We prayed that God would give them a clear vision of justice and a deep commitment to the freedom of conscience and faith that we believe are critical elements of Canada's values. These biblical principles had made our country the envy of people around the world, and we hoped that they would not be lost.

---
[1] Proverbs 21:1, (NKJV)

I arrived back in Canada toward the end of September; and the very next day, jet-lagged but energized, I joined the rest of the public relations team for a seven-day, 10-city tour. In each city, we had organized three events: a radio or TV interview, a press conference, and a prayer rally in one of the larger churches. We flew from place to place so fast that it was hard to keep track of where we were. More than once, we checked into a hotel at 2:00 a.m., only to check out by 5:00 a.m. after a quick shower and a short nap. Somewhere along the way, someone on the team began calling our adventure "Mr. Toad's Wild Ride." As a result, I acquired the handle "Toad"; Doris Olafsen became "Ratty" and the others of our team were referred to as "Mole", "Badger", "Rabbit" and others.

It was during a radio interview in Edmonton, Alberta, that I was asked the one question in five years for which I was not prepared. Perhaps trying to throw me off my points, the radio host asked: "How much money do you make?" I went blank for a moment, then responded, "How much money do *you* make?"

The interviewer laughed and said, "Let's move on." This was one of the many occasions on which I felt that God gave me quicker wits than I would normally possess.

The ambush

A similar incident occurred in Toronto, as I was being interviewed on the largest noon-time radio show in the city. It seemed to be standard practice that when we arrived at a studio, the radio host would greet our team warmly. (After all, they don't build audience numbers by interviewing intimidated, tongue-tied guests.) In addition, the other members of the public relations team typically would be invited into the studio with me. But not this time.

The team members were confined to the control room, and the hosts—a husband-and-wife team—were cold and efficient. They began to pepper me with the usual questions about 'Why is Trinity Western hostile to homosexuals?' I was prepared for these, explaining that we welcome all to study at Trinity Western, but our community is committed to observing the traditional view of marriage between a man and woman, and to behaviour that helps to maintain in the community an atmosphere of scholarly decorum and study.

Not long into the interview, I discovered the reason for our cool reception. The hosts had also arranged for John Fisher, the president of EGALE (Equality for Gays and Lesbians Everywhere) to phone in to the program for an on-air debate. No one had informed us of this; we were ambushed! I prayed silently that God would give me a calm spirit, and help me to avoid any damaging confrontation.

"Mr. Fisher," the male host asked, "what do you think of what these people at Trinity Western are doing?"

"It's terrible," he responded, "the way these narrow-minded religious bigots are forcing their views down the throats of children in the public schools. This should never be allowed!"

Turning back to me, the host crisply said, "Well, what do you say to that, doctor?" He clearly thought we'd been pressed to the wall, yet I recall thinking, "God, you've given my opponent into my hands!"

I responded by saying, "I couldn't agree with your caller more. There are Christian children, Jewish children, Sikh children, Muslim children and even children of no faith at all in our public school classrooms. It would be a terrible abuse for any teacher to force religious views on them. We train our teachers to respect each student's unique background. So I think your caller has made a very important point."

This wasn't the response they'd expected! The female host then picked up the thread by asking Mr. Fisher for his response. Still somewhat befuddled by my comments, he said, "Well, I'm not convinced that their graduates will be gay-positive."

At this point, God did something remarkable again. "What's that—gay-positive?" the male host asked, "A blood type?"

Before Mr. Fisher could answer, I jumped in: "That's the wrong thing to say! Mr. Fisher has raised a serious concern: that gay and lesbian children are sometimes mistreated and bullied in the schools. You've just made fun of his very serious concern. I think you should apologize."

Rattled, Mr. Fisher just made a few additional comments, then hung up.

At that point, the hosts said, "Tell us about Trinity Western University," and I went into full promotional mode. Then they opened the phone lines, and we began to receive calls from Trinity Western alumni and teachers from local schools, who all affirmed that Trinity Western-trained teachers were exceptional and highly valued.

The public relations team sitting in the control room told me later that the technicians had been doubled over with laughter. The ambush had gone badly, and had resulted in a benefit to our cause. My replies had been perfect, and I recognized that they were the type of responses that typically only come to mind hours or even days after a conversation. But on that day, the Lord had placed the words right on the tip of my tongue.

The prayer campaign

City by city, large numbers of Christians came to our prayer rallies. We started in Vancouver, then went to Calgary, Edmonton, Winnipeg and Steinbach, Manitoba; Thunder Bay, Toronto and Montreal. The prayer rallies were enormously encouraging. God's people and their prayers were truly with us.

We had two outstanding Trinity Western alumni travelling with us: Amber Pashuk was a brilliant young alumna, with a razor-sharp intellect and a winsome personality. Her heart and mind were set on attending law school at the University of Toronto the following year. As such, she was taking a significant risk by joining our team as, at that point, her association with the Trinity Western University case might compromise her chances of gaining admission. But, in the end, she gained admission, graduated and went on to clerk at the Supreme Court of Canada.

Now, as we gathered in churches, Amber explained why our legal case was so important for Canada's freedoms.

Also with us was Tanya Steinhilber (later to become Tanya Price), the founder of a ministry called DRIME (Disciples Ready In Mobile Evangelism). Tanya knew how to move a crowd with warmth, enthusiasm and her deep love for God. She talked about Trinity Western, what it meant to graduates, and why it was important.

The impact of Amber's and Tanya's presentations was enormous. When it was my turn to speak, I would say, "You've just met two of our Trinity Western students. There are two thousand more like these back in Langley. We need your prayers and your donations as we take this important case to the Supreme Court of Canada."

One evening, we spoke at Peoples' Church in Toronto, where a large audience was present to hear our presentations and pray for us. After the service, people came to the front to talk, as often happens at such events. Eventually, the crowd dwindled until there was only one woman left at the front of the large sanctuary. I'd noticed previously that she appeared to be hanging back, somewhat shyly. Now, with others no longer present, she stepped forward.

"Dr. Saffold," she began, "I left the homosexual lifestyle two years ago." She went on to explain that for more than ten years she'd been deeply attracted to the Christian faith. "I loved God," she said, "but every time I tried to join a church, I found people saying such harsh things about homosexuals that I'd run away." She unfolded a painful story of failed attempts to join a congregation, repeatedly frustrated by the painful things people would say.

As she talked, I anticipated that she would eventually explain that these hurtful experiences were the reason she couldn't agree with Trinity Western's position in our legal battle. But to my surprise she said: "Two years ago, my desire to be closer to Christ became so great, I decided that I'd endure whatever people said. It was more important for me to worship Him. But if people had spoken about these issues as kindly as you did tonight, I would have come to Christ years sooner!"

I felt heartbroken. How many people, I wondered, have we Christians driven away from God by speaking without love? We had taken great care to keep our message positive and focused on what we believed about marriage. I resolved then that we would have an even greater resolve to guard our words, and to ensure we always spoke with respect and love for others.

Praying at Canada's Peace Tower

At last our team arrived in Ottawa, the very city where we'd be just one month later for the Supreme Court Hearings. For our press conference, we'd booked the Press Gallery in Parliament's Centre Block. It was a dramatic setting; and we felt the significance of all we were doing as we stood on that historic platform, in front of an array of Canadian flags. Just 500 metres to the West was the Supreme Court. We were so close to what would be the final arena in our battle for justice!

We made our usual presentation, then answered reporters' questions. As we emerged from Centre Block and took in the significance of our surroundings, our team had a desire to pray, and I knew what I wanted us to pray about. For many years, our leadership team at Trinity Western had held discussions in strategic planning sessions regarding the vision of establishing a centre in Ottawa where we could provide Trinity Western students with high quality, personally impactful training in public service. The difficulty had been that we needed a base in Ottawa, close to Parliament Hill, where students could live and study. But there was simply no space of that kind available in the crowded downtown of Canada's national capital.

So Doris Olafson, Tanya Steinhilber, Amber Pashuk, Steve Reimer and I stood in the warm sun at the base of the Peace Tower and prayed: "Lord, coming to Ottawa at this time has not been our choice. We've had to come here to defend our rights; but we have a dream to come back to Ottawa for our own reasons. Lord, would you make it possible for us to find the place we need?"

As we looked up from our prayer, our eyes turned to Metcalfe Street, which stretches south from Parliament Hill. We didn't know it then, but within two months Trinity Western would have an opportunity to purchase the historic Laurentian Club building at 252 Metcalfe Street. It would become the Laurentian Leadership Centre of Trinity Western University—a small campus in Ottawa where, each semester, two dozen students could live, study and participate in internships in various government offices.

The Supreme Court of Canada

At 9:45 a.m. November 9, 2000, the large doors behind the high bench of the Supreme Court justices opened, and an official called out: "The Court. *La Cour.*" Mme. Justice Beverley McLachlin, Chief Justice of the Supreme Court, stepped toward her seat in the centre, followed by the other justices splitting left and right toward their positions at the bench. The hearing would be one day only—and, to a legal outsider, it hardly seemed sufficient, given the gravity of the case. Yet the resulting decision would be the final word on our legal case, and would determine the status of Christian freedoms in Canada.

It's impossible to ignore the weight that one bears, the moment one's case goes to the highest court in the country for a final decision. "Finality" is the legal language for such a judgment, but it would also be the occasion when the last word in our defense—and the last words against us—would be spoken, and then the final judgement made. From that judgement, there could be no appeal. I was drawn to think of the final judgment before God, when the righteous Judge of all the earth issues His final verdicts.

As in the past, Bob Kuhn was there to present our case, along with Kevin Sawatsky and Kevin Boonstra. Harro Van Brummelen and Joy McCullough were with us again, as well as Donna Lindquist, the Trinity Western alumna who had partnered with us in the legal case from the very beginning. A number of other current and former Trinity Western students had joined us, so we had a very full contingent.

Thomas Berger and his daughter, Erin, had also come to the Court. Bob Kuhn told us that Mr. Berger was highly experienced in appearing before the Supreme Court, and pointed out that the number of times he had argued a case in this room would exceed the combined total of all the other lawyers present! Clearly, we were up against a lawyer well-practiced in this environment.

In stark contrast, none of our team had ever presented in this Court before.

Mr. Berger spoke first. The College of Teachers, he said, had properly and carefully exercised its rightful administrative discretion when it determined that Trinity Western University's proposed program did not adequately prepare students to be teachers in public school classrooms. Yes, he conceded, the correctness of that conclusion can be challenged; but in the end, it is up to the College of Teachers to make the decision, as they understood schools and classrooms in a way judges do not. The Court should allow the decision of the College of Teachers to stand, because it represented the wisest and best-informed decision available. It was, in any event, a modest decision that didn't bar Trinity Western graduates from becoming teachers. It only required that they take one year of their five-year program at a public university.

We could all see that presenting before these justices was a considerable challenge. The justices interrupted constantly with pointed questions that shifted quickly among points of law and evidence. It was apparent that the justices were greatly concerned that the BCCT lacked any evidence showing that Trinity Western teachers would be unprepared. Mr. Berger replied that there *was* evidence: one had only to read the Trinity Western Community Standards that prohibited homosexual behaviour. The document itself was the evidence that concerned the College of Teachers, and it should concern this court, too.

The justices didn't seem to buy his argument. They consistently pointed out that the Community Standards also called for showing respect to all people. That may be true, Mr. Berger replied, "But at the end of the day, there's a risk of sending these graduates into the world without a broader exposure to a wider set of values." In any event, he persistently asserted, a judgement about the potential risk to students in the classroom should be made by the members of the College of Teachers, not by judges.

As he wrapped up his argument, Mr. Berger turned to the issue of what action the Court should direct. The B.C. Court of Appeal had directed the College to approve the Trinity Western program. According to Mr. Berger, even if the high court were to agree with that decision, it should order a different remedy. Instead of requiring the BCCT to give its approval, it should direct the BCCT to give the matter further consideration. This led to one of the more fascinating—even humorous—exchanges of the morning.

Chief Justice McLachlin said, "So your suggestion in the alternative is that if the Court were to disallow the appeal, it should send it back to the Council for further decision?"

"Yes," Mr. Berger replied, "because the Court of Appeal Justice goes 'galumphing' into academic issues that are beyond his expertise."

"Mr. Berger," Chief Justice McLachlin intruded, "I must interrupt you. In this Court we do not refer to the honourable justices of the of the B.C. Court of Appeal as 'galumphing' anywhere."

"It was indiscreet of me, Chief Justice," Mr. Berger said. "I apologize."

During Berger's presentation, seven of the nine justices had very aggressively probed his arguments with critical questions. For our part, we were pleased that the Court seemed to have it clearly in mind that the Trinity Western standards contained extensive language urging respect and tolerance. They seemed to recognize that there had been unclear and probably faulty procedure by the College of Teachers (since no evidence was reviewed other than policy statements) and that Trinity Western's program may have been scrutinized unfairly (compared to the standards that had been applied to others).

Now Bob Kuhn stepped forward to present Trinity Western's argument. He had told us that he had great peace about the presentation he was going to make, although he admitted that it was impossible not to feel apprehensive about presenting your argument before nine of the best legal minds in the country.

Bob argued that the BCCT had ignored the most important parts of the Trinity Western University Community Standards, and focused instead on one narrow element—and on that element alone. It is also clear that the document requires respect, unselfishness, and behaviour as good citizens. What characterized the BCCT's decision was not sound educational reasoning, but rather a decision to express moral disapprobation of the Trinity Western code—and that was wrong.

Madam Justice L'Heureux-Dubé, whom we suspected would be unsympathetic to our case, began to question Bob. She had been silent all morning, probably not wanting to slow Mr. Berger in the presentation of his case. Now, however, she began to press Bob heavily, again and again.

"Are you saying," she asked, "that the BCCT is not entitled to take into account the laws of Canada? We have said everyone **must** take into account the *Charter*."

"No," Bob answered, "the *Charter* applies. But if they are going to apply *Charter* values, they must apply **all** the *Charter* values—including respect for religious liberty." He pointed out that the BCCT had admitted that Trinity Western was not guilty of any breach of law. "It had properly to focus on a single point: *were the* [TWU] *graduates being prepared to teach in the public schools?* Instead, it turned itself into a human rights tribunal."

Through all the questioning, Bob stuck steadfastly to his argument. At length, time came for him to sum up.

First, he said, there was no identified need for the BCCT to more fully review the matter. The teacher training program would have gone ahead, but for the issue of allegedly "discriminatory" practices; and there was no evidence that Trinity Western teachers would discriminate in any way. Trinity Western had waited six and a half years for the BCCT to develop standards for a private university and, when those standards were ready, it had made an application within six weeks. The BCCT then took 16 months to review the program—and the reviewers had recommended approval. Then the BCCT Council took just 24 hours to overturn the recommendation of its own investigators! In all, Trinity Western University had waited 13 years! It was time to be done with this matter.

Second, the record was clear: the case had been reviewed by two courts, both of which said there are no issues remaining. There is no purpose in returning this matter to the BCCT, as it would certainly lead to further delay.

Finally, this case had unfairly cast a shadow of prejudice over Trinity Western University and its graduates, and that needed to be dispelled.

With this, we broke for lunch and did our best to analyze every question of the morning. It was unanimously agreed that Mr. Berger's reference to "galumphing" was likely to be a memorable moment! More importantly, however, the justices overall did not seem inclined to agree with Mr. Berger's arguments. This gave us hope.

The afternoon session was taken up with presentations by six interveners who supported Trinity Western's position, and felt that the issues at stake were significant enough that they should also have their arguments heard. The interveners included The B.C. Civil Liberties Association, the Canadian Civil Liberties Association, the Canadian Conference of Catholic Bishops, the Christian Legal Fellowship, the Seventh Day Adventists, and the Evangelical Fellowship of Canada. This significantly outweighed, at least in number, the two interventions earlier in the morning by EGALE Canada and the Ontario Secondary Schools Teachers' Federation.

Our "day in court" (as it quite literally was) had ended. Now we had to wait for the decision, which would come at some future date. We learned that we would have no more than 48 hours' notice of its release.

The final decision

Six months later, I was in Tianjin, China, where Trinity Western was developing an educational partnership with the Tianjin University of Technology. It was May 15, 2001 in China when word came from Canada that the decision would be released May 17. The 48-hour-notice clock had begun to tick, and President Snider asked me to return to campus as quickly as I could.

But there was one problem—all possible flights were booked. There was no flight with an available seat that would get me back to campus in time to field media inquiries when the decision was released. If our case failed, managing the fallout would be especially important.

At this point, God provided a way forward, just as He had done so many times throughout the past five years. The President's Office of Tianjin University offered to intervene and, within an hour, I was booked on a flight to Vancouver that would arrive in time for me to carry out my duties. Not only that, but it was an executive class seat, and I would be able to get some sleep on the long hop over the Pacific. Tianjin University then extended one final courtesy: they would provide two graduate students to drive me to the Beijing airport the next morning.

On May 16, I left China for Vancouver. Flying east from Asia, one gains a day by crossing the International Date Line, and typically arrives on the same date as the departure; so I arrived in Vancouver May 16. I quickly joined my team on campus to prepare for the judgement that would follow the next morning.

The amazing news hit the following morning: The Supreme Court of Canada, by an overwhelming vote of 8 to 1, had ruled in favour of Trinity Western University! Not only had they rejected the arguments of the College of Teachers, but they had agreed that there was no point in asking the BCCT to reconsider. They flatly directed that the BCCT approve our teacher training program!

In the ruling, the Court made its reasons clear:

> *There is nothing in the TWU Community Standards, which are limited to prescribing conduct of members while at TWU, that indicates that graduates of TWU will not treat homosexuals fairly and respectfully. The evidence to date is that graduates from the joint TWU-SFU teacher education program have become competent public school teachers, and there is no evidence before this Court of discriminatory conduct. In addition, there is no basis for the inference that the fifth year of the TWU program, conducted under the aegis of SFU, corrected any attitudes which were the subject of the BCCT's concerns.... In considering the religious precepts of TWU instead of the actual impact of these beliefs on the public school environment, the BCCT acted on the basis of irrelevant considerations. It therefore acted unfairly.*
>
> (Source: SCC ruling)

It had been a long journey from 1987, when we made our original application to offer the final year of teacher training, to the decision in 2001. It had cost Trinity Western 13 years of time and effort, five years of legal challenges, and more than $1.5 million. Some said it was the most significant religious freedom decision in Canada in the last fifty years. The truth of that statement would be known in time; but for all of us at Trinity Western, it meant that our program could at long last move ahead.

The case had been won through the hard work of Dr. Van Brummelen and the Trinity Western Education faculty who had, for years, turned out exceptionally well-qualified teachers to join the public school system. Not once during our long journey through the courts, had there been even a hint of one of our teachers demonstrating anything less than the highest professional standards.

The case had also been won in part by the truly exceptional work of a legal team led by Bob Kuhn, a Trinity Western alumnus who, with skill and passion, stepped forward at the University's moment of need with the high quality legal expertise necessary to win against exceptional opposition. Time and again over the years, I have pointed out that this was the very reason an institution like Trinity Western University is desperately needed in our country—to graduate committed believers who are well-prepared in mind and heart to serve God and people.

Finally, and above all else, the case had been won through the consistent effort of God's people to pray throughout the lengthy process, and to give faithfully so that this challenge could be sustained. From time to time, someone would observe that it was good that this challenge had come to Trinity Western, because we were strong enough (in terms of credibility, people and resources) to fight it. I was not always sure we were as "fortunate" as some thought, but the essence of that statement was true. We had been enabled by God to carry the cause, from beginning to end.

In short order, the B.C. College of Teachers, as directed by the Supreme Court of Canada, approved our proposed program. The first five-year students enrolled four months later, in the fall of 2001, and—in the words of our heartfelt theme—began earning their teaching certificates "***to the praise of His glory!***"

53

A bridge to the future

It's astonishing as I look back at all that happened between 1974 and 2006—to remember the people whom God prepared and brought to Trinity Western; to recall the plans they developed and executed to bring the "campus in a cow pasture" to a place of recognition by external authorities as one of the best universities in North America—a pioneer in leadership development and training, in nursing, in business, and with an A+ academic rating, year after year, in the liberal arts and sciences.

It has truly been glorious to see how God prepared people, implanted His vision in their hearts and minds, and then performed miracles to bring His plans to fruition!

Looking back, I realize that all along, God had planned more than we dared to dream—and that even the very best of our planning was simply walking in obedience to His vision for our future.

And above all, I realize that faith—true biblical faith—is active: faith means trusting God—enough to step out, even when we cannot yet see where the next step will land.

The pioneers who envisioned a "campus in a cow-pasture" laid a foundation of that kind of faith. The teachers and professors who shaped the institution that grew up around those pioneers' faith, and the students who enrolled in classes, in faith believing that one day there would be a diploma or a degree for them—they, too, were people of great faith.

The planners, who envisioned an institution of a quality worthy of the name of our Lord, cast dreams that were far beyond their grasp—and then set out in faith on the path towards those dreams.

Neil Snider

In every case, their actions bespoke real faith—their trust in the God who "calls into being that which does not exist."[1] The dream in their hearts—of a biblically Christian university of the liberal arts and sciences—did not then exist in Canada; but their hunger for it, to the glory of God's Name, surely did exist… and such a hunger in the human heart is like a prayer "too deep for words"—and that's exactly when "*the Spirit also helps our weakness; for we do not know how to pray as we should, but the Spirit Himself intercedes for us…*"[2]

Then, after we hear the appeal by the Spirit, is the time for action, not for passive waiting! When the Spirit of the Living God stirs our hearts, it's His dream that's waiting to be born—and we must respond!

Universities are the places where leaders are trained for their various callings: in the media, in law, in education, in politics, in medicine, in business, in the arts, in the church—and more. If the universities of our nation lapse into Secularism and Materialism, they will perforce train leaders who will lead their nations away from the God of the Bible—which history shows us always has disastrous results.

But universities that commit themselves to the God Who spoke the whole universe into being will be able to train leaders who can set their nations towards God's vision.

So it will be in the future for Trinity Western: we cannot know, yet, what God's dream is for His University; we can only know that because the dream is His, its realization will be glorious! And hope, firmly rooted in faith, will provide that bridge to the future.

---

[1] Romans 4:17
[2] Romans 8:26

Sod Turning for the new Science Centre, October 23, 1992.

BELL TOWER—The Campanile and Library Gardens were constructed in 2000. At fifty feet it is a campus landmark. The Campanile's 15 bells, which ring every hour, were imported from the Royal Eijsbouts Company of the Netherlands. It was dedicated to the memory of Norma Marion Alloway, in whose honour the library was named.

TWU Archives

PART IX

Epilogue

By Bob Kuhn, President, Trinity Western University

President Bob Kuhn

Epilogue

Much has happened since 2006, the termination point of the story told in these pages. The weaving of the Trinity Western tapestry continues to reveal daily challenges, as it always seems to have done. Some of these challenges threaten the very existence of TWU as we know it. But as we read the chapters in this book, and remember the remarkable way God provided, we can be reassured. Although once again we stand on the brink of a new era we have learned from those who went ahead how to look beyond our present circumstances. Our history teaches us to question the apparently insurmountable circumstances we face. We gain clarity of insight because we are able to stand on the shoulders of those who have gone before.

When I first arrived on the campus of Trinity Junior College (as it then was known) in the late summer of 1970, I was young, immature and naïve; my world had been an apple orchard outside of Vernon, a small town in central British Columbia. Perhaps understandably, I was both excited by the "college days" that lay ahead, and frightened, even overwhelmed, in the face of the uncertainty and expectations I felt. I was a mediocre student, inexperienced in leadership, a second-string soccer player (at best), socially insincere and spiritually confused. But despite my rather ordinary beginning, my two years at Trinity proved to be transformative beyond what I and many others had thought possible.

A passion for learning literally exploded under the caring instruction of Benno Friesen, Frank Mansfield, Allie Caldwell and others, which led to top marks in my graduating year. I became the President of the student body in 1971/72 and played goalie for the Trinity Spartans soccer team. And, thankfully, I began to understand the invaluable concept of commitment in relationships. In 1974, this newfound relational perspective led to marrying my lifelong 'growth partner' and fellow Trinity student, Renae (Guinett). But, most importantly, I came face-to-face with my need for the grace and forgiveness found only in a relationship with my God, the God of the Bible. I acknowledged then, and still affirm, that He provides purpose and perspective, wisdom and insight, and the strength and persistence necessary to stand firm in the face of adversity. Truly, living life "on purpose" began during my years at Trinity. Little did I know then that I was beginning an education in preparation for an unexpected career path that was to begin more than 40 years later.

It is still somewhat difficult to explain, but since July 1, 2013, I have had the privilege to serve my *alma mater*, Trinity Western University, as its President (first interim, and then for a five-year term). Although I have had the undeserved blessing of practicing law for more than 35 years, I never had any intention nor dreamed of serving in the position I now hold. But, over time, I can begin to see, "in the rearview mirror" how God has taken my small, inadequate thread of life to weave it into the pattern He planned at TWU.

As happened with each of the three Trinity Presidents before me (Dr. Cal Hanson, Dr. Neil Snider, and Dr. Jonathan Raymond), I was entrusted with the torch of leadership for a time. It was placed into my trembling hands with the message of Esther 4:14, the haunting words which reverberate in my head whenever I wonder, "Why me?" and "Who knows but that you have come to your position for such a time as this?"

The Trinity Western community is dearly loved by many. And for many like me, the University has succeeded in doing what Trinity does best; "inspiring hearts and minds". The integration of faith and learning and commitment to "total student development" is referenced throughout this book. The "complete champion" concept of holistic development has successfully proven that TWU Spartans are of national calibre, mature character, and extraordinary competence. Like David confronting Goliath, Trinity Western has taken on larger Canadian universities often more than ten times our size.

For the many who know us only by reading newspapers or listening to television reports, the reputation of Trinity Western University since 2000 has been largely characterized by our legal defense of religious freedom. As I write, we are standing up for the right to have the first private Christian law school in the country. While not seeking attention, our small University is being called on once again to take the lead in standing up for freedom of religion on behalf of all Canadians, regardless of their faith background.

We seem to be living in a time warp. It is a period of human history when dramatic change is happening very quickly, and our social environment gives diminishing credence to the moral values of Christian heritage of the past. It is a time when our predominantly secular society questions the current state of the law, and would disregard the 2001 Supreme Court of Canada decision that was thought to guarantee protection of the evangelical Christian distinctives of Trinity Western University, which had then been challenged by the B.C. College of Teachers.

The most recent legal questions facing TWU, and all institutions that seek to maintain the Christian traditional definition of marriage, may yet again require the final word to be spoken by the Supreme Court of Canada. This should not surprise us. Both our history and the present are replete with evidence that the identity of TWU and its God-given mission will continue to be misunderstood and, to some extent, disregarded by the world in which we live. Pluralism, by popular definition, seems to have been redefined to exclude the participation of evangelical Christians. To some extent, Christians have become dependent on the courts protecting religious freedom from the secularism that has overwhelmed popular thinking. The rhetoric of debate taken up by public and influential leaders often seems to betray an evangelical zeal that puts evangelical Christians to shame. Justice Campbell, of the Nova Scotia Supreme Court, in his 2015 judgment in the case of Trinity Western University and the Nova Scotia Barristers Society, warned that a free society must acknowledge that "The society is secular, but the state does not have a secularizing mission."

Despite new challenges and continued criticisms, Trinity Western can remain confident in its purpose and mission. There is solace in the words of Joseph who, recognizing God's bigger purpose, was able to extend grace and forgiveness to those who hated him by saying, "You intended to harm me, but God intended it for good to accomplish what is now being done, the saving of many lives."[1]

Surprisingly to some, new students continue to enroll at Trinity Western University in increasing numbers. They have heard about the extraordinary reputation for excellence in education delivered by highly regarded and internationally recognized faculty who actually care about each of their students. Those who visit the campus or hear stories from students and alumni are drawn to Trinity's student life experience. Financial supporters continue to believe in and support the mission of TWU and see economic sustainability as they invest in supplying the needs of students by supporting the construction of infrastructure, the development of new programs and increasing the student financial aid available.

The stories throughout this book are not told for the aggrandizement of the people involved. To me, these truthful accounts point to the reality of God's faithfulness and blessing of Trinity Western University. We can trust the future into His hands, just as was done by those who went before us. It is evident from the number and diversity of gifted leaders referenced in these pages that God has

---

[1] Genesis 50:20 (NIV)

used, and continues to use ordinary men and women in extraordinary ways. They never sought to be portrayed as heroes; they were submissive to being servants. Rather than hubris, they modeled humility. They cared about the well-being of the TWU community to the point of significant sacrifice. These leaders were not just mission minded; they were completely committed to the calling that brought them to this unique, often underestimated, University.

What does the future hold for Trinity Western University? What will the tapestry look like at the end of the next 50 years? If history is a foreshadowing of things to come, TWU will continue to change, adapt and grow in influence. But certain things must remain. It must retain its transformative environment; its strong sense of community; an unwavering commitment to its mission; and a continuous recognition of a touch of the miraculous.

There is a line from the 2011 movie, *The Best Exotic Marigold Hotel:* "Everything will be all right in the end… if it's not all right, then it's not yet the end." Questionable theology, but it offers hopeful thinking when current circumstances have a tendency to produce discouragement and disillusionment.

While the future of TWU will most certainly not be predictable, in all likelihood it will necessitate living on the raw edge of faith and continuing to prevail against all odds, as it continues faithfully inspiring hearts and minds.

In the words of others…

54

Remembering DRIME

By Tanya Price

I remember driving through the streets of Vancouver for the first time, in 1994. I'd just moved to B.C. from a farm in Alberta, to attend Trinity Western University; to me, the big city was captivating.

It set me thinking about a ministry to engage people in the inner city in creative and non-threatening ways; to engage them to think about spiritual things, and then to introduce them to Jesus…

Only 17, I didn't even think about possible challenges or difficulties. But I mentioned my thoughts to a few fellow students, and a couple of weeks later, our first team of ten students hit Vancouver's streets. And it worked.

That was the beginning of a student-led ministry, based at TWU, called DRIME: Disciples Ready In Mobile Evangelism. It would eventually grow to 19 ministry bases is nine countries around the world.

I remember a night, early on in our ministry, when I was standing in the crowd watching the drama team perform; I overheard a couple of bystanders as they watched and tried to figure out the message of the drama. One man seemed inquisitive and a bit concerned, because he was watching characters who represented abuse, loneliness, depression, drugs, and suicide. His friend leaned over to him, and said, "Don't worry. I've seen this team before, and it won't end this way… pretty soon, the One in White will come."

The One in White. The man speaking didn't understand all the details of the drama, but he did know that the One in White brought healing, freedom, and redemption… that the One in White made things right.

I also remember a man named Travis, in Calgary. A big, intimidating man who watched the street dramas skeptically. He seemed disengaged, until I started asking him questions. Then he began to break down and cry… and simply said, "That's me"—referring to the character in the drama who was trapped in a box. Travis proceeded to tell me his whole story: growing up in church, but having long since left his faith, he became trapped in a life of substance abuse, and had lost hope.

But that day, as his tears hit the pavement, he prayed to commit his life to Jesus once again.

In Kenya, a man named Salim accepted Christ with DRIME, and was so confident in his new faith that he prayed for his brother's healing—and his brother was healed! Salim came back and reported that he'd had a dream that night: that God was going to use him to preach the Gospel to people in the very place DRIME was doing their presentation.

There was a girl in Brazil who said she'd believed in God her whole life; but until she saw DRIME's presentation, she never knew that Jesus is still alive; that he has conquered death; that the story didn't end at the cross—that there's an empty tomb.

Back in Vancouver, Pooyan, a Muslim-turned-atheist, stopped to watch DRIME's dramas, and engaged the players in thoughtful discussion for weeks. A year later (after he'd moved to California), he called to say he'd received Jesus, and was getting baptized the next Sunday! One of the DRIMERs went to his church in California, to see Pooyan publicly declare his faith.

For 20 years, my fellow DRIMERS and I slept on hard floors, endured 35 hour flights, got sick on trips, lost sleep, raised money, and gave up their Friday nights year after year. We've sent dozens of mission trips to dozens of countries, and trained hundreds of students every year. Why? Because it's worth it.

I remember that lost people matter to Jesus… that's why we MUST remember the call, the vision, and the dream… that what God has done in those first 20 years of DRIME (and the first 54 years of TWU) is really just the beginning.

For the first decade of ministry, we were mostly just volunteers heading to the streets of Vancouver every weekend, training lots of churches and schools to use drama as a tool on their own mission trips, and in their own communities.

But in 2003, DRIME's first international base was born in Brazil. And from there, we learned, made mistakes,

Tanya Price

polished a few things... and by God's grace, have been able to launch nineteen DRIME ministry bases in nine different countries.

And so I remember the initial question I asked myself twenty years ago: "What if?"

What if our teams multiply themselves? What if DRIME Benin—that sees literally hundreds of people come to Christ each year—could help start DRIME Nigeria? And DRIME Ivory Coast? What if DRIME Paraguay and DRIME Brazil could work together to help launch DRIME Uruguay and DRIME Argentina? What if DRIME Thailand could work with our new friends in Hong Kong to start DRIME Cambodia?

WHAT IF? What if we could start 20 more DRIME bases by 2020? Then thousands of Christians would be trained to share their faith creatively, and they'd become spiritual multipliers. Hundreds more would become DRIMERS, committed to their local cities, sharing Christ regularly on their streets. Most important, thousands more would come into an active and personal relationship with Christ.

55

Redeemer Pacific College at TWU

By Tom Hamel

> *Tom Hamel came to TWU as a mature student (he'd just turned 40) with a vision to teach in Catholic schools. While here, that vision changed to one of preparing teachers to introduce students in those schools to a personal relationship with Jesus.*
>
> —Neil Snider

In the late 1980s my wife, Diane, and I were in our mid-thirties, and had been blessed by the Lord with a growing young family and a successful family business. We resolved to try to "give something back" to Him. So a few years later, we'd sold our business, and I was ready to earn an education degree so I could teach in the new Catholic high school where our children would soon attend. But where would I study?

We'd learned about the Franciscan University at Steubenville, Ohio, that encouraged students to develop a personal relationship with Jesus Christ while earning their degree. FUS, under President Father Michael Scanlan, was the first in a late 20th century renaissance of Christ-centred Catholic universities, and seemed the perfect place for my studies. In 1990, I was able to sell our business to fund my degree at Steubenville. But Jesus had other plans!

My program at FUS was to begin in the fall of 1991. However, since I wasn't working from the fall of 1990, I decided to pick up some credits at a local college or university, starting in January of 1991. I interviewed at a provincially-funded community college and at a public university, but was disappointed with their exclusively secular worldviews. That's when I decided to try Trinity Western University.

The Christian atmosphere at Trinity Western was like coming home! I was struck by the friendliness of the professors, staff and students. A kind staff member named Charlotte, who radiated Christ's love, helped me choose my courses. Then there were the faithful, skilled professors such as John Anonby, Bob Burkinshaw, Barbara Pell, Doug Shantz, Carl Tracie, Phillip Wiebe, Mark Charlton, and many others—all of whom integrated their faith in Christ seamlessly as they taught their subjects with authority.

Most surprising were my fellow students, the majority of whom appeared to be from solid Christian homes or backgrounds. I'd never before experienced such a cohesive community! The school gave the impression of being united in positive purpose: learning for the sake of serving our Lord, and bringing others to Him.

On visits to friends at public universities and colleges, I'd often seen students dragging themselves into class Monday mornings after a weekend of debauchery. But at TWU on Monday mornings, I heard students sharing stories of bringing other young people to Christ over the weekend! And then there were the chapels at TWU: every school day, around 11 a.m., the entire campus would stop: there were no classes, and most students would voluntarily trek over to the gym to worship Jesus Christ; to sing hymns of praise; and to hear solid Christian teaching from a variety of speakers, some internationally-known, and some from the TWU community itself.

The President, Dr. Neil Snider, spoke once a week at chapel; and I grew to appreciate his leadership and vision for TWU. I learned that he'd taken the school from a small junior college to an academically-excellent university of some 3,000 students.

I decided to forego Steubenville, and complete my education at Trinity Western. At TWU, I witnessed first-hand the power of students, administration, staff and faculty unified in a common mission to make a positive difference in the world through God's love. I witnessed an impressive example of the value and power of a group of people striving to follow Christ as "intentional disciples", always being "ready to give a reason for the hope that we have in Him."[1] Discipleship in Christ—knowing, loving and serving Him—was, I learned in my history studies at TWU, a Christian imperative deeply embedded in the Church from the first century.

During my final year, our oldest daughter, Jennifer, took in some classes and attended chapel as well. She was only in the seventh grade; but she told me, "I loved it!"

One day, Diane and I joined some other Catholic parents who were meeting with Archbishop Adam Exner to discuss the state of Catholic grade school education. The Archbishop commented that we needed an authentically Catholic college to train grade school teachers—the very thought I'd had!

A few days later, I was back at Trinity Western attending Dr. Bob Burkinshaw's excellent history class. After class, I told Bob about Archbishop Exner's desire to have teachers trained at a faithful Catholic college; and my hope that someday Catholics in our area would found a post-secondary institution like TWU.

Bob's reply surprised me. He encouraged me to approach TWU's administration

---

[1] 1 Peter 3:13-16 (Phillips)

and propose a partnership between a new Catholic college and Trinity Western. The college could teach, from the Catholic perspective, liberal arts courses that would count toward a TWU degree.

I graduated from TWU in April of 1995 and began classes in the teacher-training program at a large, very secular university in Vancouver. But after a short time, I decided it was not for me. I'd majored in history at TWU, and the majority of my courses were in the history of Christianity. I had a growing interest in theology and church history, rather than teaching grade school. So I started on a Masters in Theology from Steubenville by distance education.

At the same time, I did my best to get back into business so I could generate an income. Starting and running business ventures has always come relatively easily to me. But this time, I had trouble getting a new venture running.

Now, at 45 and needing an income, I began to install as well as sell floor coverings through the drapery business I'd sold to an employee five years before. One day I was on my hands and knees as I coaxed a carpet into place. I decided to pray: "Lord, I've been through four years of university and here I am, on my knees. I can't get a business going. I've tried it my way, now I'm willing to try your way. Please show me what you want me to do!"

And He did. A few days later, at the TWU campus I ran into Dr. Burkinshaw. I mentioned that I was still concerned about Catholic higher education, and was therefore interested in establishing a scholarship for potential Catholic school teachers at TWU.

Bob said, "That's a good idea. But a better idea would be to start a Catholic college here at TWU." I used to take assignments from Bob Burkinshaw as a student; now he gave me a new one: to write a proposal for the Academic Dean, Dr. Don Page; and Bob would set up a meeting. I completed the proposal, delivered it to Bob, and a week after our meeting, we were ushered into Don Page's office.

Don opened by saying: "Tom, I've read your proposal; I like it—and I've been wanting to work with Catholics in higher education for a long time." Dr. Page had enjoyed a productive working relationship with a Catholic priest while at the University of Manitoba; and he, too, had seen that, for Evangelicals and Catholics, "what unites us is much greater than what divides us." He said he'd made Dr. Snider aware of our meeting, and had been given the green light to proceed. Dr. Page told me to "Go to it!"

My first step was to establish a framework for an "Evangelical-Catholic college." I'd observed that many Catholic colleges and universities in North America were held hostage to the skeptical spirit of the age. This wasn't just my opinion; many priests were aware of the need for renewal in Catholic higher education. In fact, one of them, who later became a bishop, warned me to stay away from some of the teaching orders—which, he said, had become more secular than religious.

As I write this (in 2014) it's becoming more and more common for Catholic clerical and lay leaders to emphasize the need for Catholics to have a "personal relationship with Jesus Christ"—surely the most basic and most evangelical tenet of orthodox Christian belief.

A personal relationship with our Lord is precisely what Trinity Western seeks to foster in students; and it's what the parents who were with us wanted for their students. But if I brought this initiative directly to our Catholic leaders, without first putting in place the guarantee of the school's "Evangelical-Catholic" character, I'd risk a takeover by liberal Catholic educators who were *not* on board with the renewal that was occurring in places like the University of Steubenville.

I turned to FUS, the most renowned of the new Catholic "renewal" schools. Having its roots firmly in the Catholic Charismatic Renewal, FUS had links to orthodox Protestantism in both its Evangelical and Pentecostal forms. Father Scanlan was reputed to have a regular golf date with Charles Colson, the Nixon aide who took the fall in the Watergate affair, and thereafter accepted Christ and became an Evangelical leader, writing the bestselling autobiography, *Born Again*.

Father Scanlan, in his autobiography, *A Portion of My Spirit*, outlined his successful struggle to turn the University of Steubenville from a notorious "party school" into a campus that honoured Christ. Later, after he and I became friends, he gave me a small tract that he'd written, *Evangelizing the Catholic Campus*. In it I found a paragraph that summed up the reason why I chose FUS as the Catholic mentor for Redeemer Pacific College (my proposed name for the future Catholic college). He wrote: "An authentically Catholic campus will be an effective instrument of re-Christianization if it concentrates on adult conversion. A campus may be said to be Catholic to the degree that it creates an environment that fosters conversion to Christ and his Church. Students must be convinced of the need to own their faith, and not merely rent their parents'… students are encouraged to encounter the Lord in a personal way."

I told him about the wonderful opportunity I'd been given; and asked if FUS would partner with Redeemer Pacific College in this work. The Academic Dean, Dr. Michael Healy, told me FUS was "ready to be of service". He also pointed out that FUS was an affiliate of the largely evangelical Council for Christian Colleges and Universities (CCCU), where TWU also has membership.

Four days later, I drove to Vancouver with a 12-page letter to Archbishop Adam Exner that ended:

> In closing, I ask you, Archbishop Exner, to consider the proposal I place before you: a Catholic college that can be economically established, due to the generosity of a Christian body that recognizes the need our respective communions have for each other in this increasingly secularized society; a Catholic college guided by the University of Steubenville.... I believe that what we have accomplished so far could, with your help, lead to the establishment of a Catholic institution that will have a great impact for Christ on this province for many years to come."

Without full-time attention, the project was likely to stall or die. But by God's grace, committee-member Jim Marland (himself a Catholic TWU grad) soon found funding that would allow me to lead the initiative for another year!

The Redeemer Pacific College committee met with Archbishop Exner a number of times in 1996 and 1997. He had a high regard for Trinity Western University, because he'd earlier attended lectures by the TWU Education Department's Dr. Harro Van Brummelen, and was impressed by his approach to Christian pedagogy. As Archbishop Exner learned more about TWU's capabilities, he became more and more interested in having Catholic school-teachers trained through the proposed TWU/RPC partnership. He'd been associated with FUS over the years, and was a strong supporter of their work of putting Christ back into Catholic higher education.

About eight months later, he announced that he wanted Redeemer Pacific College to be officially recognized as a Catholic institution—the first-ever lay initiative in higher education so authorized in the Archdiocese.

In January, 1998 the Archbishop came to the TWU campus, where he and I met President Snider and his administrators. The Archbishop was looking for assurances that TWU was serious about the RPC/TWU agreement. After receiving those assurances, Archbishop Exner took in a chapel service. On that day at chapel, the campus pro-life club made a presentation. Of course this impressed the Archbishop, since the pro-life cause is deeply embedded in Church teaching. And as he was leaving the gym where chapel was held, a young Catholic student at TWU hurried over to the Archbishop and enthusiastically said how happy she was to see him there, and how much she was enjoying her time at TWU!

Three months later, the TWU Board of Governors ratified approval. Then, Archbishop Exner said the archdiocese would purchase property adjacent to the

University for the RPC campus—if we could get the owner to sell. But the owner said he was going "to stay there the rest of his life". But again, the Lord had other plans.

On September 29, 1998 I was sitting in my office at TWU, wondering what to do with my life now that the RPC/TWU association had been rendered "impossible"; while I was on the phone, my daughter, Jennifer (who was now a TWU student) heard the fax machine start up.

As the fax came out, I saw a look of shock on her face. She slapped the fax down on my desk. It was a newspaper obituary notice for the owner of the property—the man who wouldn't sell "as long as he lived"! He had died in a car accident just nine days after our real estate agent had visited him! Now RPC would have a chance of purchasing the property.

Shortly after this, TWU and RPC initialed an agreement that made Redeemer Pacific College a teaching centre of Trinity Western University.

The Glover Road property, just outside TWU's gates, was turned over to Redeemer Pacific College on August 9, 1999. We had to have the old farmhouse ready for students by September 6, 1999—just 28 days after we took possession of the property. There were at least four travel trailers in various states of repair scattered around the site, and a large teepee. I'd been told a TWU student once lived in it! There was also a small shack where the Salmon River runs past TWU. The rest of the upper level of the property had been use for storage of rocks and bark mulch. We found an old swimming pool, which was a health hazard and would have to be removed. We also discovered that a large area of the property had been used as a dumping ground for contaminated soil. Like the pool, this would have to be removed.

For the building renovations and removal of contaminated soil I again turned to Archbishop Exner, who responded by providing carpenters to do the majority of the interior construction. He also provided the money for removing the contaminated soil.

All the other work to get the College in shape for students was done by family and friends—at no charge! Due in part to all this hard work, but due primarily to God's grace, the new Catholic college at Trinity Western University opened September 9, 1999. I named it Redeemer Pacific College, because it was my intention to give all the honour and glory to our Saviour, Jesus Christ; it was my hope that every student, teacher and administrator associated with the College would come to know Him personally and deeply.

I had twelve grace-filled years as President of RPC. It was an amazing time, full of unexpected challenges, watching God work in the lives of the students.

56

Canadian Institute of Linguistics at TWU

By Michael Walrod

In late 1983, Michael Walrod was wrapping up his dissertation in Dallas before heading back to the Philippines to work toward completing the New Testament in the Ga'dang language. Realizing that he didn't have any plans for after those two big projects were completed, he thought: "If there's ever an SIL (Summer Institute of Linguistics) training program in Canada, I want to be a part of that." Here, he picks up the rest of the story…
—*Neil Snider*

The very next day, Dr. David Bendor-Samuel (Vice-President of Academic Affairs for SIL) invited me and my wife, Verna, to tea. During their conversation, he said Dr. Jim Dean, CEO of Wycliffe Canada, wanted to start an SIL training program in Canada, and added that they'd like me to lead it!

How could I refuse, after that very thought had come to me not many hours earlier? But I also needed to return to the Philippines for a couple years to finish my work there, so I suggested that they ask Dr. George Cowan, a Canadian, who at that time was President of Wycliffe International, to start the program. Jim Dean invited Dr. Cowan to serve for one summer, which later turned into two.

Where would be the best location? Jim Dean and SIL Vice-President Dan Harrison contacted Trinity Western University. President Snider invited them to visit TWU's campus; an agreement was reached for the program to start in the summer of 1985. Dr. Cowan came to TWU to get the program up and running, and they enrolled more than 30 students the first year.

Michael Walrod

In 1990, several students said they'd also like to take the advanced linguistics package being offered at TWU. That would eliminate the problems of travelling to Texas for early fall semester opening right after CSIL's summer was completed, with all its visa needs, and redundancy in course content. So in 1991, CSIL decided that if we could get enrolment back up to 30, it would warrant starting another program. Also, having 30 students in the summer program might result in 10 or 15 staying for TWU's advanced courses. So we began to pray for 30 students.

A week before summer session, we were at 28. Then Garland and Mavis Hoel's daughter, Susanne, who had studied Linguistics at the University of Alberta, wanted to try the program. She was number 29. The last day before summer session, I got a call from Kris Wilson in Oregon: "Am I too late to apply?" I took his application over the phone, and told him we'd take care of his paper-work when he arrived. So we had 30 students—on the last day before classes began!

But a week later, Susanne Hoel decided to enter SIL's program at the University of Oregon instead. Nevertheless, for a week, we'd had 30 students—and so the decision was made to expand the training program.

In the fall of 1992, advanced courses started in the old portable buildings beside the TWU gym. CSIL offered an additional set of advanced courses in spring of 1994. This completed the curriculum of training required for serving with SIL and Wycliffe in linguistics and Bible translation.

In 1993, CSIL leased offices in the Fosmark building, which had just been built to house the ACTS consortium of seminaries at TWU.

The name "Canadian Summer Institute of Linguistics", or CSIL, had suited us when courses were only offered in the summer. But in 1995, we changed the name to "the Canada Institute of Linguistics"—short form: "CanIL.".

In 1997, CanIL purchased the old portable buildings from Trinity, with the proviso that we could work there for up to three years. However, Trinity kept extending the time, as their plans for further development of the space beside the gym were deferred. In the end, CanIL used that facility for about seven years… long after we'd outgrown it!

By the late '90s, TWU offered a Master of Linguistics and Exegesis degree (through ACTS Seminary); a BA with a major and a minor in Linguistics; and the TESOL (Teaching English to Speakers of Other Languages) certificate. A Linguistics Department had emerged, and I was appointed to its chair by Dr. Phillip Wiebe, Dean of the Faculty of Arts and Religious Studies. CanIL had previously been a part of a combined Department of Communications and Linguistics, chaired by Dr. Bill Strom. This reorganization paved the way for curriculum and degree program development within TWU Academic Affairs protocols, and resulted in a major growth spurt.

CanIL had grown so much that it was becoming difficult to maintain the quality of programs, not to mention the morale of staff and students, in the cramped old portable buildings. We needed new facilities, but development on campus had major obstacles, and nearby properties off-campus were prohibitively expensive. I asked TWU's Executive VP, Dr. Guy Saffold, for advice. That conversation was pivotal.

Current estimates then were that about 2,000 languages around the world still needed Bible translations. Because Wycliffe Canada comprised approximately ten percent of Wycliffe's staff worldwide, their Canadian leaders felt a strong urging from God to commit to produce ten percent—200—of those translations. Two hundred translations would require at least 600 translators, plus many support staff; and fielding 600 translators would require training about a thousand. The CanIL staff recommended that TWU should become the main training hub for this enormous project.

TWU was enthusiastic! Years before, in 1980, they'd written the Great Commission ("make disciples of all nations") right into TWU's Mission Statement. CanIL developed a long-term contract with TWU, to have assurance that a capital campaign for building new facilities would be warranted. And CanIL benefitted by being part of a vibrant Christian university with degree-granting privileges.

Part of the agreement was a building at TWU, which would be the *de facto* home of programs in linguistics and translation. To move in this direction required incorporation as a Canadian charitable organization, separate from Wycliffe. In 1999, CanIL was granted that status. Our first and longest-sitting chair as a registered charity was Dr. William Lim, a well-known and respected Vancouver attorney. He provided guidance and leadership for more than a decade.

In 2003 our fund-raising campaign was moving forward—but not quite quickly enough to prompt the leap of faith and to begin construction. June 18 was the target date for a decision. CanIL had said we'd have to have half the resources in hand or pledged before construction could begin. We were close to the goal; but it had been a struggle, and our Board wondered whether it would take as long to raise the second half of the funds. The decision to break ground and start construction had to be made by the middle of June, 2003, because we needed 30 days after that to get all the contracts signed and start building. June 18 was when we'd make the decision.

I had a prior commitment in the Philippines, but before I left, I indicated that my vote was: "Start construction." On the evening of June 17, less than 24 hours before the board meeting by phone was to happen, CanIL got a call from Donna Staddon, who in February had lost her beautiful 15-year-old daughter, Marissa, in an avalanche while skiing at Revelstoke, B.C. Don Fama met Donna and Karl Staddon at the Wycliffe Calgary office and asked if they would consider a memorial donation, by sponsoring the CanIL library in memory of Marissa. June 17, Donna said they'd contribute $200,000 to sponsor the library. That was the biggest single donation committed to that point! As you can imagine, the board was deeply moved.

Some months earlier, CanIL had had an offer of a matching grant of $250,000, if we could raise that amount by end of June. By June 17, we'd raised only $30,000—and it didn't look hopeful! But with Donna Staddon's gift, we had only $20,000 more to raise in the next 12 days. One of the Board members said he and his wife would give the other $20,000. So in less than 24 hours, we'd gone from raising $30,000 to $500,000 because they qualified for the matching grant.

Needless to say, CanIL's board of directors voted "Yes!"

Just days later, it was announced that Vancouver was to host the 2010 Winter Olympics. By that time, CanIL had already received contractors' quotes, and they all agreed to stick with those quotes. If our decision had come after the Olympics announcement, we surely wouldn't have had such good quotes. It was another evidence that God was in control of the timetable and the process.

Construction started and stayed on schedule. Groundbreaking was July 18, with CanIL Board chairman Bill Lim officiating. CanIL finished construction and started classes the next summer (2004) in the new building.

Karen Paatan, an SIL graduate from the Philippines, taught the first class that summer. On CanIL's first anniversary, July 11, 2005, we were able to announce that all construction costs for the building were completely paid!

In 2006, TWU's MA in Linguistics program began; and CanIL experienced a significant influx in staff and faculty members. Soon after that, we set new records for enrolment, and increasing numbers of our trainees have since gone from CanIL to assignments with Wycliffe and other mission agencies.

God had brought SIL and TWU to the starting point of the CanIL story. We know God is at work. It's part of His plan for eternity, when people from all tribes, tongues and nations will be together before the throne of God, singing praises to Him.

57

Student, alumnus, administrator

By Loyal Makaroff, '85

Loyal Makaroff was a student at Trinity Western University from 1980-1985, taking a fifth year to focus on the responsibilities of Student Association President. From 1985-1988, he served at Trinity Western as first full-time Director of Extension Ministries, and from 1990-1993 full-time Director of Alumni Relations. His skills in business development, combined with his MEd and MBA, have enabled him to develop companies in Canada and abroad. Currently he resides in Vancouver with his wife Kate, their two sons, Léal and Caelen, and their daughter Elya.

—*Neil Snider*

Recently, my son began the arduous task of applying to universities for his undergraduate schooling. One of the questions to which he was asked to respond was: "How do your see yourself contributing to and benefiting from a Christian liberal arts college with a unique mission?"

As he and I discussed this, I was able to pass on to him how my experience at Trinity Western—especially through my involvement with Student Life—impacted my life.

Trinity Western was more than just a nice Christian university for me. The integrated efforts of staff and faculty to instill in the students a passion to become godly Christian leaders—emissaries of the risen Lord, equipped to serve the Body of Christ everywhere they went, and through everything they did—was powerful.

As a Resident Assistant, I'd watched and worked with the Student Life staff to help create an environment through which this passion could be taught and caught. I'd watched as these servant-leaders established

Loyal Makaroff

relationships with student leaders, and helped to influence their worldview, primarily through their example of servant-leadership. I quickly recognized that godly leadership is counter-intuitive to what the world refers to as "leadership": it's serving, rather than dictating; loving rather than imposing. The Student Life staff lived this counter-intuitive life, and changed the lives of students with whom they worked. I recall the Student Life staff, as well as the maintenance staff, gathering to intercede for students who were struggling with classes, or dealing with difficult situations. Then I saw them serve these students with all their strength.

I also saw this through the life and leadership of President Dr. Neil Snider. In my senior year—as the Student Association President—I approached him and asked if the Student Executive could "sit in" with the University's Administrative Committee, to learn from them and to be mentored by them. He agreed, and we were privileged to be able to participate in futuristic planning, and the decision-making process for the University. I don't know of any other university that does this.

As student leaders, we were then able to integrate what we saw and learned into our work with the Student Association. More important, we saw that the University's leadership, from top to bottom, had a heart that longed after God, and demonstrated dependence on Him. In a small but life-changing way, we—as a student executive—were able to experience God's transformational power as we saw the impossible become possible.

Trinity Western was more to me than just an academic education. Through the relationships that were developed with the administration, faculty, and Student Life staff, I was able to observe "God with us." I was prepared to go into the world as a Christian leader, equipped to make disciples of Jesus Christ and to serve people, regardless of their position, in the various marketplaces of life that God has in store for me.

58

'Learning about myself by learning about Him'

By Dr. Simon Moore

> *In the final analysis, the best performance indicator of Trinity Western University—by which I mean every component of the University: faculty, staff, students, Board, administration, parents and supporters—is how well TWU achieves the goals stated in our Mission Statement. That's best evaluated by considering the product: generations of graduating classes comprising thousands of 'godly Christian leaders, university graduates with thoroughly Christian minds, serving God and people in the various marketplaces of life.'*
>
> *So let's let the final voice in this remembrance be that of Dr. Simon Moore, MD, CCFP, as he relates how his time as a student at TWU, and as an intern in the President's office for part of that time, affected his life.*
>
> —*Neil Snider*

I never expected to perform at Carnegie Hall in New York City. But on an icy day in January 2005, along with 50 other choir members from Trinity Western University, that's exactly what I had the opportunity to do.

I'll never forget the surprising turn of events that led to the opportunity to stand on that stage. During the first week of my studies at TWU, I wrote my name on a sign-up sheet for a musical group. I'd played violin for years, and with some prompting by my sister—who had already been involved in the TWU choirs—I figured playing with the choir would be enjoyable.

A few days later, I auditioned for the choral professor, Dr. Wes Janzen. At the end of the audition, Dr. Janzen asked me, "Now, please sing *Silent Night*."

I laughed. I was there to demonstrate my skills as a violinist—I didn't have much experience as a singer. "That's no problem," Professor Janzen said. "Just sing, and then you can go." Apparently, he was serious.

I'll never forget what happened at the end of my attempt at singing that day. As I sang the last note, he was silent.

Dr. Janzen leaned back slowly in his chair. He put both of his hands together, looked into my eyes, and said, "Simon… you have a very beautiful voice."

I was stunned. Nobody had ever said that to me. I didn't think I'd sung particularly well. But that day, I was offered a position in the TWU choir.

Dr. Janzen, I later realized, wasn't looking for a polished vocalist with extensive singing experience. Rather, he'd seen that my musical experience, combined with the right environment and mentorship, gave me the *potential* to excel.

If this unexpected opportunity was a one-off situation, then I probably would have considered it a charming coincidence and not much more. However, this was just one of many opportunities I encountered while studying at Trinity Western University; most of them unexpected—such as athletic broadcasting, archaeology studies at original biblical sites, and—most meaningfully—volunteering at hospitals around the world.

God's exciting plan became even more apparent several years later, when I was elected to lead a national organization for Canadian resident physicians. I looked back and realized that many of the experiences I'd had at TWU, such as interning in the office of the President, and working with the TWU Board of Directors, had specifically prepared me to excel in such a role.

This wasn't only my own personal experience. Time and time again, in the lives of my friends and in the lives of many other people who attended TWU, I saw people who were presented with incredible opportunities that ultimately glorified God.

In science, when they see enough similar things happen, researchers wonder if there's an explanation for the pattern.

I might be tempted to say that these opportunities just "fell into my lap", or that it's a coincidence that TWU graduates have such exceptional experiences. But when a pattern develops, then clues of a greater plan or purpose begin to emerge.

Would I have had these opportunities at any other university? I'm sure I'd have received a standard, maybe even excellent, educational experience at any one of thousands of universities; but would I have fully developed my potential to where God has brought it today?

To be honest, I'm not so sure.

The university years are a very formative and vulnerable time in a young person's life—neuroscience research has recently discovered that the human brain is still developing and changing, well beyond age 20. On many occasions, I've wondered where I'd be today, had I lived out those formative years in an environment that wasn't as positive as TWU. And very often, I conclude that had I studied elsewhere, I wouldn't have experienced such a dramatic pattern of exciting opportunities.

What is it about Trinity Western University? Why was the environment there so richly suitable for developing unforeseen interests, passions, and opportunities?

I don't think it happened by accident. It has to do with the people who make up TWU—the intent and mission of TWU, and the blessing that TWU has experienced.

Many of the opportunities I had while at TWU—in research, teaching, travel, and so many other experiences—helped me find my passions, and opened doors for me later in life. Many of these experiences happened because staff, colleagues, or professors at TWU approached me directly and asked me to become involved. In fact, today I could still call up any one of a number of professors I studied under at TWU, and I *know* that they would not only remember me, but would be more than eager to lend a helping hand.

It's the *people* who make TWU the incredible place it is; and the relationships I've built with those people will last a lifetime (not to mention my incredible wife, whom I met at a TWU alumni event!).

I never hear friends and colleagues who studied at other universities say anything like that about their academic experiences. But over and over again, when I found myself needing advice, guidance, or support in a crisis, my TWU professors were willing to go well beyond simply teaching, and share their experiences and advice; to tell me stories about their own mistakes and failures; or to go out of their way to vouch for my character.

And it wasn't just one professor, but several—Dr. Van Dyke, Dr. Paulton, Dr. Stringham, Dr. Montgomery, Dr. Clements, Dr. Venema… Some of my most meaningful moments as a student were because of these professors—even professors like Dr. Friesen, from whom I'd never taken a single class! Like Dr. Janzen, they all helped me to discover talents I never thought I had.

With a pattern like this, it's worth looking for an explanation.

These incredible professors wouldn't have been called to serve at TWU if it weren't for the foundational work of a core group of leaders who'd heard God's call to start a Christian college in B.C. With God's blessing, that institution was born—and eventually became a university with a mission "to prepare godly Christian leaders to serve in the various marketplaces of life."

Since then, there's been a pattern of overwhelming influence; a pattern that suggests a much greater God-ordained purpose. Thanks to this "ripple effect", the pattern extends far beyond just me and the patients and students I have the honour of serving every day; but much further, through the lives of thousands of other TWU graduates. Indeed, the vision of those early leaders, with God's blessing, has resulted in influence that touches the lives of many others in Canada and around the world.

Our genes are vital to much of who we are; but just because someone is born with the right DNA doesn't automatically make them an Olympic medalist! Similarly, just because God gave me an aptitude for science doesn't mean I would automatically be granted a medical degree. So much effort and training goes into both. But even more important, so many influences in our environment also play a role.

There's certainly a strong presence of God's blessing at Trinity Western University. Thanks to the incredible leaders and professors who give TWU its character, it was undoubtedly the perfect place for me to discover talents and passions I never thought I had; and more important, to learn to use them to serve others and to glorify God far beyond anything I ever expected.

Manufactured by Amazon.ca
Bolton, ON